# THE BATTLES
# OF THE GENERAL

# THE BATTLES OF THE GENERAL

## Ken Glazier

Capital Transport

## Author's Note

In this book I have attempted to tell the story of London bus operation between 1918 and 1929, a complex and sometimes turbulent period which paved the way for the establishment of the London Passenger Transport Board in 1933. The decade was one of extremes, marked by a series of battles between the LGOC and the traffic authorities, and with a tide of new competitors. The struggles started with the dire circumstances in which bus operators found themselves after four years of total war. The LGOC and its associates in particular had been forced to sacrifice a large proportion of their buses to the war effort, leaving them ill-equipped to provide anything approaching an adequate service once the 'war to end all wars' had finished. The response was a rise in competition to heights not hitherto witnessed, only for that to be curbed in the most draconian way by Government action. Interwoven with this was a continuing thread of campaigns for some sort of unification, which eventually bore fruit in a way that many had wanted to avoid. London also went on growing rapidly, as did the bus services to serve the new populations, and there was a steady improvement in the buses used, as designers made their way towards the modern era, often despite the reactionary attitudes of the Metropolitan Police.

In a book of this nature it is not possible to give a detailed account of all the events and changes that took place in the period under review but rather, by selection of key indicators, to give a picture of what happened and, if possible, why. The vehicle developments of the LGOC and its associated companies are covered as fully as available material will allow but it has been necessary to cover the comparable history for the Independent operators in a less detailed but I hope still adequate fashion. Route developments are confined to those which expanded the network or, in the immediate post-war period, restored services to their pre-war levels. In due time the more detailed information will become available in the series of publications from the London Historical Research Group of the Omnibus Society, 'Motor Omnibus Routes in London'.

The rise and fall of the Independents is covered in detail so far as the basic events are concerned but because of the sheer number of operators involved it is only possible to offer a selection of typical examples, while covering more fully those who made a more significant contribution to events. For those interested in mining this subject further, the book to read, if you can find a copy of it, is 'London Buses Volume 1' by Ken Blacker, Ron Lunn and Reg Westgate, which can only be described as the definitive work on the subject and from which I have drawn much information. Sadly, it has been out of print for many years.

Other important sources of information which have helped me in my research are: the London Transport Archive, from which much of the detailed information concerning Frank Pick's activities was drawn; the Public Record Office at Kew; the Metropolitan Archive; and the library at London's Transport Museum. Among individuals who have given help, my special thanks must go, as ever, to Dr Andrew Gilks who not only made available valuable vehicle information from his personal archive but also spent much time checking my text. Others who have helped with information and photographs include Laurie Akehurst and David Ruddom, both of whom also slogged through my manuscript to check it for accuracy. Help and information has also been supplied by John Gent, Malcolm Papes and Reg Westgate.

Apart from the standard works of reference, other books which are an important source of information for this period include:

London Buses Volume 2 (Blacker, Lunn and Westgate)

East Surrey (Durrant, King and Robbins)

Tilling in London (George Robbins)

The London B-type Motor Omnibus (George Robbins)

General Motor Buses of the Twenties (George Robbins)

KEN GLAZIER
January 2003

*Right* A policeman does point duty in Strand at its junction with Wellington Street (now Lancaster Place) probably in the spring of 1923, judging by the presence of two NSs on route 9 and a horse-drawn cart delivering goods from Bricklayers Arms Station, still labelled 'South Eastern and Chatham Railway Company'. The SECR was absorbed into the new Southern Railway company on 1st January 1923 under the grouping provisions of the 1921 Railway Act, while the NS first appeared in the spring of 1923. Between the two NSs is a B-type on route 39 and there are also K and S-types present, the one nearest the camera being Chalk Farm's S 568 on route 77, heading for Tooting. (London's Transport Museum)

*Title page* Two types of bus that dominated the 1920s, with fleet names that did not. S 16, owned by the Tramways (MET) Omnibus Company but worked on its behalf from Hammersmith garage by the LGOC, awaits the signal from the constable on point duty at Trafalgar Square, alongside British Automobile Traction's 523 (later NS 2401). (London's Transport Museum)

The cover painting is by Glyn Kraemer-Johnson.

First Published 2003

ISBN 1 85414 269 0

Published by Capital Transport Publishing
38 Long Elmes, Harrow Weald, Middlesex

Printed by CS Graphics, Singapore

# Contents

# Introduction

At the end of what was then known as the Great War of 1914–1918, the London General Omnibus Company had a virtual monopoly of bus services in Greater London. It was by far the largest single operator, having consolidated its position some ten years earlier when it amalgamated with the London Road Car Co and Vanguard, and it had been a subsidiary of the Underground Electric Railways Company of London since 1912. This association had brought under its wing the other bus operating companies in the Group, all subsidiaries of the London and Suburban Traction Company: The Tramways (MET) Omnibus Company, the Gearless Omnibus Company and the buses of the South Metropolitan Electric Tramways and Lighting Company. Although these companies continued their independent statutory existence, their buses were supplied by, housed and operated by the LGOC. In 1918, MET had 175 buses (painted blue with the newly introduced fleet name 'METROPOLITAN'), while Gearless (grey) and the South Met (dark blue with the fleet name 'SOUTHERN') had ten each.

Other operators had working agreements with the LGOC, the details of which varied from company to company but which determined the extent of their operations and enabled a unified network of services to be operated. Receipts were shared in an agreed proportion from what was known as the London Omnibus Pool. Perhaps the most prominent of these was the venerable Thomas Tilling Ltd which had been operating buses in London since at least 1851, and was therefore the senior company by five or more years. Tilling had entered a series of agreements, starting in 1911, which allowed them to run a total of 150 buses in London and at the end of 1918 these were operating from garages at Croydon and Lewisham on eight routes, five of them jointly with General. Tilling was more obviously independent of the Underground Group than others because it had its own distinctive rolling stock, the famous TTA1 Tilling-Stevens petrol electrics. It remained independently owned throughout the period covered by this book and its London business was eventually acquired by the LPTB.

The Associated Omnibus Company was another former horse bus proprietor but of more recent genesis, having been formed in 1900. Its agreement with the LGOC covered 55 buses but these were all operated by General from LGOC garages as part of the Pool. They were painted LGOC red but carried the fleet name ASSOCIATED. General acquired the company in December 1919 and its buses were then absorbed into the LGOC fleet.

Mayhem at Aldgate tram terminus in 1919 alongside Aldgate East station whose UNDERGROUND sign can be seen at the top of the building on the right. B 925 on route 42 has come from Finsbury Park and is finding some road space between the two tram terminal stubs, overtaking of trams being allowed on either side. The West Ham Corporation bogie car, waiting for the cart to clear the track, was built in the same year as the bus, 1911, but was nearly twenty years ahead in the standards of comfort and cover supplied to its passengers. The infancy of the motor vehicle is well illustrated by the commercial vehicles, all but one of which is horse-drawn. (London's Transport Museum)

The British Automobile Traction Co Ltd, which had started bus operation as the Amalgamated Omnibus Co in 1907, was a subsidiary of the British Electric Traction Co Ltd. BAT had entered an agreement with the Underground Group in December 1912 to operate 33 buses (including three spares) as part of the Pool, its fleet of Daimlers, painted green with the fleet name 'BRITISH', being operated on route 24 from a garage in Rochester Mews, Camden Town (AQ). BAT remained independent until absorbed by the LPTB in 1933.

The National Steam Car Co had been the largest competitor of the LGOC in pre-war days but by an agreement of 1914 it had become part of the Pool. It lasted only a year beyond the armistice and ceased operation in November 1919, its services then being covered by LGOC buses.

The only major competitors of General at this time were the municipally owned tramways and the Metropolitan Railway. The three private tramway companies, Metropolitan Electric, London United and the South Metropolitan, and all the other Underground railways were part of the Underground Group, or 'Combine' as it was frequently known. The largest municipal by far was the London County Council, the others being (clockwise around London) Walthamstow, Leyton, West Ham, East Ham, Ilford, Barking, Dartford, Erith, Bexley and Croydon.

The war had had a devastating effect on bus operations in London. On the last day of peace, the LGOC and its associated companies had 3,286 buses licensed for service but by Armistice Day 1918, that total had fallen to 1,978. In the first eight months of the war over 1,900 buses had been commandeered for war service, the army at that time having no motorised troop transports of its own. There were some additions to the fleet during 1915 and 1916 but this amounted to only 230 buses and fifty of these were converted to lorries for the army in 1917, leaving a net gain of only 180. The additions came from three sources, a small number were new vehicles, some of the requisitioned buses no longer needed by the army were bought back and some acquired lorries and vans were fitted with bus bodies. Tilling's addiction to petrol-electric propulsion protected them from this onslaught. The result was the mass withdrawal of bus services, with thirteen daily routes disappearing overnight on the day war broke out and a total of twenty-six going in the first fortnight. There were many ups and downs in the succeeding four years but the standard of service being operated at the end of the war was substantially less than it had been.

Sir Albert Stanley (later Lord Ashfield), Chairman of the Underground Group from 1919, had foreseen this state of affairs as far back as 1915. An approach was made to the Government with a proposal that the company should be guaranteed a monopoly of operations in the capital for at least five but preferably for ten years after the end of the war. The justification for this remarkable idea was that the LGOC had acted patrioti-

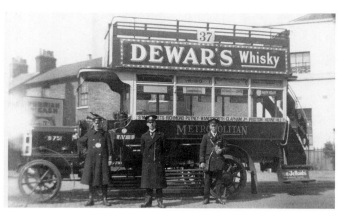

The Tramways (MET) Omnibus Company had owned 350 buses at the outbreak of the Great War but 240 of them had been commandeered by the War Department and there was still a shortfall of 165 in 1918 despite some additions during the war. B 751 was one of 63 which were transferred from the LGOC in August–September 1920 to fill part of the gap. (The Omnibus Society)

cally in supplying so many buses for military use during the war and therefore deserved some protection from opportunistic operators while it was recovering in the post-war period. The point was raised again when the London County Council submitted a private Bill seeking powers to operate motor buses, although this did not come to a head as the council withdrew the Bill. Government ministers had shown some sympathy towards Ashfield's application and there was some informal debate on the matter but nothing ever came of it. The most likely reason for this is that they were unable to define how a company could be prevented from operating unless there was special legislation which would effectively introduce public regulation. This might have had far reaching implications which they were not at that time prepared to contemplate. Ironically, by not making the decision at that time, the Government allowed circumstances to develop which laid the foundations for even more far-reaching legislation in 1924 and again in 1933.

As things turned out the five-year period

was a fairly accurate estimate of how long the recovery would take and, in the event, General did enjoy nearly four years of unmolested monopoly. However, recovery was too slow for passengers struggling with inadequate services and their patience had been exhausted long since so the door was open for competitors to step in, which is precisely what happened when Arthur George Partridge put his Leyland into service on route 11 in August 1922. This started a sequence of events leading to the passing of the London Traffic Act which introduced draconian statutory controls for the first time these in turn paving the way for even more revolutionary changes nine years later.

This book takes the story from the end of the First World War, when public control was out of favour, to the end of 1929 by which time far-reaching proposals for a total public monopoly in London were before Parliament. It was an eventful period full of 'might-have-beens', and the cockpit for the battle of ideas which ultimately settled the fate of London's transport for over fifty years.

Two B-type buses at Streatham with a still essential horse trough supplied by the Metropolitan Drinking Fountain and Cattle Trough Association in the foreground. B 1825 on the right has just arrived on route 49 from Ealing and the conductor has already changed the destination board, while the other is en route to Liverpool Street on route 34 from South Croydon, to which the route had been extended from Streatham in June 1919.

## CHAPTER ONE

# Post-War Bus Fleet Rejuvenation 1918–1922

The Combine's fleet on Armistice Day, 11th November 1918 was dominated by the B-type, with LGOC listed as having 1,639 units, the Associated Omnibus Company 46, the Metropolitan Steam Omnibus Company 94, MET 175, Gearless and SMET ten each, and there were nineteen Private Hire vehicles in store. This gave a grand total of 1,993, leaving the balance of 105 to be made up by 41 X-type (four of which were licensed), 25 Y-type, all in store, and 39 former New Central Leylands, also in store. The unlicensed vehicles in store provided the most fruitful source for adding buses to the fleet quickly but not all were in a fit enough condition to be revived for bus service. In the couple of weeks up to the end of November, therefore, this source was depleted by the conversion of ten of the Y-type and one Leyland to lorries and the sale of one Leyland. Two of the X-type were sold at the beginning of December and the remaining Ys were reduced to chassis in January 1919 but a start was made on relicensing the remaining Xs on 11th December and all 39 were in service by mid-March 1919. Twelve of the former New Central Leylands were also brought back into service on 13th December, others being added from the end of January 1919 until all 41 were in operation by 19th June. This exhausted the supply of unused vehicles from within the fleet.

Meanwhile a slow start had been made on getting extra buses onto the road by adding new or 'made-up' vehicles, using several expedients. One useful source of supply came from the substantial stock of spare double-deck bodies which had been removed from chassis requisitioned by the government for conversion to lorries during the war. Thirty-two were mounted on B-type lorry chassis (not to be confused with the famous lorry buses) and another 165 were used on renovated chassis bought back from the government following war service. General also placed an order for the supply of 250 new Bs, the expedient in this case being that AEC intended using many spares from stock manufactured in the USA in 1914. These had been part of an order for 500 chassis whose completion was interrupted by the onset of hostilities. The resulting bus, known as 'Type 7', was based on the B-type design but was more powerful than the standard type and, crucially, also heavier. Consequently the company became embroiled in lengthy negotiations with the Police to get it accepted. A prototype, B 4879, was built in November 1918 and the Police decision to sanction their construction was reported to the LGOC Board on 12th December. Work on the batch B 4883–5132 started immediately, the missing numbers, B 4880–4882, being lorries built for the Underground. The

bodywork for these buses included 172 whose construction had started before the war and was now to be completed, the remaining 78 being second-hand. The Type 7 Bs could be distinguished from others by the polished aluminium dashboard which was unique to them. Delivery of the former lorries had begun with B 1419 in October 1918 and the remainder came slowly, the last arriving in April 1919. The 250 new buses started to arrive in February 1919 and the last three were licensed on 1st July, while the former War Department buses went into service between March and August 1919.

In May 1919 the Metropolitan Police agreed to relax their fierce licensing standards and allow the temporary operation of 'sub-standard' vehicles. The LGOC immediately approached the War Department to buy another 230 complete vehicles which had been on military service overseas.

The absence of any white relief colour shows that B 537 was one of the 'khaki emergency' buses recovered from the War Department and restored to a lower standard than would normally have been accepted by the Metropolitan Police. It had been new in the autumn of 1911 but was swept into the voracious military maw within four years. (E.G.P. Masterman)

Twenty-seven of the thirty single-deck 'bentwood' Bs did not return after the war, among them B 2706 seen in more placid times clambering up the hill past Muswell Hill station. (Capital Transport collection)

B 6887 was one of twenty-five Bs built in 1916, using stored bodies, which bore high fleet numbers (B 6865–6889). It is on the Sunday extension of route 68A to the countryside at West Wickham. (The Omnibus Society)

B 28 was one of those which had been taken by the War Department in 1914 but bought back and restored in 1915. It is working from Merton garage on route 67, a new route introduced on 24th September 1919. (H.C. Casserley)

Twenty-three former lorries (fifteen wartime conversions and eight new in 1917) and twenty-four surplus single-deckers were also given double-deck bodies and used for this purpose. Most of the sub-standard buses were painted khaki, a shade of green, and were labelled 'Traffic Emergency Bus' in small white letters above the rear wheel but there were also over a hundred painted red with similar labelling. Although the red ones also had sub-standard chassis, they differed from the khaki variety in having bodies recovered from store. The first twenty had originally been on Straker-Squire Y-type chassis and differed from the B-type in having a curved white canopy while some of the remainder had been on former MET Daimler chassis. Four of the red emergency buses were all that remained of the thirty single-deckers bought new in 1914 which had been among the first buses to be requisitioned by the government. Most of the khaki buses were licensed between June 1919 and January 1920, with two more in May 1920, and the red ones between November 1919 and May 1920.

Among these emergency vehicles was B 43 which was chosen to attend a ceremony at Buckingham Palace on 14th February 1920 to represent the buses used in active wartime service. It carried a party of ex-servicemen who were to be inspected by King George V. When the bus was finally withdrawn it was given a different body, in better condition, and was specially embellished with a shell-case mounted atop the dash-board and a figure representing 'Ole Bill' mounted on the radiator. It was presented to the Auxiliary Omnibus Old Comrade's Association and was then to be seen for many years taking part in appropriate ceremonies, including attendance at the funerals of Old Comrades. It is now in the Imperial War Museum.

More or less simultaneously with the operation of the emergency buses, an even more drastic stop-gap was launched on the public with a great show of publicity, the lorry bus. These have since become legendary but their effect on the service provided was less significant than the other measures already described and, although welcomed when they started, were not popular in the longer run. The origin of the idea of adapting lorries for use as emergency buses has not yet been discovered but it may have been inspired by emergency measures the Government adopted during the strike of Tube workers between 3rd and 9th February 1919. This threw immense strains onto the already struggling bus, tram and other rail services which were simply unable to cope but the Government needed to ensure that its essential staff could get to and from their offices in central London and therefore authorised the use of army lorries. On these, the bowler-hatted gentlemen and elegantly dressed secretaries were conveyed in primitive conditions, without benefit of any form of seating, very little in the way of support while standing and with only a simple ladder on which to climb aboard. There were reports that they carried some other passengers unofficially and it was not long before a number of services were set up by volunteer drivers from the Royal Army Service Corps specifically to carry the general public. According to Press reports these services had been carefully designed, which implies that they were part of a contingency plan, but they did not last long as the strike was settled and full services resumed on 10th February.

The first public indication that something similar was being considered for more controlled application, came in a statement to the House of Commons by the Minister of National Service and Reconstruction on 28th May. This coincided with the announcement by the Metropolitan Police, already mentioned, that they would be prepared to license buses which were 'sub-standard' and this was swiftly followed by a report that 'lorry omnibuses' would start working on Monday 31st May. The speed with which these decisions were pushed through is remarkable by any standards but all the more so in the light of the usual reluctance of the Metropolitan Police to agree to anything new without months or years of deliberation. There were obviously negotiations going on behind the scenes but it is a remarkable fact that there is no recorded discussion of the subject by the LGOC Board until 5th June 1919. They were told that the details of the scheme had not yet been settled, yet by that time the first ten had been licensed.

On 14th February 1920, H.M. George V passes B 43 in the inner courtyard of Buckingham Palace on his way to inspect the war-veteran busmen. B 43 was a war veteran itself and had been chosen to represent all those buses that had served at the Front. (Ken Glazier collection)

The vehicles supplied by the government Disposal Board were AEC ¾ ton chassis fitted with Tylor 45hp engines of a type supplied in considerable quantity to the armed services during the war. Their lorry bodies, painted in War Department dark green, were treated to the minimum of alteration to enable them to carry 27 passengers safely but in minimum comfort. Access to the lorry platform was through a gap in the rear panel and the tailboard was adapted to support a simple cantilevered staircase, at the top of which a crude grabrail was added to the framework of the roof. Although this framework was meant to support a canvas cover, these were not used. An extra plank was added to the sides of the body as a safety measure to remove the temptation for passengers to use the sideboard as an armrest with parts of their arms projecting. Under-frame lifeguards of the type fitted to B-type buses were also added between the two axles on each side. The lorry buses also carried the words 'Traffic Emergency Vehicle' on the nearside and the GENERAL fleet name in white on the body sides. There were no destination and route boards but paper bills were applied to both sides of the body showing the destinations and route followed and another on the dash panel showing the route number.

A prototype was prepared by the LGOC using one of its own lorries of the same type and this was licensed on 31st May and demonstrated to the company Board. It differed in several ways from the 'production' vehicles, notably in lacking the safety boards on the side and the underframe lifeguards. It was also still carrying the WD markings rather than the company's fleet name. It entered service at Mortlake garage on route 33 on 2nd June but later in the month returned to its intended duties as a lorry. The first of the main batch were licensed on 4th June and the numbers then built up gradually until all 180 were available for service on 5th July. Known operations of the lorry buses are shown in Appendix 1.

*Above* Type 7 B 5128 when allocated to the Private Hire fleet and allocated to Willesden garage. (The Omnibus Society)

*Above right* B 4973 heads north along the London-Carlisle road at South Mimms on a long-established country run on route 84 out to St Albans, its polished aluminium dashboard acting as a useful recognition feature. The chassis of B 4973 was one of those used as the basis for 74 new single-deckers in 1921. (Photomatic)

After the initial enthusiasm for the novelty, attitudes became more jaundiced as the realities of travelling in such uncomfortable conditions began to dawn, particularly when autumn and winter set in. Passengers soon sought alternative means of travel, including walking, and the income from the enterprise began to sink to unacceptably low levels. Even when their capacity was used to the full, the lorries carried twelve fewer than a fully laden B-type double-decker but they were not used to anything like their full potential because passengers were reluctant to travel on them outside peak hours. The LGOC drew attention to this in an advertisement of their own which baldly announced that the company was bearing an average loss of 5d a mile on lorry buses because they so often operated nearly empty. Their use gradually dwindled, although all 180 remained licensed, until the whole lot was delicensed on 14th January 1920. Their withdrawal was certainly not related to any improvement in the availability of buses as the total licensed fleet was reduced by the same number to a total of 2,659. This wiped out the entire increase achieved since 6th September 1919 and left the available fleet still 627 below the August 1914 figure. Eight of the lorry bus chassis were retained and fitted with new char-a-banc bodies for Private Hire work and twenty were allotted to East Surrey in 1921/1922 for hilly north Surrey routes then being introduced. Fourteen were fitted with spare double-deck bodies from Bs (ESTC 62–65, 78–83, 87–90) and the other six with new 28-seat single-deck bodies built by the LGOC (ESTC 1, 2, 35, 36, 40, 41).

The first five of the former London Central Leylands were withdrawn as early as November 1919 but the rest remained licensed until the beginning of February 1920, after which they slowly began to slip away until the last five were delicensed on 14th May. The X-types remained intact until 19th May 1920 but then disappeared quickly, the last five of this landmark design being delicensed on 1st June 1920.

The long term solution to the company's problems obviously lay in the rapid production of as many new buses as possible which met the standards set by the Metropolitan Police and could be used to augment the fleet. A quick immediate solution might have been to resume production of the proven B-type while improved designs were developed but it is certain that the Metropolitan Police would not have approved, despite the undoubted qualities of the design, because they were already looking for lighter and quieter buses. In fact they would have been looking for a successor to the B four years earlier had the war not intervened and it seems that design work on a new model had started in 1914 but had then lain untouched until 1917. By then the end of the war seemed to be in sight and the LGOC was well aware that its standard of service would be seriously compromised by a shortage of vehicles. The LGOC Board therefore decided to make itself ready to move the project forward as soon as conditions returned to normal, by employing an American engineer S.G. Averall to prepare fresh proposals. This foresight obviously paid off because only five months after the end of the war on 10th

April 1919, the LGOC Board minutes record that tests were being carried out on two chassis of the '8 type' and to drawings being almost complete for the '9 type'. In passing it is worth noting that these type numbers, which appeared to continue the series that had ended with the 7 type Bs already described, were not used subsequently by AEC who started a new classification system in 1920 using model numbers 301, 401 and so on, with engines numbered in the 1xx series.

By the 9th May Board meeting a sample of the new model was expected to be on the road for testing the following week. This was K 1 which was duly taken into stock and licensed on 14th August 1919. Its main claim to fame was the redesign of the front end to put the driver alongside the engine, a layout generally known as 'forward-control' and claimed by some to be revolutionary. It was certainly a landmark in the development of the double-deck bus but it was not the first to have this layout as SMT had their full-fronted Lothian design in service in 1913 and there had been even earlier designs with the driver perched above the engine, horse bus style. Nevertheless, the K was the first to go into production in quantity and did introduce the concept of the half-cab which gave the driver an unsurpassed view of the road ahead and of the kerb. This set a pattern which was to remain the national standard until the arrival of underfloor- and rear-engined models thirty or more years later, with some half-cab double-deckers still being produced nearly fifty years after the K was launched.

The final body design was chosen from several samples built to test the practicability of various seating capacities and layouts. The completed vehicle had a wheelbase of 14ft 2½ ins, fully 3ft 6in longer than the B, its overall length was 22ft 9ins, just within the 23ft limit, and its unladen weight was 4t 4cwt giving a nominal laden weight of 6¾t, the limit being 7 tons. It was also 2½ins wider than the B, at 7ft 1½ ins, although it looked a lot more because of other changes in the design. The body had completely straight sides with the rear wheels inset into the body side, whereas the wheels were outside the body on the B. This arrangement increased the width of the lower deck as well as its length, giving enough space for most seats to be in forward-facing pairs each side of the gangway, rather than on longitudinal benches along the side. Both decks were longer, as the upper deck was carried forward in line with the new position of the front bulkhead. The result was to increase the seating capacity, compared with earlier motor buses, from 34 to 46, proportionately greater at nearly 36 per cent than any individual increase achieved in later years. The rear platform was also enlarged to about double the width, wide enough to allow two passengers to board or alight at the same time, something that would have pleased the Metropolitan Police who liked anything that helped reduce the amount of time buses spent stationary. The division was marked by a vertical grabrail which was attached to the projecting lower-deck roof. This was also larger and effectively provided a roof over the front half of the platform.

Mechanically the K did not represent such a great advance. Its four-cylinder engine (classified A101 in the new system then being adopted by AEC) was smaller than even the earliest Bs, with a swept volume of only 4.4 litres and an output of 28–30 hp. It had a multiplate clutch which gave a smoother start than the cone clutch used on the B but the three-speed chain gearbox was unchanged and the worm-drive rear axle was little different.

The K was the first bus type to have transverse seating in the saloon, arranged in pairs of doubles either side of a central gangway in the fashion which has remained broadly standard ever since. This view looking towards the front shows how the chair frames and backs were wooden, the only concession to comfort being the upholstered cushions on the seats.
(London's Transport Museum)

K 1 went into service on route 11 from Hammersmith garage in August 1919 and the second prototype, K 2, was licensed for service on route 25 from Seven Kings garage on 15th September. A third prototype chassis, K 3, was not bodied at this time but was used as an instructional unit until 1928. The operation of the two prototypes must have been an immediate success because, at its meeting on 16th October, the LGOC Board authorised the purchase of 500 chassis at an estimated cost of £642,500 (£1,285 each). The bodywork contracts for these was authorised later and called for 250 to be built in the company's own workshops and a like number by Brush. Another 500 chassis was authorised on 7th October 1920, and the

bodies for these were to be supplied by Brush (35), Short Bros (300), Strachan (100) and the remainder by the LGOC at North Road, Islington or Seagrave Road, Fulham. The last two orders for the initial run of Ks was for an additional forty, authorised on 5th May 1921, and another twenty on 8th August, although only nineteen of the latter were delivered and, in any case, by then all 1,059 production buses had been delivered, bringing fleet numbers up to K 1062.

The first six production Ks were licensed on 6th May 1920 and the rate at which they entered service gradually built up from an initial six a week to a peak of 38 a week in February 1921. They were quickly spread around the principal central London routes

and by August 1921 they were allocated to seventeen garages and were operating on twenty-one routes penetrating every quarter of the Metropolis. Two garages, Hackney (60 buses) and Seven Kings (100), were stocked entirely with K-types.

*Above* K 1 in service on route 11 on 3rd September 1919, a day short of three weeks after it was first licensed. The straight body sides and inset rear wheels, so clearly seen in this view, enabled an increase in seating capacity on the lower deck. (Capital Transport Collection)

*Above left* The driving seat of the new K, with the additional protection and warmth of the engine alongside and a higher dash panel, looks a little cosier than the unmercifully spartan exposure of earlier types but was still open to nature's extremes. K 2 entered service at Seven Kings on 15th September 1919 and is seen here in service on route 25 near its home base. (Ken Glazier collection)

*Above right* This offside view of Twickenham's K 221 in Upper Richmond Road shows the high driving position which gave an excellent view of the road ahead, and the extra protection given to the driver's legs and knees by the curved dash panel. On the K, the route number stencil was attached to the front of the driver's canopy, instead of hanging down from it as on the B, and the use of side route boards was discontinued. (Ken Glazier collection)

*Left* K 812 takes part in a demonstration of an early automatic washing machine at Willesden garage. This viewpoint shows the hard seat provided for the driver and the layout of the passenger seats on the upper deck. The 'police lights' were carried under the canopy on these buses instead of the dash. (John Aldridge collection)

Even while the K itself was barely off the drawing board, further evolution of the design was already being studied well ahead of any change in regulations that would allow the idea to become reality. This may have been the type 9 referred to at the Board meeting on 10th April. A prototype chassis was built by AEC some 2ft 3in longer than the K, for which, in April 1920, the LGOC built a special 56-seat body, an almost unimaginable capacity at that time. This vehicle, numbered T 1, never saw service but a photograph shows it as being a clear forerunner of the S-type, although with its front axle set back so that the wheels encroached into the body at the front, presumably to keep the turning circle as tight as possible. Some sources have suggested that this design was developed specifically to cope with the tight corners on route 25, but there appears to be no surviving evidence to support this. The chassis, which was owned by AEC, was sold for conversion to a lorry but the idea was not still-born because the LGOC successfully sought the agreement of the authorities to an increase in the permitted overall length and weight for double-deckers. The maximum permitted length was increased to 25ft and the laden weight limit was raised from 7 to 8½ tons. General immediately placed an order for 250 S-type vehicles. There was also a side order for fifteen, which General asked AEC to build 'with the utmost despatch' so that they could be put to the Police for approval and tried out in service before a final decision was taken about the design of the other 250.

The new body was ready on 19th September 1920 and the completed vehicle ready for inspection in November. The body was in essence an enlarged version of the K, the extra length of the body structure being achieved simply, by inserting an extra narrow bay in the centre of the body and by widening the window at the rear of the saloon. However, the upper deck was not only lengthened, it was moved back so that there was shorter overhang beyond the lower deck at the front while at the rear, instead of ending in line with the lower saloon, the structure was carried over part of the rear platform. This seemingly minor change helped give the S a rather less antique look than the K.

*Top* The ephemeral T 1 was photographed with route boards for the 123 when it was shown to the Metropolitan Police at Scotland Yard in April 1920. The side view shows clearly the way in which the front axle was set back, leaving the engine to project in a snout reminiscent of Berlin buses into quite modern times. (Capital Transport collection)

*Right* As yet unregistered, S 1 has been made ready for presentation to the Public Carriage Office for approval. The body is essentially an enlarged version of the K with an extra short bay in the middle of the saloon. This has been used to provide a new position in its fanlight panel for the side route number stencil. The bulb horn, looking like some elegant musical instrument of the brass family, can be seen just behind the dash, and a fire extinguisher looking much the same as others down the years is attached to the bulkhead beside the driver. S 1 joined the Metropolitan fleet, where it remained all its life. (LT Museum)

The enlarged bus had seats for 57 passengers (28 up and 29 down), including a rearward-facing bench for five across the front lower deck bulkhead. The remaining seats on the lower deck were arranged in five forward facing pairs with a longitudinal seat for two over each of the rear wheel arches. All seats upstairs were forward-facing. When it was presented to the Police they appear to have been unhappy about the rearward-facing lower-deck seats, or maybe wanted a longer section of longitudinal seating to give more space in the gangway near the door. In any event, the bulkhead seats were then removed and the rest of the lower deck rearranged to seat only twenty-six. The transverse seats were moved forward slightly and the longitudinal seats enlarged to seat three on each side. Although this reduced the capacity to 54, this was only two fewer than the figure which was later to be the standard for nearly thirty years up to the 1950s. There was to be one modification to this design during the production run. On the later bodies, the lower side panels curved inwards in a fashion which was to become a feature on all standard bodies.

S 1 went into service at Turnham Green garage, operating on route 17 between Ealing and London Bridge, on 29th December 1920. All fifteen were in service by February 1921 and were operated until the following month from Hammersmith garage, to which S 1 was transferred in January, on routes 11, 32 and 88 All were then dispatched to Turnham Green where they ran on route 88.

These first fifteen chassis were in effect enlarged Ks, presumably because that was the only way that AEC could meet LGOC's wishes on speed of delivery, but the main production run from S 16 onwards had a number of differences. They were heavier in construction and had the larger A108 four-cylinder 5.1 litre engine rated at 35 hp, although this was still smaller than the one used in the later Bs. Indeed, the S was never to be renowned as a sparkling performer on the road. The original fifteen were soon modified to the same mechanical standard, the work being completed by May 1922.

The first of the production S-type buses to arrive was S 17, on 15th June 1921 and this was licensed at Merton for operation on route 88 on 6th July. Deliveries then continued at a rate varying from six to eighteen a week until the first order for 250 was completed in April 1922. There was then a three-month pause until July when deliveries were resumed and continued to flow until the last three were licensed for service in August 1923. The rate of delivery was rather erratic, with a peak of thirty-eight a week achieved in March 1923, contrasting with three a week in February. It was only at this late stage in post-war affairs that the total number of buses licensed for service by the LGOC at last matched the August 1914 figure of 3,286, this important landmark being passed on 8th May 1923. It is only fair to add that the 1923 figure includes 1,896 K and S types which were larger, so the carrying capacity of the fleet had passed the 1914 level some time earlier.

The new buses were used at first to replace the Ks on the busiest of the central London routes, Merton, Hammersmith and Dalston garages receiving large quantities to run on routes 88, 32 and 11. The Ks in turn went to less busy routes to replace the smaller Bs. Later in the programme Bs were replaced directly by the S and by the time they were all running, the type graced most of the important central London routes.

Further orders for the S were authorised between December 1921 and 6th April 1922 which brought the total of double-deckers on order to 850, in addition to the fifteen prototypes. The supply of bodywork, which included the spares float, was shared between the LGOC itself (260), Brush (1), Christopher Dodson (150), Ransomes (31) and Short Bros (415). There were also thirty single-deckers, which will be described later. Soon after the S went into production, the LGOC opened its new overhaul factory at Chiswick and all bodies built by the LGOC from July 1922 onwards were assembled at the new works.

The proposal to set up a Central Overhaul Depot had been recommended to the General Board on 6th May 1920 by the Manager for Maintenance, following a favourable report from consultants Kendal, Palmer and Tritton. The proposal was approved by the Board on the basis that, initially, the depot would cover the work of only half the garages but in the event this proved to be a short-lived precautionary decision. Approval was also given to the purchase of land at Chiswick and the construction of the works went ahead almost immediately, enabling them to start functioning as soon as August 1921. Over the next twelve months Chiswick Works (as it came to be known) gradually

built up to full production. It brought together in one place all the facilities needed for the major overhaul of the company's buses which had been carried out until then either at individual garages or, for major work, at AEC's Walthamstow factory. The factory was very advanced for its day, being designed around an early example of flow-line operation, a concept more famously associated in the public's mind with Ford's Works at Dagenham built nearly ten years later, and one which was to reach its culmination for bus overhaul at Aldenham Works thirty years later. It was claimed that this process reduced the length of time taken to overhaul a bus from sixteen to four days, which effectively increased the number of buses available for service by 3½ per cent. There were also considerable cost savings in manpower input. In time Chiswick also took over the body building work from North Road (Holloway) and Seagrave Road (West Brompton) works, the training school moved there from Milman's Street Chelsea and associated work, such as licensing of vehicles and the manufacture of destination and route boards were brought onto the new site too.

Later deliveries of the S had an improved body style with the rocker panels curving inwards, setting a fashion which was to prevail for over thirty years. S 493 would not have had one of these bodies when new but had been fitted with one at one of its overhauls before being photographed at the time-honoured Kensal Rise station stand. (W. Noel Jackson)

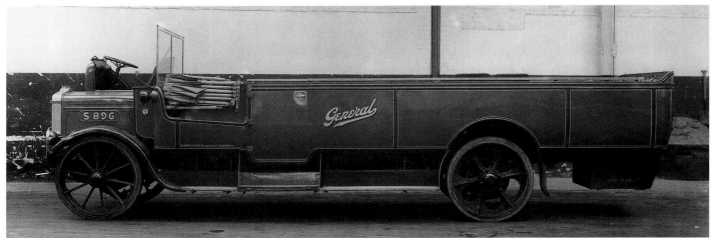

One of the 'rogue' vehicles numbered in the S series was S 896 which started life as a lorry but received this char-a-banc body in June 1924. It was photographed with its hood folded down into the area between the bulkhead and the hinged entrance door. It was mounted with a double-deck body in May 1927 (London's Transport Museum)

Three months after the last of the orders for S-types was authorised, on 6th July 1922, Lord Ashfield decreed that no further orders should be placed for existing types, including the S, because work was then in progress at AEC on a new type. This was to materialise as the NS. The edict did not prevent the fleet numbers drifting above S 895 because Chiswick built up another seven chassis between June 1923 and May 1924, of which three were double-deckers (S 897–899), one a single-decker (S 901), and two were lorries (S 896 and 902). The other (S 900) may also have been a lorry but no record of its history has come to light. S 896 was later fitted with a char-a-banc body in June 1924 but was to finish life with a double-deck body which was fitted in May 1927.

While these important improvements were being made to the double-deck fleet, single-deckers were not being neglected. These were not a major element in the fleet at the time as it was the company's policy to run double-deckers wherever they could be accommodated. However, there were some busy routes which were confined to single-deck operation either because of overhead obstruction or because of weight restrictions or because they traversed steep hills deemed unsafe for double-deckers. The company was also looking ahead to the possibility of opening up new routes in the outer areas using single-deckers in the development phase of operation. A prototype body based on the contemporary K-type, with 26 forward-facing seats, was built by the LGOC at the end of 1920 and mounted on the chassis of B 4900, in place of its double-deck body. Instead of the large indicator boards which had been carried on the roof at the front and back of the pre-war vehicles, these had a roller blind for the destination and intermediate points at the front only. In line with

Prototype single-deck B 4900 posed with a destination blind for north London route 41 but a route stencil for the 80A from the southern extremity. These were the first LGOC buses to have roller blinds instead of boards at the front. (London's Transport Museum)

the new practice adopted on the post-war double-deckers, there were no side route boards, instead there was a route number plate mounted centrally one on each side of the roof, as well as the customary stencils hanging from the front canopy and at the back.

The successful operation of the prototype led to an order being placed for another 74 which were mounted on type-7 chassis whose double-deck bodies were put in store, but the company does not seem to have had a clear idea of what its needs were as subsequent events were to show. These 74 replaced 61 older Bs, 47 twenty-seaters and fourteen sixteen-seaters at Athol Street (route 108), Chelverton Road (79), Holloway (routes 41 and 111), Plumstead (99), Streatham (109) and Tottenham (41). A matter which seems to have been overlooked was that routes 41 and 111 crossed railway bridges at Crouch End Hill and Crouch Hill both of which had weight restrictions for which the new buses were too heavy. The vehicles at Holloway and Tottenham therefore had to be withdrawn and replaced by fifteen resuscitated pre-war 20-seaters. This episode had an interesting companion event, according to

*The Times* of 26th May 1921. This recorded that the LGOC and two drivers were summoned for running double-deckers over the GNR bridges at Muswell Hill and Crouch End. The company had done this because the route had become very busy but had apparently overlooked that when full they would exceed the weight limits. The LGOC was fined £4 and the drivers 10s each, the company promising to return to single-deck operation. Some of the unused 26-seaters were used to open up new routes 93 (Uxbridge to Hounslow), 112 (Kingston – Esher – Hersham – Weybridge) and 115 (Kingston to Guildford) and for three route extensions (79 Church Cobham to Byfleet, 99A Erith to Crayford, 109 Penge to Sydenham) but this still left a surplus. Four were found a home with National but the remaining eight got their double-deck bodies back.

Within a matter of months, between January and June 1922, another eighteen 26-seat bodies were built and mounted on older chassis. These were fitted with more powerful engines and most were used on new outer London routes but five were sent to National to join the other seven already on

loan. Even before the last of these had been delivered, in May 1922, alterations were made experimentally to one of the earlier 26-seat bodies to make it lighter, its seating capacity being reduced to twenty. The same type of modified body was then fitted in November 1922 to six earlier chassis which had been lengthened for the purpose. Between then and the end of 1923 no fewer than forty more were treated in the same way and the ranks of twenty-seaters expanded even more by the addition of eight new bodies. These were of a slightly different design which had inward curving lower panels, instead of the straight sides which had been normal until then. This brought the total of twenty-seaters to 55, many of which had been needed for substantial increases in frequencies on routes 41 and 111 and for new route 110 (Finsbury Park to Golders Green).

Of the depleted 26-seater fleet, six were lent to Thomas Tilling between April and November 1922 for operation on route 71 (Croydon to Lewisham via Beckenham) from Croydon garage, foreshadowing a more enduring arrangement on route 109 which was to start in 1924.

B 442 was one of the 46 single-deck Bs built between November 1922 and the end of 1923 which used earlier chassis and had the new style of body with inward curving rocker panels. This rear view at Grove Park Station shows the platform arrangement and demonstrates the problem presented to boarding passengers by the high steps. (The Omnibus Society)

While the LGOC were indulging in these costly and untidy comings and goings, they were already working on the next generation of single-decker which would replace many of the larger Bs during the early autumn of 1922. An experimental 32-seat body was built for S 265 at Farm Lane, some time between December 1921 (when the chassis was delivered to the factory) and 14th March 1922 when it was submitted to the Noise Committee. The body was similar to the lower deck of the double-deck body but with the saloon extended the full length to contain the entrance, platform and six extra seats. The unladen weight was only 5cwt less than the double-decker, which shows how little weight was represented by the seating and side panelling of the open upper decks. It went into service at Kingston on route 115 on 3rd April. Thirty-four similar bodies were built between July and October but these were thirty-seaters, presumably because as many as six seats in the rear extension had proved impracticable in service. Their numbers were scattered through the S series between 303 and 531, except for one interesting oddity, S 9, which was an overhauled chassis which happened to be available when the new bodies were being built. Most of these buses were used to replace the 26-seat Bs at Athol Street, Kingston and Streatham and to operate the new Chiswick local route 55 (Acton to Chiswick, Grove Park) based at Acton garage. Nine, including the prototype S 265, were sent to National to operate on new or extended routes N8, N13, N14, N15, N15A and N16 which started that summer.

One single-decker built at this time, S 327, was of unusual interest in having an experimental 30-seat body designed for one-man operation. It was built in the summer of 1922 and delivered to National on 11th October, when it received the Hertfordshire registration NK4473. It was returned to Chiswick on 17th November and then went for a spell with East Surrey between 1st and 31st December. The experimental body was then removed and it was fitted with a standard S-type 30-seater instead. It did not return to National but on 23rd August 1923 was allocated to Kingston and remained in the LGOC fleet where its Hertfordshire registration marked it out as an oddity.

Only three days after prototype S 265 had started running, the LGOC Board authorised the purchase of another thirty, complete with sprag gear, at a cost of £1,825 each. These were delivered between April and August 1923 and were numbered between S 776 and 893. Two of these went to East Surrey (S 835 and 841) and five to National, (S 839, 855, 859, 865, 872), while the remainder continued the replacement of the single-deck Bs.

There were a few other single-deckers in the LGOC fleet which played their part in the post-war story. General kept a small fleet of vehicles for Private Hire and touring work which, at the end of the war, comprised fifteen double-deck M-type (De Dions) and four chars-a-banc. The De Dions did not operate after the war and were eventually sold in May and June 1921, while the chassis of the

chars-a-banc were used in the programme of conversions to emergency buses. The char-a-banc fleet was gradually built up again, using the Tylor chassis which had been lorry buses and a total of thirty-six had been licensed by the end of March 1922. In June and July 1922 four B-type chassis were fitted with Daimler engines and pneumatic tyres ready to receive new 19-seat char-a-banc bodies, the complete vehicles being numbered C 1–4. Only C 4 remained as a permanent member of the LGOC Private Hire fleet, the other three all being sent on loan to National. Six more were built in June 1923, using AEC YC (Tylor) chassis, four

The prototype single-deck S 265 was allocated to Kingston for a short time in 1922 before being allotted to the National Omnibus and Transport Company for operation on new route N13 in August. The body was similar to the lower deck of the standard double-decker but with a different window layout and the saloon extended to incorporate the platform area.

One of the East Surrey S single-deckers parked at the Red Deer South Croydon, showing the offside prospect of the body. The bus carries both its LGOC and its East Surrey fleet numbers S 841 and 43. The S3 normally ran to West Croydon but this picture was probably taken during the tram men's strike in 1924 when the Trade Union advised its members not to run buses over tram routes. (The Omnibus Society)

The production batch of thirty S-type single-deckers built in 1923 had the same window layout as the double-deck version and the new design of inward curving rocker panel. S 882, seen parked in a Poplar Street, was one of the batch which replaced the Bs on Blackwall Tunnel route 108 (London's Transport Museum)

C 9 was one of the six 19-seat chars-a-banc built in June 1923 on AEC YC chassis but sold in 1926 to Paragon Motors in the Channel Islands. It has an early form of windshield for the driver and a very impressive looking horn. (Ken Glazier collection)

(C 7–10) were 19-seat chars-a-banc and the other two were fitted with B-type twenty-seat bodywork for operation as one-man buses (C 5 and 6). These were all registered in Hertfordshire and were lent to National.

The arrival of the first batches of S-type single-deckers had completed the main developments in the immediate post-war period but the K and S types were far from finished. There were to be further batches of single-deckers of both classes in the second half of the decade, details of which can be found in chapter seven.

## CHAPTER TWO

# Service Developments 1918–1922

In November 1918 the LGOC was in a precarious state. During the war years the working population of London had been swollen by the needs of war work of all kinds and passenger traffic had grown by nearly one-fifth. Because of the loss of so many buses to government service the capacity General was able to offer to serve this demand was 36 per cent less than had been available in 1914. Many services had been cut or withdrawn altogether in the intervening five years, the severest cuts being concentrated on roads also served by trams. This process continued for a while after the war but it was not long before a leavening of increases began to appear among the cuts and eventually the trend began to be all one way.

Services in some areas had been expanded during the war where there was a need to meet the needs of essential workers in the munitions industry, particularly in the Woolwich area where the workforce at the Arsenal had grown from 11,000 to 65,000. Some of these services had attracted a government subsidy, a fact which was not well received by the tramway operating municipalities who did not receive any equivalent payments. These subsidies were withdrawn at the end of hostilities when the munitions industry began to be run down and the special services were then speedily dismantled. The first things to go were the special early morning, evening and Sunday journeys which had been put on to serve factories where longer working hours and Sunday working had been practised during the war years. At Woolwich, where there was the greatest concentration of such journeys, the Sunday short workings on route 109 from Chislehurst to Woolwich were cut from 17th November and early journeys on routes 21, 99, 99A, 101B (which served North Woolwich) and 109 were removed on 1st December. Other services which had been created specially for munitions workers at Woolwich were withdrawn completely. Route 92 was an interesting curiosity, as it comprised only one journey from Hammersmith to London Bridge early on Sunday mornings to connect with a specific train for Woolwich. It ran for the last time on 24th November, to be followed into oblivion a week later by routes 75A (Plumstead to Lower Sydenham) and 93 (Woolwich to Sidcup and Foots Cray). Routes 99 and 99A (Poplar to Erith/Crayford), whose strategic importance had been recognised during the war, enabling General to build additional single-deckers to operate them, were subjected to a series of cuts after November 1918 until they were withdrawn altogether on 31st March 1919. This removed buses from the top road through Upper Belvedere to Erith but only temporarily as they were to return in July 1920. The single-deck buses released by this cut were used for conversion to double-deck as described in chapter one.

War materials had been produced at factories all over London, with particular concentrations in Croydon, Hayes (Middx), Hendon, the Lea Valley, Park Royal and Watford, so there were many other areas where special services were now withdrawn or frequencies reduced. On Armistice Day itself new schedules started on routes 59, 59A and 59B (serving Croydon) and 85 (serving Kingston Vale), which reduced frequencies by between sixteen and forty per cent. On 14th November, special evening journeys on routes 16 and 142 were withdrawn and further withdrawals followed on 17th and 25th November. The dismantling of special wartime measures continued into 1919 with the withdrawal of route 11A journeys between Hammersmith and Park Royal and the special journeys on routes 101 and 142.

The potentially lethal combination of solid tyres and the slimy surface of Farringdon Road tests the skills of the driver of B 967 as he threads his way between the street market and lorries horse-drawn, steam-powered and motorised. The Metropolitan Cartage Company lorry on the left is towing an old horse cart, an interesting example of motive power in transition. Route 63 was one of the early post-war new routes and re-introduced buses to Honor Oak in September 1919. (London's Transport Museum)

By the end of 1918 a few extra buses were becoming available, some of them released by the cuts just described. The privilege of being the first service to see an increase went to route 8 where the frequency was given a modest uplift of two buses an hour from 2nd December. Route 103 (Cubitt Town to Blackwall Tunnel) got an even more puny increase on 18th December. Similar small advances were made during the next couple of months but anything more had to wait for the thin trickle of new and relicensed buses to build up to a useful total. By early February the fleet size had increased by 63 and this enabled service increases of real substance to be started, the first being on LGOC/Tilling joint routes 36/36A, on 10th February. Route 36A (West Kilburn to Grove Park) was rerouted to start from Kilburn, thereby providing a useful boost of four buses an hour through Maida Vale, while the service on route 36 (West Kilburn to Hither Green) was doubled in frequency. This needed no fewer than thirteen extra buses. Another five were spent on giving a boost to route 68 (Tulse Hill to Chalk Farm).

A fortnight later on 24th February, by which time the fleet had grown by nearly a hundred, the first weighty programme of improvements went into operation. Two substantial routes were reinstated, one rerouted and eleven were strengthened. Route 35 had not operated on Mondays to Saturdays since 5th August 1914, the bulk of its route being covered by the 35A. It now returned in extended form running from Walthamstow (Wood Street) to West Norwood (Rosendale), the route south of Loughborough Junction following the tram route through Wanless Road, Milkwood Road and Herne Hill. The

other route to be reinstated was the 45 (Kings Cross to Clapham Common) which was closely associated with the 35 as the section between Elephant & Castle and Clapham Common had been replaced by the 35A when the 45 was withdrawn in 1917. These changes represented a considerable increase in the service along Walworth Road, as well as lesser improvements over the rest of the routes. The altered route was the 34, which was withdrawn between Brixton and West Norwood (Rosendale), being replaced in part by the 35, and extended instead to Streatham Common adding another eight buses an hour to Brixton Hill and Streatham High Road.

Another important reinstatement came on 17th March when route 73 re-appeared, running from Highbury Station (extended from its pre-war Kings Cross terminus) to Barnes (Red Lion). Twenty buses were needed at Mortlake to provide the 7½ minute service. The introduction of new Monday–Saturday route 80 on 10th March 1919 between Charing Cross and Belmont not only provided a small boost to route 88 between Charing Cross and Mitcham but was also the first post-war example of expansion into new areas. Belmont had been served at weekends for some years but on Mondays to Fridays for only two weeks in 1916. This was therefore the first time a sustained all-year-round Monday–Saturday service had penetrated the area south of Mitcham. As Sunday services did not normally need extra buses above the peak requirement, it was possible to make improvements to them more quickly and fourteen more routes were strengthened during the rest of March, when improvements to Monday–Saturday services were slowed down awaiting more vehicles.

Another two important reinstatements came at Easter, when route 74 (Putney to Camden Town) reappeared on 20th April after an absence of two years, followed two days later by a Monday–Saturday service on the 27A which was virtually an extension of part of route 27 from Twickenham to Teddington. A Sunday service to Hampton Court had been running since 13th April. These coincided with the introduction of the first peacetime summer programme, an event of some significance because, although there had been summer Sunday special services and extensions throughout the war years, these had been on an increasingly diminishing scale whereas those for 1919 were a good deal more substantial than in 1918. Sunday services which had not operated in the 1918 season included two new operations, a revised version of route 32 (Trafalgar Square to Hampton Court) and an entirely new 112 (Cricklewood to Hampton Court). Other long-lost Sunday services which were now reinstated were: route 81 (Hounslow to Windsor), 105A (Ealing to Leatherhead), 117 (Heston-Hounslow Station to Egham) and 120 (Finsbury Park to High Beach). New summer extensions were: route 15 from Forest Gate to Wanstead Flats and 43 from Brixton to Kenley. Several other routes had operated for a much shorter season in 1918.

Route 35 was restored between Walthamstow and West Norwood in February 1919 but later exchanged numbers with the 35A. This happened in two stages, the West Norwood route being withdrawn in February 1920, re-appearing as a limited supplementary from Liverpool Street in March 1921 and then extended to Walthamstow in May 1921. B 273 is on the latter version. (The Omnibus Society)

After a gap of three years, a Monday–Saturday service was restored to the Whipps Cross–Woodford road from 4th June 1919 when route 38A became daily (its weekend service continuing to Epping Forest). B 1418 is on the stand at The Castle in Woodford, one of the many public house forecourts used as terminals. (Photomatic)

The service to Dorking had survived throughout the war, although on Sundays only until May 1915 when the 107A became daily. B 2609, like most buses on the route, was supplied by the Tramways (MET) Company from Streatham garage. (Ken Glazier collection)

With the second part of the summer programme on 25th May 1919, the seasonal extension of route 88 to Kew Green was reinstated and the 112 was extended to start from Golders Green. Further additions took place in June and July when route 27A was extended to Hampton Court on Saturday afternoons, the 74 to Wimbledon (Saturday afternoons), 74A to Epsom and 74B to Belmont (both Saturdays and Sundays), 103 from Blackwall Tunnel to Chingford and the 117 was diverted and extended to Virginia Water. There was also a new 103A from Cubitt Town to Epping Forest (Warren Wood House) and a 116 to the same point from Cricklewood. Also resuscitated were the 155 (Golders Green to Hatfield) and, from 3rd August, 175 (Hounslow to Burnham Beeches). Further additions were made to the seasonal operations as the summer wore on and by the end of the season the following had joined the list: 118 (Elephant & Castle to Godstone), 123 (Greenwich to Sidcup), 151 (Woolwich to Chislehurst) and 176 (Finsbury Park to Wormley).

The flow of new or emergency buses was now beginning to reach substantial proportions, helped out from the beginning of June by the lorry buses, so that no fewer than 462 additional buses and lorries became available for service between 1st May and 31st July. More routes were reinstated, many routes were able to enjoy increased frequencies, some routes were extended to augment others and there were more new routes. One of these was the 44 which ran from King's Cross to Victoria via Woburn Place, Covent Garden (Long Acre), Leicester Square and Piccadilly from 28th May 1919. Another, which started on 4th June, was the 20 which ran from Ladbroke Grove to Ebury Bridge, following the 15 to Queens Road (now called Queensway), then Bayswater Road and Park Lane. Routes reinstated included the 1 (Kilburn to Tower Bridge, with twelve buses), on 4th June, and National Steam service 65 needing fifteen buses for its route from Putney to Stroud Green, a modified amalgam of the previous 65 and 65A (14th July). The

extensions included route 36A from Kilburn to North Finchley via West Hampstead and Golders Green (renumbered 39), 59 Croydon to Kenley and 73 from Barnes to Richmond. The pace then eased as the first rush of deliveries of new or renovated buses were fulfilled but this did not prevent the even more substantial route 5 (Clapham Junction to South Hackney) which needed twenty-four buses, starting on 6th August.

Buses were not the only things that had been requisitioned for war service; twelve LGOC and two Tilling garages had also been closed. The Government now began to release these properties and the first to be re-commissioned was Upton Park, on 28th May 1919, initially to operate routes 9 and 23. Twickenham followed on 4th June and was soon running buses on routes 27, 33 and 79. At the end of the same month, 25th June, Tottenham resumed operations on route 76, followed by Camberwell (9th July – routes 10 and 40A) and Hounslow (30th July – 105 Mon–Sat and 81 Sundays). When Clayhall (known then as Old Ford) re-opened on 9th July it was earmarked as a base for the operation of lorry buses, the routes allocated being the 23, 56 and, later, the 103. It was the only garage to have an exclusive allocation of lorries. It closed again on 11th August 1920 when its buses were transferred into the newly enlarged Dalston. Shepherd's Bush also re-opened on 9th July but in rather curious circumstances as its sole purpose at the time was to provide somewhere for route 11 to terminate, in place of The Lawn at Shepherd's Bush Green. It did not

resume its operational role until 4th July 1923. When Catford (AN) re-opened on 8th October 1920, it was occupied by Tilling buses which had been transferred from Lewisham, hence the new code TL (Tilling Lewisham). Plumstead opened its doors again on 19th November 1919 but Crayford had to wait until 10th August 1921 when route 99 was restored. Farm Lane (Fulham) and Kilburn LGOC garages and the Tilling premises at Acorn Street and Victory Place did not re-open.

Summer Sunday route 155 between Golders Green and Hatfield 'The Dray Horse' had operated for a couple of summers during the war but had not run since 9th July 1916 when it was re-instated on 29th June 1919. (Ken Glazier collection)

A daily service came to the stretch of road between Surbiton and Hook on 16th July 1919 when a Monday–Saturday service was introduced on route 105A. Unlike the summer Sunday service which ran from Ealing Broadway to Leatherhead, this started from the 105 terminus at Argyle Road, where Tramways (MET) Omnibus Company B 737 is parked.

The section of road through West Green between Turnpike Lane and Tottenham was served by an extension of single-deck route 41 to Tottenham (Swan) from 20th August 1919, closely followed by a further diversion to Tottenham Hale on 10th September. By this time, inspired perhaps by the delivery of the first K, the LGOC felt itself to be in a strong enough position to stretch out beyond its main core of operations and reinstate the Watford – Stanmore – South Harrow route which had been a war casualty. It had borne the number 173 but returned as 26, with a Sunday variant 26A which took the direct route from Bushey Heath to Harrow Weald. Two other routes were restored on the same day (10th September). The 46A mostly strengthened other routes, running between Kensal Rise (Cricklewood Sundays) and Elephant, but taking the route via Kennington Lane between Vauxhall and Elephant which had not seen a bus for three years. The 97 ran from Ealing Broadway to Northfields via Eaton Rise, Cleveland Road and Argyle Road and restored a service to these areas, also dispossessed since 1916. Two other September rebirths were (17th) the 109 between Bromley and Penge and (24th) 67 between Stamford Hill (extended from Liverpool Street) and Raynes Park, which restored a service to sections of Kingston Road between South Wimbledon and Raynes Park. Two other areas of south-east London were given new services in this fruitful month. The section from Peckham Rye to Honor Oak got its first regular service when new route 63 started running between Gospel Oak and Honor Oak on 17th September, although there had been a short-lived special service while Honor Oak and Lordship Lane stations were closed. The route through Kirkdale between Forest Hill and Sydenham was covered from 1st October by new route 71 running between Greenwich and Sydenham (Cobbs Corner).

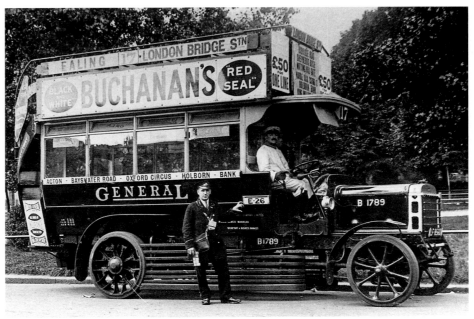

*Top* The route from Bromley to Penge had been numbered 112 before the war but had been included in a route through to Woolwich numbered 109 in 1916, which had been withdrawn in February 1919. It was re-instated between Bromley North and Penge on 17th September 1919. B 2705 was one of the three 'bentwood' single-deckers built in 1914 which survived to be bought back in 1919. (Ken Glazier collection)

*Centre* When route 67 started on 24th September 1919, it reintroduced buses to parts of Kingston Road, Merton but was later modified in various ways. By the time of this photograph at Wandsworth Common in May 1924, it was running between Stoke Newington and Merton Park. (H.C. Casserley)

*Right* Soon after the end of the Great War, the Combine adopted a policy of minimising competition between its buses and trams, a natural consequence of the acquisition of the LGOC by the Underground Electric Railways Company in 1912, but probably delayed by the war. The Shepherd's Bush to Ealing section, served by London United Tramways route 7, was also covered by route 17, which had its service over this section halved on 21st January 1920, when, in addition, the 49A was withdrawn between the two points. B 1789 is on the stand at Haven Green, Ealing. (Ken Glazier collection)

Night service 94A between Liverpool Street and Willesden was reinstated on 17th August 1920 after a lapse of just over four years. This posed photograph of K 76 was taken about three years later. (LT Museum)

Despite this impressive list of improvements bus services in London were still severely depleted at the start of 1920 and the travelling public was becoming increasingly restless about the conditions which they encountered daily. A little over 700 extra buses had been licensed since Armistice Day but the total was still nearly 1,200 short of the August 1914 figure, there were, as yet, only two of the new K-type in existence and the use of emergency lorry buses, already at a low ebb, came to an end completely after 13th January. This led to some retrench-

ment and several important routes, some only recently restored, were again withdrawn, running for the last time on 30th December 1919 (74, 91), 20th January 1920 (27A, 71, 97, 105A), 27th January (33A). Other routes were curtailed or had frequency cuts. On 14th January the 26 lost its Watford to Stanmore section and was renumbered 140, the 26A was renumbered 141 and became Daily instead of Sundays only, the 105 was withdrawn between Kingston and Surbiton, the 17 had its service halved between Ealing and Shepherds Bush

and the 49A was withdrawn between the same points. The cuts on routes 17, 49A and 105 were severe but both affected stretches of road were served by the LGOC's fellow Underground Group company, London United Tramways, with a frequent service of trams. On the brighter side, enough resources were garnered on 21st January 1920 to open up a small bit of new territory in southern suburbia when route 49A was extended to forge the link between Crystal Palace and Sydenham, continuing on from there to Catford and Lewisham.

Shortly before these events The National Steam Car Company had decided to close down its London operations and transfer its activities to Essex where it believed there was greater scope for expansion. National Steam had been operating as part of the Combine since 1914 so when the closure came in November 1919 its routes were absorbed by the LGOC who ran them from their own garages. The National garages at Nunhead and Putney were bought by the LGOC for £95,000 but as both were in need of alteration to house petrol buses and to comply with London County Council regulations, they closed when NSCC ceased operating. This work added another £19,800 to the cost of acquisition, the work at Nunhead being the more expensive to complete at £12,260. Putney Bridge garage (F) reopened on 21st January 1920, operating routes 14A and 96 but work at Nunhead (AH) took another three months and it was not until 21st April that routes 12A, 37 and 63 took lodgings there. No buses changed hands. The Shepherd's Bush (Becklow Road) garage remained the property of National in its reconstituted state as the National Omnibus and Transport Company, who in later years used it for storing coaches, but it may have continued to be used by LGOC route 12A as a terminal point for some time.

The number of buses licensed for service hardly varied in total from the time the lorry buses were withdrawn until the end of 1920. In fact, on 31st December there were twenty fewer than on 14th January because the arrival of the Ks had enabled vehicles unfit for further service to be withdrawn. At least the larger capacity of the K meant that there was the equivalent of another seventy or so buses on the road. This state of affairs continued well into 1921, sometimes dropping even further below the January 1920 figure. It was not until the production run of S-types got under way that the numbers began to show a consistent increase but even then progress was slow. Until that time, service improvements could only be given by careful husbanding of resources.

The biggest beneficiaries were those who travelled on Sundays and this was reflected in the seasonal programme which was again bigger than in 1919. Routes which had not operated in 1919 were the 119 (Chalk Farm to Chislehurst, a revised version of the prewar 159), 146 (Golders Green to Boxmoor), 152 (Stockwell to Caterham), 160 (Stockwell to Reigate) and the extension of route 85 from Kingston to Leatherhead. Routes which had longer extensions than in 1919 were the 43 which continued beyond Kenley to Caterham and the 116 which went to High Beach instead of Warren Wood House, Epping Forest.

The gradual expansion into new areas was not stalled completely. On 10th March 1920 the recently reinstated 109 was extended from Bromley through the suburban and semi-rural greenery of Bickley to Chislehurst, penetrating an area hitherto served only by summer Sunday routes or extensions. It was to be joined there on 21st July by a Monday to Saturday service on route 119, which had been running on Sundays since 2nd April, coming in from the north from Charing Cross, through Elephant, Camberwell, New Cross, Lewisham, Eltham and Mottingham. The 119 changed from being a summer Sunday only service to one running daily all the year round and in the process lost its most northerly tail between Chalk Farm, Euston and Aldwych. New route 80A similarly pushed the boundaries of daily operation south of Belmont to Lower Kingswood on 9th June 1920 and the 38B, which started on 30th June 1920, covered new ground between Buckhurst Hill and Leyton on its way to Victoria. The following month saw the return of the 99 between Woolwich and Erith, on 18th August, restoring the service from Plumstead through Upper Belvedere to Erith.

The Caterham–Godstone road got its first regular Monday–Saturday service when route 59A (Camden Town to Caterham Valley) was extended on 11th August 1920. August 1920 was a significant month for services into what the LGOC called the London Country Area because it was on 25th August that two new routes started in the Watford area (143 Croxley Green to Garston) and 145 (Bushey Station to Boxmoor), operating from a new garage at Watford (Leavesden Road). These became entangled in events which eventually led to their operation by the National Omnibus and Transport Company on behalf of the LGOC. A similar arrangement was also set up in the south using the East Surrey Traction Company as General's agent. A full account of these developments and what followed is in later chapters.

In Essex, route 26, which had started running between Stratford and Romford on 2nd February 1921 restoring the pre-war service on route 93, was now pushed on along the main road to Brentwood from 4th May 1921. Later in the year, on 7th September, associated route 26A started working between Stratford and Upminster, extending General's sphere to another area east of Romford. Further north in Essex on that day, the road from Woodford Bridge to Abridge was blessed with a new route running daily from Elephant & Castle. It was numbered 10C at first but took the more logical number 10, of which it was a straight extension, from 5th October, coinciding with the introduction of a daily service on route 10A north of Loughton to Epping. Since the earliest days of route numbering, the LGOC

had been inconsistent in its use of suffix letters, sometimes using them, as in the case of 10C to indicate an extension of the main route, sometimes as a short working and sometimes as a bifurcation. In at least one case, route 101A, it was simultaneously an extension and a bifurcation, the number being used for two different routes from North Woolwich to Lambourne End and to Ilford.

Closer into the built-up area, in the Borough of Walthamstow, route 35 was extended on 26th October from Wood Street into the newly developing area north of what is now the North Circular Road, to finish at Highams Park. A little to the west the 38 was also extended, on 9th November from Hoe Street station to the Crooked Billet, although the roads were not new to public transport as there had been trams running there since 1905.

At the opposite extremity of Greater London, a long way from any other LGOC operation, red General buses began to roam bucolic Buckinghamshire from 16th March 1921 when new route 95 began plying between Uxbridge and High Wycombe. At Uxbridge it met the Combine's London United trams from Shepherd's Bush as well as the non-Combine Metropolitan Railway. It needed only one bus to furnish the three-hourly service and this was supplied by distant Acton (E) garage. It was obviously a success because just over three months later, on 29th June, it was extended to West Wycombe and simultaneously increased in frequency to every 50 minutes, a typically LGOC awkward headway designed for schedule efficiency rather than easy recall. The four buses needed for this were now worked from Turnham Green garage. The Uxbridge web was given another strand on 27th July by a new route 93 which came up from Hounslow every 65 minutes (!) through a very rural west Middlesex. It followed the old Bath coaching road out from Hounslow to The Magpies, then turned north to serve the villages sitting alongside the Grand Union Canal in the Frays River Valley at West Drayton, Cowley and Cowley Peachey.

The direct road from Hackbridge to Wallington passing Beddington Park and Wallington Green, Woodcote Green and Foxley Lane were all newly served by route 87 from 7th September 1921. Merton ran B-type single-deckers until March 1922 when the route was reallocated to Streatham garage and later allocated new S-type single-deckers, one of which, S 875 new in 1923, is seen standing outside the garage. (The Omnibus Society)

Further south, the development of suburbia in northern Surrey prompted a number of changes in the first half of 1921. On 13th April a new route 89 started running between Charing Cross and Wallington, following route 88 as far as Mitcham and then along unserved roads through Hackbridge and Carshalton. The direct route through Wallington Green was covered from 7th September by new route 87 Streatham via Mitcham to Purley, which also put Woodcote Green and Foxley Lane on the bus map. A little further east, on 27th July, new route 49B was an extension of 49 from well established South Norwood to West Wickham, introducing Spring Lane and Shirley Road to the rattle of the B-type bus. The introduction of single-deck route 113 between Kingston and Lower Kingswood followed on 7th September. Still recognisable eighty years later as the modern route 213, the 113 brought motor buses to the route from Norbiton, through Coombe, New Malden, North Cheam and Cheam to Sutton. The availability of additional single-deckers also enabled further extremities of Surrey to be brought within the LGOC fold during 1921 with a network spreading out from Kingston. Former New Central route 79 had been running beyond its original Esher terminus to Church Cobham variously on Wednesdays, Thursdays, Saturdays and Sundays since August 1920 but this became a daily, if relatively infrequent, operation from 18th May 1921. It was pushed on further to reach

Byfleet from 29th June. The Portsmouth Road beyond Cobham through Ripley to Guildford was served by new hourly route 115 from 20th July and a week later a branch was established by route 112, which took off at Esher for Hersham and Weybridge every half-hour. A few of the special instructions to drivers on route 112 were typical of many to be found all over the system and give a fair illustration of the kind of terrain into which these buses were venturing. Walton-on-Thames Urban District Council imposed an 8-mph speed restriction between Esher Road, '…where the roadway touches the river…' (after passing Lammas Bridge) and the junction of West Carr's Lane with Queen's Road. The Company drew attention to narrow sections of road in Esher and Hersham where care had to be exercised and to dangerous telegraph poles in the vicinity of Lammas Lane. It imposed its own 6 mph restriction on Monument Hill. It was no picnic driving a 'country' bus in those days.

Eastern Hertfordshire was surprisingly neglected by General in all this expansion but this changed in May 1921 when a new route 132 was introduced between Waltham Cross and Ware in response to potential competition from Harvey & Burrows of Hertford. This started a significant chain of events involving the National Omnibus and Transport Company which are described in chapter five.

General was also much less active in protecting its eastern flanks both north and

south of the Thames and this was to be reflected in the shape of the company's area and that of the LPTB that followed. However, route 99 played a small part by having an extension, numbered 99A, from Erith to Crayford via North End on 10th August 1921. A fortnight later, the area east of Sidcup through Swanley to Farningham was opened up by a new route 21B, coming all the way through from Wood Green (Wellington) at 64 minute intervals, on what was really an extension of part of route 21 from Sidcup. At a time when long routes were common, this was one of the longest examples to be found operating daily, the through journey taking about 2½ hours at a fare of two shillings (10p).

Inner London was not entirely bereft of such developments. A number of small sections of road were knitted into the network, perhaps the most significant being a change made to route 1 on 10th August 1921. It was withdrawn from its traditional terminus at Tower Bridge Hotel and rerouted through the heart of Bermondsey through Grange Road, Southwark Park Road, Lynton Road, Galleywall Road, Rotherhithe New Road and Surrey Docks to Greenwich. This more or less replaced the horse tram route (London's last) which had been withdrawn in 1915, although the single-deck trams had gone under the railway bridges in Southwark Park Road, which the double-deck buses studiously avoided, and then via Raymouth Road.

There was a full programme of summer services again in 1921 but Lord Ashfield (Albert Stanley had been ennobled in January 1920) began to ask questions about their performance. Day to day operation was in the hands of Frank Pick who had been Commercial Manager of the Underground Group since 1912. He had been appointed Assistant Managing Director in 1921 and it is worth dwelling on the exchange between the two men that followed as it reveals several interesting aspects of the way things were done at the time. Ashfield wrote on 8th August about his experience on '...two or three recent Sundays...' when he had motored through the country, particularly the west and south-west, and had been surprised at how few passengers were being carried considering the attractive places which the routes served. He wondered if the buses were suitable for this class of traffic, or were the fares too high? As ever, Pick was ready with his answer. By some remarkable coincidence (or was it two great minds thinking alike?), during the second half of July three summer services which ran outwards from Hounslow had been extended to start from inner London points with the express intention of improving their appeal. The 81 to Windsor now started from Hammersmith but did not follow the obvious route through Chiswick and Brentford, where it would have competed with the LUT trams, preferring instead to meander through Barnes, Richmond and St Margarets shadowing the 37. The 117 to Virginia Water and a new 117A going even further out to Ascot were both extended to start back from Clapham Common, and the 175 to Burnham Beeches now came from Putney Bridge station, all again following the route through Richmond and St Margarets. Over these roads they followed route 37 which had been extended to Maidenhead two weeks earlier under the number 37A, running all the way through from Nunhead Garage every fifteen minutes on a journey that took 3 hours 24 minutes and needed a total of 28 buses. Someone obviously thought that these inner suburban areas were ripe with suppressed demand and ready for picking, because on the five routes combined the total service going beyond Hounslow was thirteen an hour and that was additional to the twelve an hour working locally on the 37/A.

When Pick told his Chairman about these changes, he was quick to point out that the services had not run at a loss, although not doing as well as they should. He also accepted that fares from town, with a break of journey, were 'quite appreciable', especially as bus fares in outer areas were more expensive. A typical example was a rail fare of 1s single to Hounslow and a further 1s 6d or 2s for the onward bus journey. Under the new arrangements the bus fares were reduced but remained quite high, a through ticket from Peckham to Virginia Water, for example, costing 3s (down from 3s 4d). Coaches, whose proprietors had not entered into restrictive agreements with the LGOC, were charging 4s 6d return, a saving of 1s 6d even on the reduced bus fare, the heaviest

competition being on the Windsor and Virginia Water roads. Pick therefore recommended that all fares should be brought down to the uniform level of 1d a mile which already applied in the central area. In the event, the new arrangements ran for only one more season, the problem being solved in later years by having special through rail-road 'excursion' tickets. Ashfield's strictures had extended to the new single-deck routes out of Kingston but Pick defended these on the grounds that they had been operating only for a few weeks.

Through ticketing of a different nature came under review a few months later. In 1920, the London County Council sought Parliamentary powers to operate buses to link up the northern and southern areas of its operations and enable its passengers, without financial penalty, to reach areas of central London to which trams were denied access. Following objections from the LGOC, the application was withdrawn but the matter did not end there as the chairman of the House of Lords Committee recommended that the LCC and LGOC should

A B-type has arrived in a bustling Wandsworth High Street from Virginia Water on the extension of summer route 117 from Hounslow to Clapham Common, introduced in 1921 in an attempt to improve its financial fortunes. The tram stop is of the standard design used by many municipalities in the early days and it is interesting to see that avoidance of clutter or simple economy has caused it to share its post with the gas-lit street lamp. (Ken Glazier collection)

consider the introduction of through tickets by bus and tram. The Council then entered into negotiations with the LGOC and a three months experiment was agreed, a number of changes being made to bus services to accommodate the new arrangements. Two variants of route 25 were introduced on 16th February 1921, both designed to connect with trams at Victoria. The 25A was an extension of route 25 beyond the LB&SC

Apart from Ellis & Company's hand cart parked outside their wine shop on the right, the only vehicle to be seen on this peaceful Sunday in East Sheen is B 1167 which still has well over two hours to go before it reaches its destination at Maidenhead.

Route 19 was given a frequency boost in June 1919 and route 39 was a completely new route which started on 16th November 1921, and ran from East Sheen to Moorgate via Wandsworth, Wandsworth Road, Vauxhall and Southwark Bridge. It received major surgery on 8th February 1922 after which it ran from Clapham Junction via Battersea Bridge, Victoria and Waterloo, serving Royal Hospital Road for the first time. K 368 on the 19 leads B 513 down Falcon Road, Clapham Junction where an LCC tram can be seen outside Arding & Hobbs department store. (Ken Glazier collection)

Railway station to Ebury Bridge, routed to pass the tram terminus in Vauxhall Bridge Road, and the 25T a new route running from the tram terminus to Oxford Circus. Through bookings were made available from Bond Street to points as far as Balham, Clapham Junction, East Dulwich (Whateley Road), Peckham, Telford Avenue, West Norwood and to intermediate stops up to those points. Other routes brought into the scheme were the 2, 16, 36 and 36A (from Park Lane, Mount Street connecting at Victoria), 11, 46 (Sloane Square via Victoria), 11, 24, 24A, 29, 29A, 76 (Parliament Square via Victoria), 25, 38, 38B, 44 (Bond Street, Piccadilly via Victoria). The facility to book through from Parliament Square via Victoria looks odd, as there were trams to all the destinations from Victoria Embankment, but they would have been useful from intermediate stops in Victoria Street. The scheme was extended on 20th July to include bookings via Charing Cross, Euston Road, Holborn, Moorgate and Southwark Bridge tram terminals. New route 20 had been introduced ahead of the new arrangements on 7th June, running from Camden Town to Moorgate Tram Terminus via a circuitous route taking in Euston Road, Holborn, Blackfriars and Southwark Bridge tram terminals. Two other new routes served the south side trams at Charing Cross (Embank-

ment) from 20th July, the 16A from Cricklewood via Marble Arch, Oxford Circus and Trafalgar Square and the 24A from Hampstead Heath (the earlier route 24A had been withdrawn by this time). At the same time, route 25T was modified to run from Victoria to Charing Cross (Embankment) via Bond Street, Oxford Street, Great Portland Street, Euston Road, Tottenham Court Road, Charing Cross, Horse Guards Avenue and Northumberland Avenue. From the northern side terminals, through tickets were available out as far as Archway, Harringay and Amhurst Park.

On 8th December 1921 Frank Pick told his Board that the experiment had been a failure and that the time had come to consider the withdrawal of the through bookings. The immediate result of the review was that a large number of the bookings were withdrawn and a few new ones introduced on 1st February 1922. The bulk were allowed to continue until the end of 1922, by which time it was clear that the scheme was not a success and the last day of issue was 31st December 1922. The special routes were not all withdrawn immediately, although the 25T had already run for the last time on 13th December 1921. The 20 had been altered on that date to run from Elephant & Castle to Moorgate and then survived right through to 27th March 1923, when route 24A also ran for the last time, the 16A having gone six days earlier. Although it is possible to see this as a bit of a charade, the scheme covered a large number of journey possibilities and was not abandoned without some attempt being made to refine it. The problem was less likely to be the way the scheme was operated than the fact that most of the journeys could be done directly by bus and there was no real incentive for people to incur the inconvenience of changing. Perhaps the most bizarre example of this was on route 24, where there was a through booking

from Charing Cross or Cambridge Circus to the Cobden Statue (Mornington Crescent Station). This would have meant getting off the bus at Euston Road, leaving it to go sailing on to the Cobden Statue only a few minutes up the road, which it would probably have reached by the time the passenger had taken a seat in the waiting tramcar. What was really needed was for trams to be allowed into the West End and the City so that they could carry their own passengers right through to their objectives and compete on equal terms with bus and Underground but this was never to be granted during the lifetime of the first generation electric trams.

At the LGOC Board meeting on 8th November, Frank Pick was able to report that 149½ miles of new road had been occupied during the summer of 1921. He claimed that this, together with developments agreed with East Surrey and National, had resulted in the 'effective occupation' of the whole of the area at present attributable to London, 'except for a small operation in the west'. Given the large gaps in the security fence already mentioned, this sounds like hyperbole but was broadly true. This had been achieved by redeployment, rather than the availability of extra buses, the extra capacity of the K and S types being used to slim down vehicle requirements of some routes to make extra buses available for others. This was underlined by an important milestone which was passed on 3rd November 1921. From that date, for the first time, the total seating capacity of the licensed LGOC fleet began to exceed the total offered at the end of July 1914, although the number of buses in service was still appreciably lower. Nevertheless, this set the scene for the next phase of development and, ironically, for the emergence on the scene of the small Independents just when the LGOC thought it was out of the wood.

*Left* There was always a small fleet of buses assigned to Private Hire work, which seems to have been a thriving business. At least five buses seem to be involved in the transport of this party from The Crown Cricklewood, the three at the front being 'Type 7' Bs 4976, 5053 and 5011.
(Ken Glazier collection)

*Below* One of the busiest days for Private Hire operations was Derby Day, when the buses doubled as grandstands while they were at the course. Of this mass of buses huddled together at Epsom, the two that can be identified are B 5128 and B 2003, behind course bookie George Hewitt's stand.
(Arthur Ingram)

## CHAPTER THREE

# Independent Heyday

The LGOC's fear that it could be faced with strong competition in the early post-armistice years while it was struggling to repair the ravages of the war, were not realised straight away. Although the number of buses licensed was not to reach parity with the August 1914 figure until May 1923, the K and S-types had more seats than their predecessors and the carrying capacity of its fleet had drawn level towards the end of 1921. As more 54-seat S-type came onto the road this gradually built up to show a sizeable surplus over 1914 and General's position by then might have seemed secure. However, there had been a considerable increase in demand for bus travel during and immediately after the war and even the extra capacity still left the standard of service well short of what the public expected. Three years of inadequate services and miserable travelling conditions had alienated the London public who were not slow to criticise the shortcomings and had little sympathy with the LGOC's difficulties, however genuine.

The long queues and heavily laden buses which characterised the London street scene in those years had been observed from the driving seat of his taxicab by a man whose name has now become an indelible part of London's transport history, Arthur George Partridge. He came to the conclusion that the situation was so bad that there was scope for others to operate in London at a profit and provide a better standard of service and

with the help of two ex-service friends he raised the capital to buy a bus. Using the services of Christopher Dodson (who supplied the body) they ordered a Leyland, the first of the LB type which had been designed specially to meet the particular requirements of London. Like most of the small proprietors who were to follow their lead, they used a hire purchase agreement to pay for it. The bus was not given approval by the Metropolitan Police when it was first presented in July, because they wanted a number of minor changes to be made, but it was eventually cleared for service on 2nd August 1922. The handsome chocolate and primrose colour scheme with gold lining-out gave the bus an air of high-class quality, and ensured that it stood out boldly from the standard red and white of the LGOC. The company was incorporated as the Chocolate Express Omnibus Co Ltd on 22nd September 1922, having run as a partnership until then. The original choice of plain 'Express Omnibus Company' had been disallowed by the Registrar because a similar name had already been registered but the simple name 'EXPRESS' was adopted as the fleet name and remained so, although the buses were nearly always known as the Chocolate Expresses.

The bus entered service on 5th August 1922 on route 11 and was the immediate target of a relentless campaign of action by the LGOC to drive it off the road. It was normally 'nursed' by two General buses, one in front and one behind which, in the early

days, ensured that it carried only a handful of passengers on each journey. Although Partridge was determined to keep going, this state of affairs, repeated day after day, could not be sustained for long without the company going out of business. All was changed by an interview given reluctantly by Partridge to the Daily Herald, which resulted in a sympathetic article describing the efforts of an ex-serviceman trying to earn an honest crust while struggling to combat the full brutal force of the Combine's tactics. It soon became a national story which cultivated a wave of public sympathy. The bad press and the public reaction persuaded the LGOC to withdraw its chasers within a few days and the Chocolate Express was left to make its own way in the world. This Partridge did with some success, although ambitions to develop a larger fleet were thwarted by lack of funds in the early years and by the stranglehold of the London Traffic Act later.

*Above* The infiltration of the London bus scene by Independents is symbolised in this photograph of Charing Cross showing the Pembroke Dennis on route 59 flanked by an LGOC S on the 177 and Tilling TS3A 896 on the 59. Behind the Tilling is LGOC K 17 on route 3, another route favoured by Pembroke, whose bus started running on the 59 on 6th September 1924. This small company survived the turmoil of the late 1920s and was acquired by the LPTB on 10th November 1933. (London's Transport Museum)

Strictly speaking, Partridge had not been the first Independent to start operating in the Metropolitan Police Area after the war, although certainly the first to stab at the heart of LGOC's operations. In January 1920, a motor engineer with premises at Waltham Abbey, Charles Waymann, started a service between Waltham Cross and Waltham Abbey using a B-type single-decker. The route was extended later to run from Enfield Town to Epping Forest (Volunteer) and at least two double-deck buses are known to have operated, a B and a Straker Squire. Most of the route was covered later by National working on LGOC's behalf, on routes N13 from Waltham Cross in about October 1923, and N30, which was run at first by Harvey & Burrows, from 7th June 1924. Waymann withdrew on 1st July 1926 and his premises in High Bridge Street Waltham Abbey were leased to National.

On 5th September 1922, Frank Pick reported to Lord Ashfield that George Shave (the Operating Manager and Chief Engineer) had come by information about pending competition fostered by 'the Leyland people' who were financing a large number of small owners to acquire buses for use in London. He also reported that some of the people interested in Samuelsons, which was a public company in liquidation, had also bought buses. He recommended that one measure that would 'justify our position' would be a general reduction in fares and this came in 1923, when the charge per mile was reduced

from an average of 1.05d per mile to 0.95d. The threat from Samuelson proved real enough, although in the event short-lived. Some of the assets of the failed company had been acquired by Sydney Hole, a former LGOC Garage Superintendent, who started a new business, trading as Samuelson New Transport Company. On 7th September 1922, he started running on General's route 97 between Northfields and Ealing (Argyle Road) but running via Argyle Road which had been unserved up to then. The buses had former charabanc chassis, two Daimler Y and one Dennis, and were mounted with

The rolling stone that started an avalanche. Chocolate Express XL7513 was the first Leyland LB1 and the first Independent bus to go into service in the inner London heartlands. Its smart turnout and neatly uniformed driver typify George Partridge's desire for quality which, on this journey at least, encouraged good business.

*Below* A nearside view of XL7513 before delivery.

34-seat bodies which had come from Thomas Tilling TTA1s, painted brown all over. The service appears not to have prospered, in the face of the strong presence on the route of General buses, and was withdrawn in December 1923.

*Below* The Primrose Straker Squire XM3527 operates a short working of LGOC route 11 pursued by General's own S 381. The prominent advertisement for the manufacturer on the side panels is notable, if unsurprising, but the double front adverts have a quite different association as LGOC chairman Lord Ashfield had an interest in The New Gallery, then recently opened in Regent Street. (Ken Glazier collection)

The next assault on the inner area heartlands was carried out by a man who had a long and distinguished career in the transport industry, Percy Frost Smith, perhaps best remembered for being the Chief Engineer at Tilling-Stevens. After leaving Tillings, he had designed a new petrol-electric chassis, and it was the first six of these, bodied by Christopher Dodson, that were to be the rolling stock for his new bus operating venture. They were painted in a blue and white livery with the fleet name 'PETROL F.S. ELECTRIC' and the first three were licensed, as 44-seaters on 30th October and 3rd November. They started running on 12th November plying two unnumbered routes between Lee Green and Liverpool Street both via New Cross and Camberwell to Victoria, then one went via Hyde Park Corner, Marble Arch, Oxford Circus and Holborn and the other via Westminster, Trafalgar Square and Fleet Street. A third route running via Piccadilly Circus and Shaftesbury Avenue started in December when the other three buses were licensed. Although these did not follow any existing route exactly, they were not to the liking of Thomas Tilling, who ensured that they were nursed unmercifully. The Frost Smith buses were moved onto route 11 soon afterwards, running between Victoria and Liverpool Street but this did not run long either and the buses were switched in January 1923 to a long straggling route running from Ealing Broadway to Farnborough (Kent). It was not long before this venture was abandoned too and FS buses were then to be found for a time running on the more lucrative sections of many different routes, before settling down on route 88. The pressures of competition were augmented by the unreliability of the petrol-electrics and the business was soon in financial difficulty. Bus operation ceased on 1st December 1924.

Two days after the first FS service began running, on 14th November 1922, another unnumbered service started, this time between Edmonton and Victoria, via Tottenham, Stamford Hill, Hoxton, Moorgate, Bank, Fleet Street, Trafalgar Square and Westminster. The new proprietor who had launched this venture was George Adams and the bus was a Straker Squire, carrying the appropriate fleet name 'PRIMROSE' to go with its cheerful yellow and white livery. Adams later gave the route the number 8, although it only waved to the LGOC route of that number as their paths crossed at the Bank junction. After some time, the Primrose bus was to find its way onto a variety of routes, including such important LGOC routes as the 6, 9, 11, 29 and 33 among many others. Adams seemed to like operating composite routes and there were many of these, perhaps the most spectacular being a Wormley to Victoria service. Primrose also ran out to Wembley for the Empire Exhibition in 1924, following General routes 6 and 8. No doubt with the needs of the Wembley traffic in mind, the Straker was joined in May 1924 by a Dennis 4-ton with Strachan & Brown 48-seat bodywork. It was painted in a red and primrose scheme that had already been applied to the other in March 1923. Primrose was to survive into the regulated era after December 1924, settling down to operate on route 69 running between Camberwell Green and Wormley.

Straker Squire ME 7240 was one of the first two buses to be owned by A.T. Bennett, which joined the two Cosgrove pioneers on 20th February 1923. The high standards set by the new company are evident in the neat uniforms of the driver and conductor and the smart appearance of the bus. The slogan displayed on the upper deck side panel makes clever use of the different spellings of 'fare' and 'fair'. (D.A. Ruddom collection)

The last company to get started during 1922 was Admiral, a name which had been chosen by its founder Bernard Cosgrove as a naval antidote to all the Generals parading the streets of London. The company was to become a force to be reckoned with, although not with Cosgrove at the helm. In time it became a model of how an independent private operator could be forward-looking and enterprising while establishing the highest standards of comfort and service for its passengers, but this was all in the future as Cosgrove's first two Admirals set sail on route 29 on 14th December 1922. They were brand new Straker Squires, a type of which he had gained some experience when working for Harvey & Burrows of Ware, who

feature in the National story in chapter five. They were smartly and handsomely finished in an appropriate navy blue livery, with brightly shining radiators and chromium-plated hub caps. The buses were housed at the premises in Willow Walk, West Green, where A.T. Bennett & Co carried on a variety of activities, including motor engineering and taxi operation. Bennett was impressed by the success of Cosgrove's enterprise and joined in as the second operator of Admiral buses with two more Straker Squires, which were licensed on 21st February 1923. Cosgrove added two and Bennett four more during the next three months, bringing the total to ten. Two more proprietors joined the association, Lyle Newstead whose first

Straker Squire (of two) was licensed on 17th May, and G.J. Heast whose single Straker went into service in June 1923. This brought the total Admiral fleet to thirteen but only for a few weeks. In July 1923, Cosgrove started a new enterprise, The Edmonton Omnibus Company, for which he bought two new Strakers. His four Admiral buses were sold, two each to Harvey and Burrows and C.W. Pallant. Newstead also went off to work on his own account in December 1923, leaving Admiral with six Bennett buses and one owned by Heast. Further expansion took place after March 1924, with three more Strakers for Bennett and one for Heast, after which Bennett decided to switch to Dennis. Heast withdrew in January 1925.

MF5397 was the fourteenth bus to join the Admiral fleet but by the time Bennett bought it there were only seven other buses bearing the name. This and two other Strakers were the last of the marque to be bought by Bennett who turned for his later requirements to Dennis. The Green Dragon, Winchmore Hill was the northern terminus of the 529 which Admiral started under the terms of the London Traffic Act in February 1925, building it up to a 12 minute headway, with additional buses supplied by up to seven other Independents. (W. Noel Jackson)

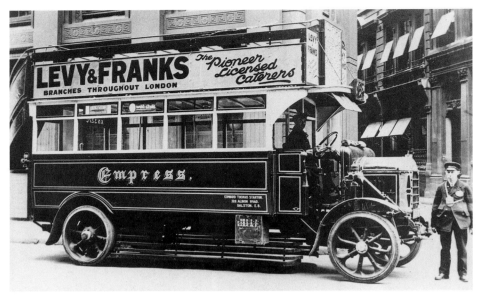

One of the companies that had a long and successful life was Empress Motors Ltd, founded by Edward Thomas Stanton, and operating from the Empress Garage at Canal Sidings, Cambridge Heath. The company's first two buses were Straker Squires, the first of which was delivered in a brown and cream livery, but this was later changed to red and white. This Straker is on route 8 but the first route operated was the 42, in March 1923, and it was the 42A and the 6A on which Empress Motors were to be found after 1924. Empress Motors operates coaches to this day from its premises at Cambridge Heath. (Ken Glazier collection)

At the end of 1922, when Admiral was still a purely Cosgrove enterprise, there were six Independents running thirteen buses in total, the largest being Frost Smith with six. The LGOC's worst nightmare became reality from the end of February 1923 onwards when the lead given by these pioneers was taken up enthusiastically by a host of new proprietors whose buses began to appear at an average rate of six every month for the rest of the year. The total then reached 75 and the number of buses owned 184 but to the alarm of the LGOC, the pace quickened to an average rate of two a week during 1924. By the end of that year another 105 companies had put 320 more buses on the road, but the introduction of the London Traffic Act stifled further development and the sixteen names added during 1925 brought the total to its maximum of 196 (625 buses). The new companies varied greatly in size and in the relative success of their enterprises. Although some were offshoots of existing businesses, including twenty-two

established coach operators and at least forty-two who were motor engineering companies or had road haulage interests, many were started by individual or groups of individual former ex-servicemen either disillusioned by their post-war working lives or unable to find suitable employment. For many of them the starting capital for their businesses was provided by the gratuities they had received when they left the Forces, topped up by helpful hire-purchase terms from manufacturers, notably the Independent's friend, Christopher Dodson. Many came from a wide range of activities with no transport connections and were therefore innocent of the complexities and vagaries of bus operation but also, in many cases, lacked basic financial or business skills. There were some with a transport background, including former LGOC drivers and conductors who were instrumental in setting up at least twelve companies, and former taxi drivers or owners, like Partridge, who were involved in fifteen.

An early example of an ex-servicemen's partnership was the X Service, started by three ex-officers, whose single khaki and red Dodson-bodied Straker Squire went into service on 20th February 1923, the first of a torrent of new operators. The company had six of its own routes but by at least April 1923 was running on LGOC routes such as the 2, 13, 31 and 84 and by January 1924 had settled onto the 29. Two of the three proprietors had left the business within a year, leaving it in the sole ownership of Lionel Punnett. He added a second bus in April 1924 but sold out in 1925 to E.E. Farwell, who unfortunately gained nothing from the sale as he was unaware of the restrictions imposed by the 1924 Act on the sale of schedules.

Similar tales could be told of many other companies whose periods of operation were sometimes spectacularly brief, sometimes fraught with financial or operational problems but often enough blessed with success for a significant number of concerns to become established and flourish. By London Independent standards some became large and prosperous concerns, others, like Partridge's pioneering operation, remained small but also flourished and continued to provide a professional service of high quality until they were compulsorily removed from the scene by the 1933 London Passenger Transport Act.

Several companies which started in 1923 were destined to claim a permanent place in the Independents' 'Hall of Fame', the first such to appear being Premier, which was started by William Allen, Augustus John Schiffer and Frederick Charles Schiffer. Three Dodson-bodied Straker Squires, turned out in a mauve and white livery and the fleet name Premier, started working between Cricklewood and Liverpool Street on 3rd March 1923. The buses were housed in a former aircraft hangar in Somerton Road, Cricklewood. The original order had been for Leylands but their delivery was delayed and Allen cancelled that order. However, when additional buses were needed, Leyland returned to favour and two Dodson-bodied examples were licensed in March and April 1923. Further growth was made possible by the intervention of three new investors who, in conjunction with Allen and the Schiffers incorporated the Premier Omnibus Company on 12th October 1923. Four new buses were added to the fleet in September-November 1923, the choice of chassis having switched again, this time to the Dennis 4-ton, of which another five were added during 1924, two being used to replace the Strakers. All had Dodson bodywork. Premier's twelve buses roamed far and wide over London in the early days with regular appearances on the 6, 9, 12, 33, 51, 73 and 142 but in the second half of 1924 they were normally on the 11, 18, 60 and 73. By this time, after a brief sojourn at Thackray's garage in Ledbury Mews, the fleet was housed at a garage in Leysfield Road, Shepherd's Bush.

Only three days after Premier's buses started work, the company which eventually

Dennis 4-ton MF3319 was the tenth bus to join the Premier fleet, being licensed on 27th November 1923 to replace the first of the three founding Strakers. The fleet eventually rose to a total of fourteen and the company also branched out into local coach operation between London and Windsor in later years. (W. Noel Jackson)

became the largest of the London Independents to survive into the LPTB era, licensed its first bus, a Dodson-bodied Leyland LB5. The City Motor Omnibus Company was formed by Walter Crook, a one-time LGOC employee but more recently Works Manager for Leyland at Kingston, and Frederick Mallender, Leyland's London Manager. Ten Leylands were ordered for the launch of the company and all entered service between 10th March and 2nd June 1923, operating from railway arches at Queens Road station in Peckham which had once housed the horse trams of the London Tramways Company. Another twelve LB5s were bought in five small batches between December 1923 and August 1925. The buses were used on all manner of routes in the early days, in true 'pirate' style, and a total of at least thirty-five routes is known to have been host to the brown and cream Leylands. However, a pointer to the future direction of the company's operations came early in 1924 when it attempted to start its own service, jointly with United, between Oxford Circus and Putney via Notting Hill Gate, Kensington and Hammersmith under the number 65, not then in use by the LGOC. It was not a success but the looming requirements of the London Traffic Act encouraged the company to try another service of its own, the 517 between Highgate and Peckham Rye which it started on 5th December 1924. This was operated jointly with United, who supplied four of the twenty buses, and heralded a period of co-operation between the two companies lasting until the LPTB stepped in nearly ten years later. Having jumped the first hurdle of the 1924 Act successfully, the company was to show its true mettle in the years of Metropolitan Police control described later.

March 1923 was obviously an auspicious month for famous names as the next operator to license a bus was a company trading as Carlton but, more significantly, incorporated, on 20th February, as Dangerfield Ltd, with Walter Dangerfield appointed General Manager for life. The first brown and white Dodson-bodied Leyland, XN3091, was licensed on 27th March and another seven arrived during the rest of 1923. They were accommodated at Dangerfield's own Mohawk garage in Harmood Street Chalk Farm, opposite the LGOC garage, and were used on routes 24, 27, 28, 29, 31 and 59. However, in its early days Carlton was best known for what has been claimed as the first substantial attempt by an Independent to operate its own route, the line chosen being Muswell Hill to Victoria. The number 4 was allocated, the same as had been used by the LGOC for a similar route in 1912 but having no relationship to the LGOC route of that number in 1923. It was one of the routes on which Dangerfield was authorised to operate under the 1924 Act, the Bassom number 285 being allocated. The fleet name most famously associated with Walter Dangerfield, 'Overground', made its first appearance on Dodson-bodied Dennis XT3927 in May 1924. This was licensed to Dangerfield himself, had a new livery of red

Leyland LB2 XN1231 was one of the first eight buses licensed by the City Motor Omnibus Company in March 1923. The Dodson body was painted in a distinctive brown and cream colour scheme, with the fleet name 'CITY' arranged in an oval medallion shape on the lined-out side panels. The battered condition of the route 9 number stencil might be indicative of its constantly being changed as the bus was moved from route to route in the early days of City's operations. (Ribble Enthusiasts Club)

The first six buses purchased by Dangerfield Ltd were Leyland LB2s with Dodson bodywork finished in brown and cream and bearing the fleet name Carlton. The sixth, first licensed on 2nd August 1923, was XO8490, seen here dressed for operation on the company's unique route 4. (Ken Glazier collection)

The famous OVERGROUND fleet name, provocatively chosen and provocatively laid out to resemble the UNDERGROUND symbol of its chief competitor, first appeared in May 1924. Among the first twenty buses to bear the name was XW3697, a Dennis 4-ton with 48-seat Dodson bodywork, painted red and cream. Licensed on 21st November 1924. It is seen three years later at Hadley Highstone on route 284A, another number specially associated with Overground. (W. Noel Jackson)

Leyland LB2 XN4292, with the almost inevitable Dodson body, was the Enterprise Omnibus Company's first bus. Painted chocolate and primrose, it entered service on route 12 on 14th April 1923 and was housed in a railway arch in Astbury Road, Peckham. Various routes were operated in the early days but Enterprise later settled down onto the 14 group. By the time it was taken over by the LPTB it owned five buses. (W. Noel Jackson)

and white and was the first of a fleet of twenty bought between then and January 1925. The Carlton fleet also expanded towards the end of 1924 with the purchase of a Leyland and three Dennises. The success of the new name led to it and the red livery being applied to the existing Carlton buses as well. The two fleets were managed as one by Dangerfield.

Among other well-known names which appeared for the first time in 1923, some of whom were to survive into the 1930s, were Chas. H Pickup, Redburn's Motor Service, Atlas, United, Prince, Cambrian, which rose to be the largest of all, Red Line and Ambassador. Some companies did not manage to keep going even as far as 1st December 1924, when the provisions of the 1924 Act were applied. Unity had a Straker Squire which was licensed on 5th April 1923 and went into service but the company had ceased trading by July 1924. F.H. Bruce formed the London Circular Omnibus Company on 8th January 1923 and applied for licences for 25 Leylands which he intended to run on eight routes, mainly in the south-western quarter. Leyland XN5034 was licensed on 17th April 1923 but the company soon ran into financial difficulties, was given notice to quit for failing to pay for petrol or rent and had its bus repossessed by Dodson before the end of May 1924. Another defaulter on hire-purchase repayments, was Sydney Moreton who had three buses running under the name 'London' from Cathnor Road, Shepherd's Bush. Moreton was apparently a sharp operator, who had indulged in a number of questionable money-making enterprises at the expense of others and was eventually charged with fraud. The first 'London' bus was a Daimler, XP7425, licensed on 4th

*Top* When the Pioneer Omnibus Company put this Thornycroft J into service in July 1923 it was the first of the type in London and had a higher seating capacity, 50, than any other Independent bus. It is seen on route 73 in Oxford Street near Marble Arch but after 1924 the company's buses were normally to be found on routes 18 and 247, where it made good profits. Pioneer survived to hand over three buses to the LPTB in December 1933. (Ken Glazier collection)

*Centre* When George Frederick Buck bought his first bus, a Leyland LB4, in December 1923, he had its Wilton body painted in a livery resembling the LGOC's and adopted the fleet name GENIAL, a device that misled General's drivers and passengers alike into thinking that it was a Combine bus. General tolerated this for a time, even accepting Genial's return tickets, but eventually it sought and was granted an injunction to restrain Buck from using the name. The bus was relabelled Buck in March 1924. Buck's second bus was named 'St George' and by the time the LPTB took over, there were three buses. (Ken Glazier collection)

*Left* The only bus ever owned by the Phoenix Motor and Omnibus Company was this Dodson-bodied Thornycroft J. It was first licensed on 31st January 1924 operating from the Brixton Motor Works in Brixton Road but later moved to Toler's garage in Lothian Road Camberwell, the home of at least sixteen operators, among them United and Pickup, where it was the only double-deck example of its marque to be housed. The run-out to Reigate on route 59 was a favourite choice for fine Sundays but the bus also ran on many other routes. (Norman Anscombe collection)

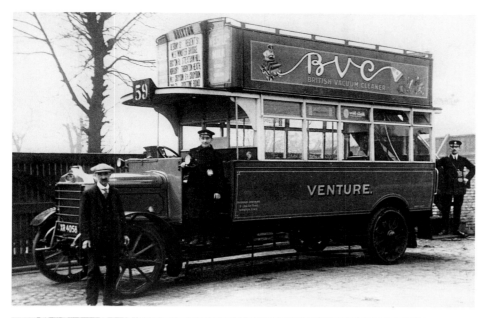

December 1923. A second Daimler followed and the third bus, XT946 was licensed in Moreton's name on 17th April 1924 and had the fleet name 'New London'. Within two months the business had ceased trading and the buses had found new homes with other Independents. CWP was the company formed by Pallant when he bought the two Admiral Straker Squires from Bernard Cosgrove in about July 1923. The association with Cosgrove continued until September 1924 when Pallant applied to operate between Victoria and Chadwell Heath but whether or not this happened is not known and CWP effectively ceased trading in October 1924. One of the Straker Squires nominally in the Premier fleet, XN513 (see page 38) was owned separately by Frederick Schiffer and a Walter Harsant. It was operated as part of the Premier fleet until 29th December 1923 but Harsant then took sole ownership and registered a new company, the Regent Omnibus Company under which banner it ran on a variety of routes. Harsant did not make a success of the venture and he went out of business in October 1924.

Of the 105 companies which started up during 1924, less than a quarter were destined to survive more than a few years. Most of the survivors were fairly small fry but operators who built up reasonably sized fleets included Renown, G.H. Allitt, Peraeque, Gordon, Westminster and Reliance. A surprising omission from this and previous lists in this chapter is the name of Birch, one of the oldest established in the industry and with a history dating back to before the formation of the mighty LGOC itself. Although the company was to blossom into one of the largest in London, at the end of 1924 it had just taken delivery of its first two new buses and its entire operational history, in this period, was confined to the regulated era.

*Top* Frederick John Nunn operated two of these Daimler Ys with Strachan & Brown 42-seat bodywork under the fleet name Venture. XR4058, the first, was licensed on 29th February 1924 and the second in April. Various routes were applied for, including the 59 which was a popular hunting ground for the Independents. The buses were kept at the Cedric Garage on Brixton Hill, a short distance south of Upper Tulse Hill. (Ken Glazier collection)

*Centre* This Dodson-bodied Dennis 4-tonner was the only bus owned by the A.A. Matthews and Ernest Vine partnership, which traded as Crest. It was licensed on 18th July 1924 and is believed to have been kept at a petrol station in Tramway Avenue, Edmonton under the nose of the Metropolitan Electric Tramways depot at the end of the road. It first ran on the 76 but later on the 69 and 73. (Ken Glazier collection)

*Left* Marcus Forno's aptly named Independent bus was another of the many housed at Toler's garage in Lothian Road, where it took lodgings in August 1924. XU4662 was a Strachan & Brown-bodied Daimler Y, painted red and white, as was the companion which joined it two years later. The number of Daimler Ys operated by Independents never rose above 33, one less than the Thornycroft J and, like the Thornycrofts, they had a short operational life in London. (Ken Glazier collection)

The public sympathy whipped up by the Daily Herald for the treatment of Arthur George Partridge by the LGOC, laid the foundation of continuing warmth towards the new operators in the early days of their growth but the unscrupulous behaviour of some soon brought first disenchantment and later outright hostility. All companies which started between 1922 and the end of 1924 operated to a greater or lesser degree as 'pirates' in the sense that they were all trying to find a crack in the LGOC network which they could exploit and were therefore inevitably 'poaching' traffic from established operations. There was always a substantial core of operators whose aims were of the highest order, who were in the business to provide a good service at a fair price, believed in fair competition and carried out their 'pirating' with a high degree of integrity. Unfortunately, there were also too many for the good name of bus operation whose sole interest was to turn a quick penny and who put high earnings far above any responsibility to passengers in their order of priorities. These were the true 'Pirates', the operators who had no compunction in ditching a load of passengers at the side of the road and switching to another destination if they saw a crowd of people wanting to travel in the other direction or on a different route. Although the abandoned passengers often got their fares refunded the inconvenience and injustice still rankled. Some conductors did not even offer this small compensation, preferring instead to mislead people into believing that their tickets would be valid on the next bus along, which of course they were not.

'Racing' was a word that came into frequent use in this period as bus drivers joined enthusiastically in the worst aspects of competition by racing each other to stops to be the first to pick up a load. It did not always stop at racing as there were some cases of drivers trying to ram another bus to push it into an obstruction or off the road altogether. These practices were not confined to drivers of Independent buses. Although there is no evidence to support the idea that any of it was positively encouraged by the Combine managements, there can be little doubt that racing, if not the more violent actions, was condoned, at least at a local level. Lord Ashfield was certainly aware of it.

A good example took place on 10th February 1923 when a passenger described an incident when he was travelling on 'one of the blue buses' (a Frost Smith petrol-electric) from Bromley to Southend Pond. It was following an LGOC bus on the 12C which was in turn following a Tilling on route 47 on Bromley Hill. The 12C is important here because it was introduced by the LGOC for the sole purpose of competing with Frost Smith's buses. The driver of the FS bus tried to pull out and overtake the General but the driver of the 12C crossed him, did not pass the 47 himself but 'zig-zagged all the way up Bromley Hill to Southend Pond', preventing the FS from passing in a most dangerous way. There were four other witnesses, one of whom said he heard the driver say 'You are

a non-union man and I'll run you down before the week is out'. In evidence the driver admitted his bus was a 'C12' (sic!), known as a 'chaser' and moved from route to route. The charge of driving dangerously was dismissed but he was convicted of wilful misbehaviour and failing to keep on the left of the carriageway, for which he was fined a total of £5 plus £4 6s 0d costs, a substantial amount in 1923. Apart from revealing the official nature of the nursing, this case also showed how the animosity was felt by individual drivers who were suspicious of non-Union staff and the motives of the operators in employing them.

There was no love lost between the two factions even when violence was not involved and workers' solidarity was the last thing on the minds of drivers who were happy to inform on others for breaches of the regulations. One example was when a Blue Bell driver reported an LGOC bus for carrying the wrong faretable. The LGOC crew had apparently been instructed by an official to switch from route 25 to route 101 'for competitive reasons' but had continued to display a route 25 faretable and route boards. Fining the LGOC driver twenty shillings (£1) and 14s 6d costs, the magistrate observed that had it not been for the presence of the Blue Bell bus, the General would have continued its journey on the 25.

Many strange and sometimes exotic fleet names were chosen by Independents one of which, Shanghai, was applied to the bus put into service in August 1924 by Evelyn Puttergill. XU5585 was a Dennis 4-tonner with Strachan & Brown body painted red and white with brown lower panels and gold lettering for the fleet name. The photograph was taken in York Road (now Way), Kings Cross after the introduction of the Bassom system, although the 73A for which it is boarded ran from Stoke Newington–Richmond. (W. Noel Jackson)

The Independents used a variety of different establishments to house their buses, ranging from rented yards, through shared purpose-built garages to premises of their own. When the partners Messrs Powell, Bray and Bunning bought their first bus in August 1923 they kept it at the premises of the furniture removal company C.L. Gooch in Chadwell Avenue, Chadwell Heath, illustrated in this publicity photograph. PU292 on the left, was that pioneer, and a special bus in its own right in being the prototype of the Daimlers that were rebuilt by Josiah Roberts of Shepherd's Bush, as mentioned in chapter 7. The other bus, a Dodson-bodied Dennis, joined the fleet in January 1925. (Ken Glazier collection)

The Police took a strong line and were pledged to take prompt action to 'nip in the bud' the tendency to revive racing and nursing as more Independents came onto the road and to do all they could to prevent the competition between companies from overstepping the bounds of legality. The Metropolitan Police Commissioner sent a letter to all plated licence holders asking them to warn staff that if they indulged in such actions, they ran the risk of conviction. Nevertheless, the atmosphere was highly charged with resentment and animosity and the bad practices became so commonplace that there was widespread concern among the public, press and public authorities. The number of convictions became so serious that the subject was raised in the House of Commons and there were many sensational newspaper stories to feed the growing public anxiety. The inevitable effect was that people started to avoid using the 'pirate' buses and preferred to rely on the stability which the Combine was desperately trying to maintain.

Some Independents tried to protect themselves by repainting their buses into General-style red but it was clear to the more responsible owners that they needed to present a united front to defend themselves against unfair treatment. They formed the Association of London Omnibus Proprietors (ALOP) which was incorporated as a company limited by guarantee on 1st November 1923 with the principal objectives of promoting, safeguarding and protecting its members' interests. ALOP also procured concessions and provided other facilities for members and supplied an arbitration service for resolving disputes between members. It was formed in the nick of time. The Metropolitan Police were unwilling to accept that the anarchic conditions on London's roads could continue and appointed its own Director of Traffic Services in December 1923. The man appointed to the post was Supt A.E. Bassom who was given the temporary rank of Chief Constable for the purpose and charged with the task of advising on how the problems should be handled. His name was destined to become part of the vocabulary of bus operation between 1924 and 1934. The Combine also had a strong interest in restoring order and stability as the Underground Group's finances had suffered severely, especially those of its tramway companies whose routes had been particularly hard hit by the competition. Lord Ashfield was in any case a strong advocate of unified management and integration and he received the support of the Transport and General Workers' Union who took the view that there was no place in London for small Independent operators.

The outcome of all this build up was the London Traffic Act which received the Royal Assent on 7th August and came into force on 1st October 1924. Its provisions covered a whole range of traffic matters but the important sections so far as bus operation was concerned were 6 and 7. Section 6 imposed a requirement on operators to deposit schedules of routes and times for Monday to Saturday operations which, once deposited, had to be observed strictly and could not be varied in any way without police approval. Sunday operations were not affected and were allowed to continue on the old basis. Section 7 gave the Minister of Transport far-reaching powers, on the advice of the London & Home Counties Traffic Advisory Committee to designate particular streets as 'Restricted', and limit the number of buses allowed to ply on them. The L&HCTAC had a number of responsibilities relating to road traffic and its membership included representatives from a whole range of interests including, at first, the Independent bus proprietors. However, their representative, F.W. Prowse, Managing Director of the Fleet Omnibus Company, was to resign in May 1925, five months after the main provisions of the Act had been activated, in protest at the way in which the Independent sector was being treated. The effective date of operation of the new system was 1st December 1924, after which the fortunes of the Independents changed materially, as chapter eight will show.

A mounted policeman controls heavy traffic at Ewell on its way to the Derby at Epsom, with public transport well represented by buses, chars-a-bancs and a large number of taxis. He seems unaware of, or does not care about, the supplies of champagne stacked precariously on the roof of the car in the foreground! The bus nearest the camera, a Straker Squire first licensed on 5th March 1923, is a Skylark owned by Arthur Herbert Ansell, whose normal hunting ground was route 11. Skylark's second bus, a Dennis, was licensed exactly a year later and the fleet eventually rose to five buses.

## CHAPTER FOUR

# General Spreads Its Wings: The South

Before 1914 the LGOC had not operated regular daily services much beyond the immediate built-up area of London, although summer services and extensions had operated, mainly on Sundays, to many parts of London's country. The exceptions to this general rule were the 81 to Windsor, 84 to St Albans, 105 to Watford and 110 from Slough to Maidenhead. In 1914 the company had entered into an area agreement with the East Surrey Traction Company which established the boundary between the two companies' spheres of influence as the so-called 'valley road' from Guildford to Sevenoaks (later immortalised as the A25). The LGOC would not operate south of that road and East Surrey would not go north of it, except that they were allowed to run from Redhill to both Merstham and Kingswood, from Westerham to Westerham Hill, Godstone Green to Caterham and on any roads within the Borough of Reigate. This was later extended to include an agreement with Aldershot & District Traction under which the Guildford to Dorking road was reserved to that company, the Dorking to Reigate road to East Surrey and Leatherhead to Guildford to the LGOC. One early outcome of the agreement was the introduction of a daily service on route 160 between Stockwell and Reigate via the main Brighton Road to Merstham and then Wray Common. Further development was stalled by the war and nothing more happened until November 1919.

The 1914 area agreement had come about in the unlikely circumstances of a dispute about the purchase by East Surrey of new Daimler buses, during which the company's founder and Managing Director, Arthur Henry Hawkins, was impressed by the LGOC managers he met when putting his case. This led to meetings with Ashfield and Pick, at their invitation, to discuss service issues, during which Arthur Hawkins's attitude swung from outright hostility to the Underground Group as a potentially ruthless competitor to one of warmth and admiration for the two men. The details are outside the scope of this book but it is important to an understanding of later events to know that Hawkins obviously recognised Ashfield and Pick as soul mates, with a similar approach to running a bus business. In particular, Hawkins was every bit as ruthless in his approach to competitors. It was this aspect of his character which led him to approach Frank Pick in November 1919, by which time the 1914 Agreement had run its course, to suggest an even closer working relationship. He was concerned about the potential for competition in the fallow area between the Metropolitan Police boundary and the valley road, which might pose a threat to his company, and suggested to Pick that East Surrey should develop routes in the area on behalf of General. Although the approach was welcomed, the time was not right to put the idea into practice because the LGOC was fully stretched in rebuilding its main London business and had no spare resources available for adventures further out.

Dorking High Street in the late 1920s, by which time the LGOC writ ran far to the south of London, with two East Surrey NSs on route 414 and motor cars of various makes and quality parked freely and randomly along the pavement edge. Although there is no Bus Stop, the passengers for the 414 to Horsham know that the place to wait is by the elegant bandstand, where the motorists have thoughtfully left a gap. (Ken Glazier collection)

East Surrey at work deep in its own territory, designated 'The Traction Company's Area' in the Agreement with the LGOC. This unidentified B-type is at Newdigate 'Six Bells' on route S26, which started running from there to Reigate on 26th March 1923 following the acquisition of Reigate Garages Ltd and its two small buses, a Garford and a Thornycroft.

A formal agreement was subsequently negotiated, the terms were agreed on 16th June 1921 and the Agreement was signed on 7th July. The three areas defined by the 1914 agreement were continued and were now named as 'The London Area', 'The London Country Area' and 'The Traction Company's area' with broadly the same rights of operation as before but with important extra provisions relating to the London Country Area. In that area and across the boundary between that area and the London Area, East Surrey was afforded the right to run bus services on behalf of the LGOC and its associates by written agreement between the parties. It was also given the right, again subject to written agreement, to run services into the London Country Area from its own area, these being designated joint services. For services operated on its behalf by East Surrey, the LGOC undertook to provide the buses and any other facilities necessary.

East Surrey had already started to work in its own right into the London Country Area a year before the Agreement was signed when it introduced its first new post-war service apparently with the informal agreement of General. This ran from Redhill to Epsom via Lower Kingswood and Tadworth and

started on 5th June 1920. It was later absorbed into the Agreement network and numbered S6 on 16th November 1921. Another venture in June 1920 which anticipated the agreement was a plan to take over the Dartford to Sevenoaks route operated by W.P. Allen. This was a joint effort by the two companies and the LGOC supplied four B-type double-deckers to East Surrey for the operation. However, Allen withdrew from the negotiations and continued to work the route so the borrowed buses were returned. Still determined to infiltrate the area, Hawkins negotiated instead to take over the Autocar service between Sevenoaks and Farnborough on behalf of the LGOC and this started on 26th May 1921.

Once the agreement was signed, developments followed helter-skelter. The Sevenoaks route was extended to Bromley North on 6th August with the brand new number S2, and a week later a new S2B was introduced between Sidcup and Farnborough via Green Street Green. On 16th August three major new routes fanning out southwards from West Croydon were inaugurated, the S3 to Sevenoaks via Chelsham and Westerham, S4 to Edenbridge via Chelsham and Limpsfield and S5 to Redhill via Purley. There were no East Surrey garages in the areas served by routes S2, S3 and S4 and it was necessary to establish outstations where the buses could be kept. Those for the S2 and one of the S3s used the Railway Hotel, Sevenoaks, those for the S4 and the remaining S3 the Hoskins Arms at Oxted, continuing an association with the

tavern trade dating back to the stage coach era. Three months later, on 16th November, the S6B appeared, running from Epsom to Guildford via Leatherhead, replacing the LGOC 85 between Leatherhead and Guildford, and on the same day the Epsom–Redhill route was given the number S6. The buses for the S6B were kept overnight at the Swan Inn, Leatherhead. East Surrey also took over the responsibility for running the winter service on the southern section of route 59B from 19th October 1921, by means of an S5B between West Croydon and Reigate via Wray Common.

After a five month pause there was another spate of changes on 14th April 1922, which brought East Surrey buses deeper into north-west Kent and saw the first example of a 'joint' route running across the valley road divide. New route S7 ran from Sidcup through Bexley, Crayford, Dartford and Wilmington to Crockenhill, covering roads between Dartford and Swanley once served by W.P. Allen whose route had not run for nearly a year. The three buses which operated this service were kept in the yard of the 'Lullingstone Castle' public house at Swanley. The first 'joint' service was an extension of the S5 southward from Redhill to Crawley and then either to Handcross or to Horsham via Faygate. Two existing routes were pushed in the other direction, further into the Metropolitan area, the S6 being extended from Epsom to Kingston and the S6B from Epsom to Sutton via Cheam. East Surrey's own routes were numbered into the S series from this date but remained outside the agreement and are not directly relevant to this account. The S6B was given the more appropriately distinctive number S8 on 5th June. Two more routes were added on 3rd June.

Another joint route, S9, filled one of the remaining gaps south of Croydon running from West Croydon through Purley and Caterham-on-the-Hill to the London Country Area boundary at Godstone, continuing to East Grinstead and Forest Row, then to either, Hartfield or Chelwood Gate. The section of General route 59A between Caterham and Godstone, which was the latest variant of a service that had operated since April 1920, was withdrawn on Mondays to Saturdays, severing the link through to Camden Town! Caterham-on-the Hill does not appear to have had a bus service of any description before 1920, despite being a well populated area and the home of the Guards, perhaps because it was perched on top of the North Downs accessible only by dauntingly steep hills. On 22nd November that year the Caterham Motor Company had started two routes running up Church Hill from Caterham Station to Caterham-on-the-Hill and to War Coppice via Stanstead Road. However, they appear to have petered out again within a few months, leaving the way clear for the more sustained service now provided by East Surrey. The buses for the S9 were stabled at two outstations, the Tally Ho! public house at Godstone and at the Crown Hotel, East Grinstead. The other new route was the S10, which ran along the valley road from Reigate through Godstone and Oxted to Westerham where it struck north up the arduous 1 in 9 of Westerham Hill to enter established LGOC territory at the top. It continued to Bromley North, replacing the Mondays to Saturday service on the 136, which was withdrawn. Although some of the buses for the S10 were supplied from Reigate garage, others were kept at The Crown, Westerham.

The increasing volume of service being provided in the London Country Area was beginning to put a strain on the outstations, especially those in Kent which were remote from the engineering facilities available at Reigate. The yard of the Railway hotel at Sevenoaks had become a virtual garage with its own engineer in charge and the LGOC therefore gave priority to finding a suitable site in the area for a purpose built garage. Authority was given on 6th October 1921 for the purchase of a piece of land in London Road, Dunton Green, just north of the bridge over the Westerham branch of the former South Eastern and Chatham Railway. A building suitable to house twenty buses was erected at a cost of £6,500, opened in April 1922 and took on the task of running routes S2, S2B and S3.

W.P. Allen finally withdrew from bus operation in Kent on 1st September 1922 when he handed over his Dartford–Farningham–Sevenoaks route to East Surrey. It was given the number S1, which had presumably been sitting in a cubby hole somewhere waiting to be dusted off ever since the first abortive attempt at take over by ESTC in 1920. Three of the buses for the S1 were

*Top* B 2126 was sent on loan to East Surrey on 2nd September 1921, three weeks after route S2B started running between Sidcup and Farnborough. (The Omnibus Society)

*Above* One of the three routes that started on 16th August 1921 was the S4 between West Croydon and Limpsfield, on which single-deckers were operated. The photograph appears to feature the maintenance crew and a manager, unhelpfully posed to hide the exact identity of the vehicle but it is one of the six AEC YC former lorry bus chassis on which LGOC mounted new 28-seater bodies. (Ken Glazier collection)

kept at the Lullingstone Castle, Swanley and the fourth at Dunton Green garage, the bias towards Swanley being dictated by the weight of service which was predominantly between Dartford and Farningham with only four journeys continuing to Sevenoaks.

Within only eighteen months East Surrey buses had become a significant part of the north Surrey and West Kent landscape, particularly in Croydon, and most of the major routes between the North Downs and the valley road had been occupied. A measure of the extent to which East Surrey had expanded northwards is that by the end of 1922 nearly sixty per cent of its buses were working on behalf of the LGOC.

The forty-nine buses needed for all these routes were supplied, under the terms of the agreement, by the LGOC. There were twenty-nine standard B-type double-deckers built before the war and therefore between eight and eleven years old, and twenty former lorry buses, AEC YC type ex-War Department vehicles which had the more powerful 40hp Tylor engine. Six of the YCs had new 28-seat LGOC single-deck bodies and the other fourteen had second-hand B-type double-deck bodies. The buses were painted in East Surrey's own royal blue and white livery but all those delivered after April 1922 were painted in General red with only the East Surrey fleet name to identify the different operator. At about the same time the ESTC Board took the decision to adopt the same red livery for its own buses, no doubt in the interests of economy although it might have appeared to some that the LGOC had taken over the company.

Four of the single-deckers were needed for routes S3 and S4 because they ran via the Red Deer and Sanderstead Road which was crossed by a low bridge carrying the LB&SCR main line. No doubt their 40hp engines were also helpful in lifting them up and over the North Downs where, at Botley Hill, they passed the highest point on the system. Ten of the double-deck Tylors were allotted specifically for use on the arduously hilly routes S9 and S10 where again their more powerful engines were put to good use. Actual operation of the buses other than these specific allocations was not always so clear-cut as the bare facts imply, partly because the introduction of the longer 'joint' services required the provision of some East Surrey buses but also for other reasons best known to the Reigate management. The S6 and S6B, for example, although agreement routes, were normally worked by the company's own AEC and Daimler buses, the LGOC-owned Bs being operated on ESTC's local Reigate routes instead. Similarly, when the S5 was extended south of Redhill, East Surrey used its own, ironically more modern, K-type buses for the whole operation, instead of the LGOC Bs.

There were few route developments in 1923 and little or no new ground was opened up. On 3rd March the S8 was extended from Sutton to West Croydon but this was merely a replacement for General's own route 34A (Wallington Green to Liverpool Street) which was withdrawn, leaving the London end to route 34. In November some journeys on route S3 were extended on Wednesdays and Sundays to what was then known as Chelsham Mental Hospital, Warlingham Park Hospital in later years.

A start was made during 1923 on replacing some of the older buses with K-type double-deckers taken from the LGOC's own fleet. The first three were allocated on 14th March and by the end of the month there were ten, all of which replaced Bs. These were joined in May by two S-type single-deckers and then a further twenty Ks were added. Only seven Bs were replaced, the other new buses being needed for the expansion of services.

The S5 was extended south of Redhill alternately to Horsham and Hand Cross on 4th April 1922 but this photograph was taken later, after K 659 had joined the fleet in June 1923. The EAST SURREY fleet name on the dash panel alongside the embossed 'GENERAL' on the radiator demonstrate the split responsibility for the vehicle. The double-front posters are advertising reduced fare char-a-banc tours to Brighton daily for 5s or Eastbourne on Sundays for 7s 6d. (Ken Glazier collection)

PC9252 was one of the fourteen former lorry buses which were given second-hand B-type double-deck bodies when allocated to East Surrey. It was licensed on 1st June 1922, just in time to work on new route S9 which worked alternately to Chelwood Gate and Hartfield from 3rd June. Their 40 hp Tylor engines were more powerful than those of other double-deckers and were an essential requirement for the stiff climbs up to Caterham-on-the-Hill. (H. Snook)

General and East Surrey embarked on an interesting initiative at the beginning of 1924 when a range of through bookings was introduced with interchange in Croydon, either at The Greyhound or West Croydon station. These started on 14th February and were available from either Earlswood or Redhill to Oxford Circus, Charing Cross or Brixton, where there was a popular, cheap and thriving market, home of the original Marks and Spencer Penny Bazaar. They were apparently not a success as they were withdrawn after 31st December 1924.

In his negotiations with General's Commercial Manager about the summer programme for 1924, Hawkins made a number of proposals which would have increased his company's penetration into LGOC's heartland and most did not meet with approval. He had applied to increase the frequency of S8 between Cheam and West Croydon but was told that the LGOC intended extending its own Kingston–Sutton service to West Croydon, which could make a joint 15 minute headway with the S8. No such extension ever took place. Other rejected ideas were to extend the S10 from Bromley to Lewisham, ostensibly to meet competition from Timpson's, and a proposed Redhill to Sutton route which General thought would interfere with its own traffic south of Sutton. Not that refusals were always in one direction. When General approached East Surrey in June 1924 asking it to extend one of its services from Bromley to Grove Park, Hawkins was prepared to do so only if it could continue to a more promising objective, such as Eltham via Mottingham. This the LGOC could not agree and introduced its own 108B later in the year instead.

*Top* The interior of the new Dunton Green garage, which opened on 4th April 1922, with three B-type buses, two of which can be identified as B 2276 (East Surrey 42) on the left and B 324 (ESTC 39) in the centre. Although East Surrey buses did not run south of Sevenoaks, B 2276 is showing the destination Tunbridge Wells because passengers were able to book through and change at Sevenoaks onto the Autocar bus. This scheme came about when East Surrey acquired the Farnborough to Sevenoaks part of the through Autocar route in May 1921. (Alan B. Cross)

*Centre* In addition to those on loan, East Surrey also bought some former LGOC AEC YCs for its own fleet, the double-deckers being fitted with bodies from B-type buses. ESTC No 20 is seen working in the 'Traction Company Area' on route S22, which was extended from East Grinstead to Hartley on 5th May 1924 to replace that section of 'joint' route S9. (H.J. Snook/Norman Anscombe collection)

*Right* K 260, also numbered 86 by East Surrey, one of the thirty K-type double-deckers which were allocated by General to replace B-types between March and June 1923. (H.J. Snook/Ken Glazier collection)

The fine Market House built in 1708 at the eastern end of the High Street has supplied an elegant back-drop to many photographs of buses in Reigate over a period of ninety years and the 18th century houses and shops in the High Street help to build the atmosphere of a typical small country town. Eighteen of the thirty PS-type delivered to East Surrey in the summer of 1924 were owned by the company, one of them being 139 (PD1372) seen on LGOC Agreement route S6, which had a tradition of using company-owned rather than General buses from its earliest days. (H.J. Snook)

*Below* The East Surrey routes which crossed the Met Police boundary were mostly given Bassom numbers which matched their former identities, as in the case of S7 which became 407, but the extension to Bromley South via Farnborough did not take place until 14th October 1925. Sidcup had developed from its early beginnings into a small suburb during the 18th century, as the frontage of the Black Horse might bear witness. This was the original outer terminus of LGOC route 21 and remained the turning point for the main service from London throughout the 1920s. K 429 (ESTC 107) was put on loan to East Surrey in June 1923.

The proposals that were accepted were introduced with the summer programme. On 17th April, East Surrey's own S25 was extended northwards from Merstham to West Croydon which gave a joint service at 7½ minute intervals between Gatton Point and Croydon on routes 59, S5 and S25. On 5th May, the S1 was extended from Dartford, via Dartford Heath, to Bexley, the S2B from Farnborough to Locks Bottom and the S7 from Crockenhill to Sidcup via St Paul's Cray and St Mary's Cray. This did not fulfil the agreement with LGOC, which had been for the S7 to go to Orpington, because approval was not forthcoming from the Metropolitan Police. This did not happen until October 1925, when the St Pauls Cray to Sidcup section was removed and the route diverted into Orpington. The S1 was further extended, to Bexleyheath, on 6th October.

An unlikely new service was introduced on 23rd April 1924 to serve the area to the east of the railway at South Croydon , deep in the heart of Tilling/LGOC territory but obviously with the backing of General. This was the S3B which did the short trip from West Croydon to Sanderstead Station every forty minutes. To enable the use of a double-deck bus, the route taken was via Park Lane, Coombe Road, Normanton Road, Lismore Road, Carlton Road and Mayfield Road, avoiding the low bridge under the railway in Sanderstead Road. The rather classy inhabitants were not impressed with this intrusion and opposed the operation vigorously but East Surrey seems to have won hearts and

minds by having a particularly smartly turned out bus and begloved drivers. Whether this trick really worked or the residents got bored as time passed by, no-one can tell but East Surrey felt confident enough to reroute the S3 that way from 6th October. The S3B was then withdrawn, which might suggest that it was put on only to test reactions before undertaking a more permanent change. Journeys to Chelsham Mental Hospital on the S3, which had run briefly between 10th November 1923 and 16th April 1924, were now restored.

Two changes in the 'Traction Company's Area' during the year affected joint routes The section of the S9 running to Hartfield was withdrawn on 4th May and the service to Uckfield doubled in frequency, and the S4 was extended from Edenbridge to East Grinstead via Lingfield and Felcourt on 1st August.

The Route Approval provisions of the London Traffic Act (1924) were applied from 1st December 1924, from which date all routes entering the Metropolitan Police District were allocated 'Bassom' numbers. Those from the north were put into the series upwards from 300, from the south in the 400-499 series and those from the west in the series from 500 upwards with all short workings given a unique suffix letter. The routes operated by ESTC for the LGOC were then re-numbered as follows:

| | | |
|---|---|---|
| 401 | (S1) | Bexleyheath–Sevenoaks |
| 402 | (S2) | Bromley North–Sevenoaks |
| 403 | (S3) | West Croydon–Sevenoaks |
| 404 | (S4) | West Croydon–East Grinstead via Edenbridge |
| 405 | (part of S5) | West Croydon–Hand Cross via Crawley |
| 406 | (S6) | Kingston–Redhill |
| 407 | (S7) | Sidcup Station circular via Bexley, Dartford, Swanley, Crockenhill and St Mary Cray. |
| 408 | (S8) | West Croydon–Guildford via Epsom and Leatherhead |
| 409 | (S9) | West Croydon–Uckfield via Godstone and East Grinstead |
| 410 | (S10) | Bromley North–Reigate via Westerham |
| 411 | (S2B) | Sidcup–Locks Bottom via Orpington and Green Street Green |
| 412 | (part of S5) | West Croydon–Horsham via Crawley |
| 414 | (S25) | West Croydon–Horsham |

This hefty wedge of services, sitting as it was on the solid base of East Surrey's own extensive network, ensured that no serious competition was to arise which would challenge General's ultimate total control of the area. At the end of 1924, East Surrey had 77 LGOC-owned buses in its fleet, including its first NS which had been delivered to Reigate on 5th November 1924. The new PS type had also started to enter the fleet in June 1924 and eighteen were in stock while the Bs had been reduced to only six examples, and there were 30 K, two S (single-deck) and 14 double-deck and six single-deck Tylors.

East Surrey 141 offers passengers on route 409 the temptation of a bottle of Dow's No 1 Port for the price of one of the company's excursions to Brighton, or perhaps a couple of journeys to West Croydon from Uckfield. New in June 1924, it was one of the AEC PS-type with NS-style Ransomes Sims and Jefferies bodywork which were unique to the company. (Pamlin Prints)

*Below* The 408B was the West Croydon to Epsom short working of route 408, the main route running through to Guildford. East Surrey received its first NS on loan from the LGOC in November 1924 but 165 (PE2425) was one of ten which the company bought for its own services in May 1925. The buses are seen passing in the section between Cheam and Epsom. (Ken Glazier collection)

One of the NSs taken into East Surrey's own fleet in 1925, operating in Kent on LGOC Agreement route 401, after being fitted with pneumatic tyres in 1928. The body of 167 also came from Kent, having been built by Short Bros of Rochester who supplied over 900 bodies on NS chassis. (Ken Glazier collection)

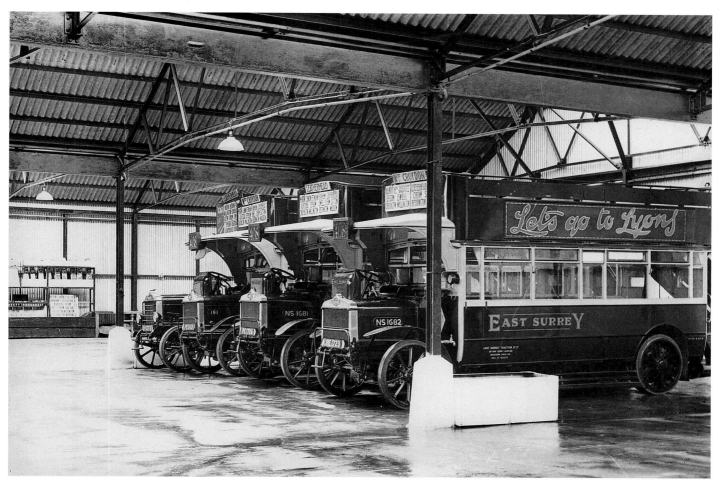

The interior of the new Leatherhead garage soon after it opened. Three of the four buses parked in the centre are NSs, 1681 and 1682 belonging to the LGOC and East Surrey's own, numbered 161, but of exceptional interest is the bus at the far end, boarded for operation on route 408. It is a former LGOC Daimler which was first acquired by East Surrey in 1914 and was not withdrawn until at least 1927. At the far end, on the left, are the racks containing the route and destination boards. (The Mike Sutcliffe collection)

Several garage building projects came to fruition during 1925. Land had been bought for garages at Warlingham and Godstone in June 1924 and for one at Leatherhead in September 1924. Another project agreed in 1924 was for a garage at Swanley and land for this was bought in February 1925. Pick wanted these structures to be of a much more simple and less expensive design than Dunton Green which had been based on the standards being used for new LGOC garages. At Swanley he went as far as saying that he wanted 'just a tin shed' because he thought that traffic would develop away from it in time and at first he rejected the proposals submitted by Newton & Hill which were based on those for Godstone and Warlingham. Following various inspections, Pick agreed that Swanley should be built to the same standard as the other two garages, a decision for which future generations over the next eighty years were no doubt grateful.

Although later known as Chelsham the original use of the name Warlingham for the new garage in Limpsfield Road was more accurate because the premises were on the corner of Chelsham Road in the Urban District of Caterham and Warlingham, whereas the village of Chelsham was across the border in the Rural District of Godstone. The cost of building the garage, which could house eight buses, was £2,150 and the work was completed in time for operations to start on 20th January 1925, the same day as the new premises at Godstone were commissioned. The land for Godstone garage, on the north-eastern corner of the junction of the Caterham and Oxted roads, was bought for £300 and the building, by J.J. Pink of Merstham, cost £2,350 and had room for sixteen buses. Chelsham took charge of routes 403 and 404, and Godstone the 409 and S24 (Reigate–Sevenoaks) as well as three of the buses for route 410 and the use of three outstations by these routes was discontinued. Leatherhead garage was sited on the north side of Leatherhead Road just west of the railway bridge, more in Fetcham than Leatherhead, and was a substantially bigger building, with a capacity to house twenty-four buses. Its total cost of £4,200 was commensurately larger. The contract was awarded to Newton & Hill, a company favoured and trusted by Hawkins and work started in January. It was used as a parking area for buses on route 408 as soon as the

concrete flooring had dried but it opened officially, for accounting purposes, on 1st June 1925. The last of this group of garages to open was Swanley, sited in the main London to Maidstone Road just over half a mile east of the centre of the town, which opened its doors to routes 401 and 407 on 21st October 1925. It had cost £3,150 to build and was capable of looking after sixteen buses.

These garages were all enlarged in later years as the volume of work grew. Godstone was enlarged to take an extra four buses in 1928, Leatherhead was doubled in size, from 24 to 48 buses in 1928 and plans were laid for the enlargement in 1930/1931 of Dunton Green and Swanley and the completion of a delayed project at Warlingham. These were all LGOC projects, but East Surrey also built garages in its own right during these years at East Grinstead and Crawley

In the case of Warlingham, the need for enlargement arose within two years because of an increased service on route 403 and new route 415. A proposal to double its size to take an extra eight buses was put to the LGOC in December 1926 but at that time it appears that General was having doubts about the extent to which East Surrey should operate in the area. Judging by Hawkins's comments to his Board, General were considering taking over the Croydon to Warlingham corridor themselves, which is hardly surprising, and had asked for a postponement of the project in January

1926. What is surprising is that the LGOC went along with the idea in the first place, of having an ESTC garage in a village on a relatively unimportant road only just inside the London Country Area where the scope for future development of services was likely to be almost wholly on the London side of the border. The extension was never built during the period covered by this book, having to wait until 1931.

This episode did highlight the strange anomaly whereby East Surrey, and ultimately the Country Bus department of London Transport, ran local suburban services in a large area of south London, a quirk that was not repeated in the north. In fact, this was the source of some tension between the two companies, although not of the bad-tempered kind which was to develop occasionally between National and General over vehicle policy. There was a lot of debate between them about the extent to which their operations overlapped, particularly in Bexley and Croydon which, inevitably, were resolved in favour of General. East Surrey even objected formally to the LGOC in 1927 when route 494 was introduced between West Wickham and Wallington, following route 408 west of Waddon. Its Sunday equivalent, the 194, was even more competitive as it ran right through to Cheam.

East Surrey started a new route on 8th April 1925 running from West Croydon to Esher, following the 408 to Leatherhead and then through Oxshott. East Surrey called it 408D, although if Bassom rules were applied strictly it should have had a new number. In fact, the Metropolitan Police had refused to sanction the operation and the company had appealed to the Minister of Transport for a ruling under the London Traffic Act. The matter was settled satisfactorily and the route was able to continue but was allocated the new 'Bassom' number 416 from 14th October. Another variation starting on the same day as the 408D was the 408S which ran between Leatherhead and Guildford via Effingham Junction and therefore not part of the LGOC network but it is mentioned because of its close association with the 408. In July 1925, the LGOC asked East Surrey to run another service in this area which, had it been agreed might have led to more expansion by the company in that quarter of Surrey. The proposed route was from Leatherhead to Weybridge via Cobham and Hawkins was prepared to comply if General supplied the buses and a garage but he made an additional condition that ESTC should also operate or expand their operations in Kingston, Windsor, Woking and Guildford. This was not acceptable to the LGOC who instead extended their own Slough–Staines service 162A right through to Leatherhead via Chertsey, Weybridge and Cobham on 31st March 1926 under the Bassom number 162B.

Another new Croydon area route appeared on 4th December 1925 when double-deck route 415 started operating half-hourly between West Croydon and Chelsham via South Park Hill Road, Normanton Road and Sanderstead station. This was the old S3B

resurrected and extended but remains a slight oddity because it followed exactly the same route as the 403 and might reasonably have been given a Bassom suffix to the basic 403. In lived to justify its separate identity by being extended to Farleigh on 1st April 1928. East Surrey made an attempt at this time to get approval for a route from Walton-on-the-Hill to Croydon via Tadworth, Banstead and Woodmansterne. The residents of this high-class district did not warm to the idea of anything as common as buses and their influential objections ensured that approval was not given. The route through Woodmansterne and Chipstead was doomed to remain busless until local operator Banstead Coaches provided a service over thirty years later.

Renewal of the LGOC-owned fleet continued during 1925 with the delivery of ten NS and two AEC 202 single-deckers with pneumatic tyres. The NSs replaced five of the Tylors and the six remaining B-type. The two S-type single-deckers were also returned to General. The new AECs had front-entrance LGOC bodywork (one with 22 and one with 24 seats) and were suitable for one-man operation, although not used as such.

By 1926, the route network had almost reached its maximum extent and most changes after that were minor adjustments of various kinds. The 404 was withdrawn between Croydon and Botley Hill and diverted to Tatsfield instead on 16th June 1926, no longer entering the Metropolitan Police District but retaining its Bassom number. A side-effect of this was that buses were withdrawn finally from the section of Sanderstead Road between the Red Deer, South Croydon and Sanderstead station.

There had been an earlier proposal, which was submitted to the Ministry of Transport in July 1925 for route 404 to be rerouted via

Selsdon Road to serve the new Selsdon Garden Village being built by Messrs Costains but this was apparently not approved. However, in July 1926, East Surrey were asked by Costains to operate a bus service under contract between the village and South Croydon station during what might broadly be described as peak hours on Mondays to Saturdays. This was agreed at a charge of 1s 3d a mile with a minimum of 60 miles a day. To ensure the legality of the operation, a condition of the contract was that Costain would sell weekly and daily tickets direct to passengers. This does not appear to have convinced the Police who warned Hawkins that they were considering prosecuting the company for plying for hire without authority. The company believed that it was within the law but offered to withdraw if that was what the Police wanted and to apply for approval to the temporary operation of single-deck buses. This was duly granted and the contract service was replaced from 8th November by a new single-deck route numbered 417 between 'Croham Heights Lodge Gates' (the junction of Upper Selsdon Road and Addington Road) and South Croydon Station via Selsdon Road, Lismore Road, Normanton Road and Croham Road. This elaborate procedure avoided the low bridges, even though a single-decker was used but this proved to be a prudent measure as it was soon necessary to substitute a double-decker to cope with increasing demand.

Route 418 started running between Epsom and Effingham Junction on 4th June 1927 and brought buses to Ashtead Station and Barnetwood Lane for the first time. PH1892 (East Surrey 179) was a 32-seat ADC416A which had gone into service only ten days earlier. (Ken Glazier collection)

Because of the original direct approach from Costains, East Surrey slipped into this operation, which was not part of the joint agreement and well within the areas served by Combine companies in their own right. The LGOC appear to have turned a blind eye while the route was in its early stages but as soon as it became evident that a more substantial service would be needed, they negotiated to take it over. East Surrey ran for the last time on 12th April 1927 and the next day LGOC route 54 was extended from the 'Swan & Sugar Loaf' to what they, more prosaically, called Selsdon running all day every twenty minutes.

A new route 418 brought a service to two of the remaining areas which were covered in the 1920s. From 4th June 1927 it started running between Epsom and Effingham Junction, leaving the main road through Ashtead to serve the station and Barnetwood Lane and absorbing the Leatherhead to Effingham section of the 408S. On 23rd May 1928 it was extended from Epsom into the newly developing area to the north-west of the Epsom to Raynes Park railway line, to terminate at West Ewell Bungalow Stores. Further east along the North Downs, ESTC started a route 33 on 26th September 1928 in rather unpromising territory between Caterham-on-the-Hill and Westerham Hill via Woldingham, Botley Hill, Tatsfield and Hawley's Corner. It lasted only four months, being swallowed up on 30th January 1929 by an extension of route 30 from Edenbridge via Crockham Hill, Westerham and Hawley to give a through East Grinstead to Caterham route. The weakest link in this chain was the section between Westerham Hill and Woldingham and it is no surprise that the route was severely curtailed within two months to run only between Caterham and Woldingham, forming the nucleus of what was to become a Woldingham–Earlswood route a year later.

The only other new area served before the end of the decade was in Kent. East Surrey introduced a new route 23 on 30th January 1929 running between Dartford and Stanhill via Wilmington and Leyton Cross. It was extended to Birchwood on 9th October.

New buses taken into the 'agreement' stock in 1926, 1927 and 1928 comprised fourteen PS, nine NS, twelve ADC 416A and the prototype AEC Reliance. In 1929 movements in the fleet slowed down almost to a stop, with the delivery of a solitary NS, an experimental LS and the prototype AEC Regent UU6610, which later became ST 1139. An important transformation was wrought in the double-deck fleet in 1928 when the S, PS and NS double-deckers were fitted with pneumatic tyres in a period of ten weeks from mid-November to the end of January 1929. Single-deckers had been so fitted for a number of years but their use on double-deckers was constrained by the restrictions placed on vehicle width by the Metropolitan Police. These were lifted on 1st July 1928, when an overall width of 7ft 5ins was allowed, but the real incentive was given by new legislation which increased the speed limit for buses fitted with pneumatics from 12 to 20 mph. From 1st October 1928 some of the ADCs were on loan in connection with a competitive enterprise on the Dorking to Guildford road, of which more later, and the rest for the new 418. So, at the end of 1929 East Surrey had on loan from the LGOC 27 K, 32 PS, 21 NS, two AEC single-deckers, 12 ADC 416A, one LS and one ST, a total of 97.

East Surrey 171 was one of the eight AEC PS-type taken into stock on loan from General in 1927. Half of them, including 171, had LGOC bodywork with NS-type styling, the rest were bodied by Short Bros. The photograph shows 171 after it had been equipped with pneumatic tyres. (H.J. Snook/Ken Glazier collection)

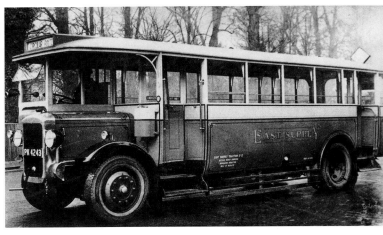

The LGOC bodywork supplied for the six ADC416A buses bought by East Surrey in 1927 was a distinct pre-echo of the classic design which was to appear on the T and LT classes a few years later. Associated Daimler was a jointly-owned but short-lived company set up by AEC and Daimler in 1926 to market their products. Daimler influence is apparent in the design of the radiator of 181, a considerable advance on the rather old-fashioned shape that had been in use by AEC until then. (Snook and Son/Ken Glazier collection)

*Above right* PK4243 was one of three prototype AEC Reliances which were based on modified AEC 426 chassis and is believed to have been the first to enter service. The 32-seat bodywork was supplied by Hall Lewis, predecessors of Park Royal. (Capital Transport collection)

While these developments had been taking place in the London Country Area, East Surrey had been assiduously expanding its own area of activity south of the valley road boundary and building up its own fleet based for the most part on the types employed in the LGOC-owned fleet. There were many skirmishes with competitors, most of whom were extinguished ruthlessly by a determined Arthur Henry Hawkins but none of this had anything to do directly with the LGOC. However, the LGOC did get drawn into two significant episodes which illustrate how close the relationship between the two companies had become and proved to be a pointer to later events. Despite the existence of an area agreement, East Surrey had been in dispute with the Aldershot & District company about running rights between Dorking and Guildford for some time. When in December 1925 the opportunity arose to acquire a local Independent, Surrey Hills Motor Services, the LGOC provided funding for the purchase jointly with Aldershot & District, in whose area most of the services ran. General took this as an opportunity to enter into a fresh agreement with the Aldershot company to ratify the rights which were in dispute and this was signed on 27th September 1926. This gave the LGOC equal running rights with A&D between Silent Pool and Gomshall, from Shere and Gomshall to Horsham via Peaslake and Ewhurst, between Dorking and Westcott and for through journeys from Guildford to points beyond Gomshall. The route through

Newlands Corner, the nub of the dispute, was also made subject to equal rights. To help East Surrey implement the agreement quickly, General lent the company four K-type single-deckers.

Another severe competition dispute between two companies brought the LGOC into the picture again, this time on the south-eastern boundary of East Surrey's activities. The fearsome battle had been raging between Autocar Services Ltd and Redcar Services Ltd of Tunbridge Wells and both companies got into a precarious financial state. The LGOC and East Surrey had been eyeing Autocar for some time, in fact both companies had approached Autocar in 1923 with proposals to acquire an interest in the Kentish company. The East Surrey offer was apparently rejected and, although the LGOC offer was at first accepted by W.O. Pritchard the Managing Director, it too was ultimately rejected. In September 1926 Pritchard offered to sell his shares to East Surrey as agents of LGOC for £65,000, plus payment of all liabilities. This was rejected and a counter-offer made jointly by LGOC and East Surrey of £65,000 free of all liabilities. This also came to nought. The changed circumstances of 1928 gave the LGOC the chance, using East Surrey as its agent, to attempt to acquire not just Autocar but Redcar too. During the negotiations it came to light that the British Electric Traction Company were considering acquiring Redcar as a

subsidiary of Maidstone & District, so East Surrey withdrew from those negotiations. A deal was then completed with Autocar, East Surrey acquiring a controlling interest on 5th April 1928 by the purchase of 15,001 preference shares, and A.H. Hawkins and A.W. Makovski joined the Autocar Board to represent East Surrey. The LGOC's interest in the matter was sealed by the negotiation of new clauses to the agreement with East Surrey. These introduced a new category of 'Joint Areas' in which the two companies had equal running rights but while the agreement was in force, the services would be run by East Surrey in joint account. This was the essence of the agreement, which included a number of other detailed provisions. The Joint area concerned was that covered by Autocar's services, which meant that the LGOC had acquired a half interest in them.

This was all a prelude to the grand finale, which took place on 12th June 1929. In 1928, the four Main Line Railway companies had been granted parliamentary powers to operate bus services but, rather than starting from scratch, they chose to exercise the powers by buying large shareholdings in existing bus companies. Autocar and East Surrey were prime targets for the Southern Railway and the Underground Group was fearful of the effect on its southern boundary if East Surrey were to slip from its grasp. Pick, who described the situation as being 'now acute',

In 1927 East Surrey bought six ADC419 normal control chars-a-bancs with 29-seat bodywork by Short Bros. On these vehicles, the framework supporting the canvas hood remained in place when the cover was rolled back, allowing the windows to be closed to give some protection from the wind while not impeding the view. PH1209 is seen in Marine Parade Brighton, apparently on a private hire trip, although East Surrey also operated excursions to the seaside town. (H.J. Snook/Ken Glazier collection)

entered into urgent negotiations with Arthur Hawkins in February 1929 aimed at the LGOC acquiring a controlling interest. These were completed successfully, what was described as 'an informal formal offer' was made on 25th April and an agreement signed on 23rd May. At the East Surrey Board meeting on 4th June 1929, three directors of the company resigned and Frank Pick and Arthur Lee Barber (Commercial Manager of the LGOC) were invited to join the Board in their place. The company and its subsidiary Autocar, both now became part of the Underground Group. Arthur Hawkins remained as Managing Director but his opposite number at Autocar, W.O. Pritchard, retired and Pick became a director of that company too. This acquisition brought into the ownerhip of the LGOC a large and flourishing network of services in southern Surrey and north Sussex, forty-one double-deck buses of the K, S, NS and PS type and twenty-five single-deckers, the majority (19) of which were AEC 416 type. The other six single-deckers comprised three AEC 202 and one each of Guy, GMC and Renault manufacture. This was an important step in the progress of East Surrey towards the all-encompassing creature that it became in 1932 when, renamed London General Country Services, it was to take over the operation of the services on the north side operated until then by National.

*Top* When PK4244 was built, the use of aluminium alloy in the construction of bus bodies was almost unknown but Short Bros of Rochester, who had pioneered the use of light metals for aircraft, did offer an all-aluminium bus body from 1926 onwards. One of these was bought by East Surrey to mount on this Tilling Stevens B10A2 chassis, an experimental vehicle which went into service on 3rd December 1928. It was also a pioneer of roller destination blinds which, when the bus was new, included a large intermediate point display which had been painted out by the time this photograph was taken. (Ken Glazier collection)

*Centre* A third experimental vehicle bought by East Surrey in 1928 was UC2265, which had a 45-seat double-deck body mounted on an ADC416A chassis, a model designed as a single-decker. Numbered 81, it made its first operational appearance on the special service to the Royal County Show Ground at Gatton Park. As it was fitted with pneumatic tyres it was confined at first to services operating outside the Metropolitan Police District. (Capital Transport collection)

*Right* When East Surrey acquired its controlling interest in Autocar Services of Tunbridge Wells, this immaculate 1925-vintage AEC503, KL7246, was one of the buses that came under its indirect control. Unlike the Metropolitan authorities, those at Tunbridge Wells must have been fairly easy-going as the bus is not fitted with underframe lifeguards and there is an alarmingly large space between the axles into which bodies could fall unhindered. (Ken Glazier collection)

## CHAPTER FIVE
# General Spreads Its Wings: The North

Meanwhile, in the northern 'country area' similar developments had been taking place but from a different starting point as General had not been looking to set up such an arrangement until they ran into some labour relations problems at Watford. Soon after the war, the LGOC had decided to expand their activities in the Watford area and, with this in mind, on 8th May 1919 the Board approved the construction of a new garage in Leavesden Road at a cost of £13,800. The routes, which were started in 1920, all operated at first as part of the company's main business but the staff were paid at a lower rate and had different working conditions. This may not have been a problem but for the fact that Leavesden Road shared the operation of route 142 with Cricklewood, whose staff were paid at normal London area rates of pay, and also operated route 140

which went some way into the main LGOC operating area. The Watford staff did not like this and applied for their conditions of employment to be the same as for their London-based colleagues. This was rejected in December 1920 and the discontent which followed led the General Board to decide that the National Omnibus and Transport Company should be approached with a view to their working the routes on the LGOC's behalf. National responded positively and the operational agreement which was then negotiated was in similar terms to that with East Surrey. As it happened it was actually signed over a month earlier than that with the Reigate company, on 13th May 1921, and came into force on 21st July. Because of the way things turned out in Watford, National were first to operate services on General's behalf, although only by a matter of days.

The attractive village of Elstree was first served by route N13 on 2nd August 1922 when it ran from Watford to High Barnet, later continuing to Enfield and finally Waltham Cross in March 1923. The photograph is redolent of the period, with only a handful of people in sight (some made ghost-like by the camera), a traffic hazard sign in the form of a red triangle on a wooden post, a haycart in the distance and a couple of contemporary cars parked. S 390, passing the timeless Plough public house, is in the red and white livery which soon replaced the old National white, and the use of a board for the Waltham Cross destination suggests that it was photographed soon after March 1923. (Laurie Akehurst Collection)

National may have seemed an odd choice but there was no company comparable to East Surrey with a base in the area and General already had close contacts with National through its operations in London as the National Steam Car Company. There was another strand of General's history which bound it to National, arising from the isolated pocket of routes inherited from New Central which it had operated around Bedford before the war. Bedford garage had been taken over by the military in November 1914, when the bus services were withdrawn, and was due for release in 1919 but the LGOC decided not to restart the services which they thought were too remote from their main sphere of operations. Instead, an Area Agreement was negotiated with the National Steam Car Company under which National undertook not to operate in the Metropolitan Police Area or within a fifteen mile radius of Charing Cross, whichever was the greater. Bedford garage was sold to National Steam for £7,000 and re-opened in August 1919, providing a handy base for expansion in Bedfordshire by the newly constituted National Omnibus and Transport Company. The withdrawal of National Steam from London took place in November 1919 as already noted in chapter two. This close association with National also operated at a personal level, as the General Manager was Walter James Iden who had been Chief Engineer of both LGOC and The Associated Equipment Company until 1917. National was therefore a natural choice as a partner in the north comparable to East Surrey in the south, although it was Arthur Hawkins who proved to be the more congenial collaborator and, in the long run, it was East Surrey that was to gain ascendancy, albeit at the eventual cost of its independence.

The Watford operations had had a shaky start even before the staff problems materialised. General had planned to start four new routes on 4th February 1920 and these had been announced in detail in the LGOC Traffic Circular. They were to have been: 143 Watford (Clarendon Hotel) to Rickmansworth via Rickmansworth Road and Croxley Green; 144 Watford to Berkhamsted and 145 Watford to Hemel Hempstead (The Posting House) both via Kings Langley and Two Waters; and 146 Bushey Railway Arches to St Albans Market Place via Garston, Chiswell Green. There were also two 'supplementary' services shown as part of route 145 serving Apsley Mills from Boxmoor Station and Hemel Hempstead. Routes 143 and the Hemel Hempstead supplementary of 145 were single-deck and the rest double-deck, except that a special note attached to the Boxmoor supplementary pointed out that if it was operated by the same omnibus as the Hemel Hempstead, it must of necessity be single-deck.

This programme never came to fruition and it was not until 25th August that substantially modified versions of two of the routes started. The 143 was now Croxley Green to Garston and the 145 Bushey Station to Boxmoor, operating from the new Watford (Leavesden Road) garage. The 143 was later extended from Garston to St Albans Market Place on 24th November and then to Fleetville on 6th April 1921, and the 145 to Berkhamsted on 24th November. They were joined on 25th October 1920 by a 147 running from Bushey Station to Hemel Hempstead. This one was interesting because it had a summer Sunday extension to Golders Green which operated between 25th March and 25th September 1921 with buses from Hendon garage, whose crews would have been paid at London rates. It did not reappear in subsequent years. These three routes (apart from the Sunday 147), Leavesden Road garage and the 15 B-type buses, which were all Tylors built in 1919, were handed over to National on 25th May. National set up a new operating area with headquarters at Watford to operate the LGOC services and, on the same date transferred one of its existing routes to the jurisdiction of the new Watford Area. This became route 200 and ran from Dunstable to St Albans. At some time before 6th August 1921, the 201, St Albans to Welwyn, was added to the set and this was later extended to Hitchin via Stevenage in place of a National Bedford Area route 13.

The Watford routes were renumbered into the LGOC's new system from 6th August 1921, becoming N1 (143), N2 (145), N3 (147), N4 (200) and N5 (201). From that date, or possibly a week later, new route N6 was introduced between Watford and Chesham via Rickmansworth and this was extended to Berkhamsted by the following June, when the N2 was also extended to Northchurch from Berkhamsted. On 12th August National's Chelmsford Area routes 11 and 14 were transferred to the Watford Area, joined together to become Bishop's Stortford to Brentwood via Epping and Ongar, and renumbered N9. There were two further innovations in the northern network in 1921, both starting on 8th September. The N7 ran New Barnet to Hatfield Station and the N8 ran Radlett to Wheathampstead via St Albans. The N8 was soon extended at both ends (from 3rd June 1922) to become Borehamwood Station to Kimpton.

The first garage to be built specifically for National to use was at Hatfield, where 10,000 sq.ft of freehold land was purchased in October 1921 for £300. Formal authority for the expenditure of £5,500 to construct the building was given by the LGOC Board on 15th June 1922 and the garage opened soon afterwards. It was sited in St Albans Road and took over responsibility for routes in the area which until then had been operated from various outstations.

The LGOC seemed to wake up rather late to the potential for competition on its north-eastern flank, even to the extent of neglecting the main Hertford Road north of Edmonton and the hitherto busless town of Hertford. Because of its strategic position running along the Lea Valley, this was one of the more developed and populated of the main roads out of London and its absence from the LGOC bus map showed a surprising lack of enterprise or awareness. This changed abruptly after 1st January 1921 when a new operator Harvey and Burrows, trading as Hertford & District Motor Omnibus Services, started running south from Hertford as far as Wormley. H&B's operations grew rapidly, prompting General to apply jointly with National to run from Hertford to Bishops Stortford and Braughing, and by General to run its own service between Waltham Cross and Hertford. The Bishops Stortford service was new territory but H&B, at that time ignorant of General's intentions, applied for the same route in March 1921. Hertford Council granted H&B's application but held off allowing LGOC or National into the town as they preferred to support the local men. Harvey and Burrows, recognising the seriousness of the threat from the powerful Combine company, sought to secure an operating agreement with the LGOC and approached Pick. The terms proposed by the LGOC at the subsequent meeting were so onerous that talks broke down on 24th April. The same fate appears to have overtaken another attempt to negotiate on 5th May, although Pick felt able to announce to the LGOC Board on the same day that a 'temporary agreement' had been entered with Harvey & Burrows.

Straker Squire chose one of the Harvey & Burrows buses to display at the Commercial Motor Exhibition at Olympia in 1923 and a fine sight it must have been in its pristine state. The main body colour was red with a white relief around the windows and some simple lining out of the panels, the fleet identity being conveyed by an 'H&B' monogram. It was the last bus to join the fleet before the company disappeared into the maw of the LGOC in July 1924, although a Daimler Y char-a-banc was purchased in April 1924. (Ken Glazier collection)

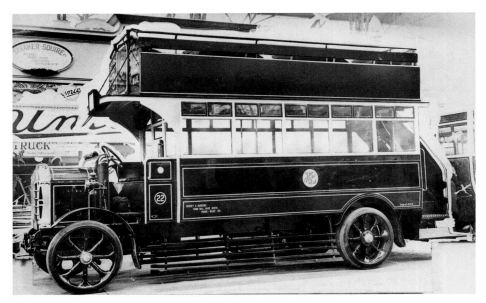

In the absence of a licence to run into Hertford, the LGOC started its new service 132 between Waltham Cross and Ware on 11th May 1921, running hourly on Mondays to Fridays, half-hourly Saturdays and every 22 minutes on Sundays. To protect themselves, Harvey & Burrows cut back to Broxbourne on Mondays to Saturdays and rerouted via Hertford Heath to avoid Ware. General was given a drubbing in the local press and soon realised that it was not going to succeed in running H&B off the road without creating considerable hostility which could damage it commercially. Negotiations were therefore resumed. On 14th July 1921, two months after the 'temporary agreement' with the LGOC, Harvey and Burrows had set up a route between Hertford, Cole Green, Hatfield and St Albans, which they ran jointly with Road Motors of Luton (who ran via Essendon Corner). National, on behalf of General, sought to acquire H&B's rights in the service and came to an agreement with

the younger company to take over their share of the operation on 8th September, numbering it N10. The H&B bus made redundant was used to start a new Bunting-ford to Bishops Stortford service via Puckeridge and Little Hadham. Meanwhile a licence had been granted to General allowing them to operate in Hertford and, perhaps to keep Harvey and Burrows on their toes during the negotiations, the 132 was extended from Ware on 1st August.

*Below* Although it was the county town with a population in excess of 10,000, Hertford did not see a regular motor bus service until Harvey & Burrows started their Hertford–Wormley service on 1st January 1921. But there are three operators to be seen in this view of Fore Street. On the left is a Harvey & Burrows Daimler Y 29-seater on the service to Waltham Cross and on the right is J.R. Street's Straker Squire, here on a private hire but also used on a Hertford–Ware bus service. In the background is a Road Motors Dennis on the route to St Albans, which became the N10A in September 1922 when they relinquished it to National.

The eventual outcome was settled at a meeting on 7th November 1921, when Harvey, Burrows and Pick signed an operating agreement under which H&B would not operate more than ten buses within a 35-mile radius of Charing Cross. These were to be confined to five routes: Hertford to Waltham Cross via Ware, Hertford to Hoddesdon via Hertford Heath, Hertford to Watton, Ware to Braughing and Ware to Buntingford. In return the LGOC agreed to withdraw from the Hertford Road, except that it retained the right to operate at weekends and on public holidays. The rights to the Hertford to Bishop's Stortford service were relinquished by H&B, the operation being transferred on 14th December to National, who numbered it N11 in the LGOC series. Almost at the eleventh hour of these negotiations, on 2nd November, General introduced a 132A running right through from Finsbury Park to Hertford on Mondays to Saturdays via Hertford Heath, another H&B route, but this and the 132 both ran for the last time on 13th December 1921. A route N12 was advertised in the January 1922 LGOC Bus Map as running from Hertford to Hitchin via Watton and Stevenage. It may have started operating in December 1921 but if so it was withdrawn again early in 1922 and as it would have been outwith the agreement with H&B, there must be some doubt as to whether it ever operated.

At the same time as the agreement was made with H&B, a similar operating agreement was signed with Road Motors of Luton which came into force on 11th November 1921. It followed the now familiar pattern, providing that Road Motors would not operate bus services within 30 miles of Charing Cross, except that the company was given sole rights to the services from Luton to Markyate and Wheathampstead. Provision was also made for co-ordination of services with National between Luton and St Albans and with the LGOC between Harpenden and St Albans. There were also provisions for restraint of competition with National outside the 30-mile limit. Finally, Road Motors agreed to relinquish their St Albans to Hertford service by 30th September 1922, which they did. National took over on 1st October and gave it the number N10A.

By the end of the first phase of expansion in June 1922, National had 37 buses on loan from the LGOC, a mixture of single- and double-deck B-type operating on eleven routes, the greatest concentration being in Watford. During the summer and autumn of 1922 the network around Watford was further fortified with the introduction of new routes to High Barnet, via Elstree and Borehamwood (N13), Uxbridge via West Hyde (N24), Bedmond via Garston (N15), Harrow via Rickmansworth and Northwood (N16) and Bovingdon via Croxley Green (N17). A little further north a new N14 filled the gap between Hemel Hempstead and St Albans. The N24, which started on 13th August 1922, was interesting in being a joint operation with Thames Valley, also working on behalf of General, who numbered their part W24 but this arrangement did not last long. The N24 was cut back to West Hyde on 7th December and Thames Valley withdrew on 31st December 1922.

The buses needed for these extra workings included the first of the new S-type to be allocated to National, eight single- and two double-deck but some of these were used to replace B-types. At the end of 1922 the total on hire was 34 B and nine S and since September, three chars-a-banc had been operating on tours and private hire work on behalf of General.

*Top* NK6089 (nominally PS 9) was one of the thirteen PSs with bodywork based on the S-type, allocated to National in June and July 1923. It is at St Albans, painted in the new livery of red and white with an underlined fleet name in the General style.

*Centre* The first five single-deck S-type lent to National in the autumn of 1923 had the straight-sided bodywork derived from the design used on the later B and K-types. S 859, seen on the stand at The Clarendon Hotel Watford Junction, has a simpler form of the fleet name, without underlining, and carries an advertisement for Pearson's shop in Enfield which continues to trade at the time of writing and does very good afternoon teas!

*Right* Harvey & Burrows introduced a Waltham Cross–Waltham Abbey–Epping Forest service on behalf of the LGOC on 7th June 1924, in competition with Charles Wayman. It was numbered N30 when National took it over and became 306B under the Bassom system. NK3459 (WD 8) was a Daimler Y 26-seater which H&B had bought in 1922. (Alan B. Cross)

There was a restrained incursion into the neglected eastern flank of the area on 3rd August 1923, when a service was started between Havering-atte-Bower and Grays via Romford, eastern Dagenham, Rainham and Aveley (N20) but the Aveley to Grays section was taken off again in November. There was already a number of General's own routes reaching out to Brentwood, Ongar and Epping, as well as the N9, but otherwise, for the time being, Essex was left to National operating in its own right or to a profusion of Independents. Hertfordshire, on the other hand, continued to receive attention, as did outlying areas of Middlesex. The N13 reached Hertfordshire/Esssex border territory at Waltham Cross, via Ponders End, in about October 1923, having been pushed on as far as Enfield from High Barnet on 19th March. A slightly surprising operation was the N18, which began running in August 1923, as this ran from Harrow (Met) Station to Uxbridge, territory that seemed rather close to the heart of the LGOC's own business and certainly within the Metropolitan Police District. In any event it was 'temporarily suspended' in October and did not run again. August 1923 also saw another service entering Hemel Hempstead on its journeys from Bovingdon to Great Gaddesden (N19) but this was swallowed up in October by a more helpful extension of the N17 from Bovingdon, to give a through Watford, Croxley, Bovingdon, Hemel, Great Gaddesden route. In Watford itself, another existing route was brought under the sway of the LGOC in October 1923 when National took over a former Rickmansworth & District route between Watford and Harefield, and numbered it N22. By November 1923 a variant of the N5 running from St Albans to Hitchin via Codicote had started.

All this expansion needed fourteen extra buses and another five were allocated for the replacement of expiring B-types. These comprised thirteen PS-type double-deckers, four S-type single-deckers and the two C-type one-man buses.

The main event of 1924, a year when no entirely new services were started, was the final chapter in the short but eventful story of Harvey and Burrows. The company had managed to continue with a degree of expansion following the 1921 agreement with LGOC. May 1922 saw new routes from Hertford to Woolmer Green (Saturdays only), and Welwyn and a Wednesday, Saturday and Sunday extension of the Buntingford route to Royston, which was outside the 35-mile limit. Other new routes were introduced later in the Royston area. Closer to home the Broxbourne to Watton service was extended to Stevenage in November 1922.

The timetable for route 313 when it started on 7th July 1926 shows a pattern found on many routes of a similar kind, with a more frequent weekend service than was operated on Mondays–Fridays. It is a direct ancestor of the route still running in 2003. The absence of any acknowledgement that the service was operated on behalf of the LGOC is noteworthy. (Laurie Akehurst collection)

National received its first NSs in January 1924 and was operating 23 by the end of that year. They seem to have been a little camera shy when in normal service in their early days but this scene shows three of them, led by NS 1149, carrying a private party which, judging by the massed hats, could have been the Women's Institute. (Ken Glazier collection)

Despite the company's apparent success and healthy financial state, Harvey and Burrows decided to realise their capital and secretly started negotiations with General early in 1924 for the sale of the undertaking. While these were in progress, H&B introduced their last new route, between Waltham Cross and Waltham Abbey with journeys onwards to Epping Forest (Volunteer) on Tuesdays, Saturdays and Sundays. This was done at the specific request of the LGOC, to confront competition from another Independent operator, Charles Wayman, a clear indication that the negotiations were going well. The sale was concluded at a meeting on 15th July 1924 and its effective date settled as 1st July. The LGOC and National agreed to pay £20,000 for the complete business, of which National contributed £2,000 in respect of the services operating outside the LGOC area. Under the terms of the sale, the two partners were prohibited from running buses within a 30-mile radius of Charing Cross or in any area where the National Omnibus and Transport Company operated. The services of Harvey and Burrows were retained in an advisory capacity for two years at a joint salary of £500 but there is no evidence that they ever did anything. The twenty buses, various cars and service vehicles and the garage behind the Town Hall at Ware, all became LGOC property but were immediately leased to National for them to operate under the terms of the 1921 agreement.

The buses which changed hands and their LGOC fleet numbers were:

### DOUBLE-DECKERS

| WB 1 | AEC B | O34RO |
|---|---|---|
| WD 1, 2, 11 | Daimler Y | O36RO |
| WD 3 | Daimler Y | O42RO |
| WD 5 | Daimler Y | O46RO |
| | | |
| WS 1, 2 | Straker Squire | O44RO |
| WS 3 | Straker Squire | O46RO |
| WS 4 | Straker Squire | O48RO |
| WS 5, 6 | Straker Squire | O52RO |

### SINGLE-DECKERS

| WD 4 | Daimler Y | B40F |
|---|---|---|
| WD 6, 8 | Daimler Y | B26R |
| WD 7 | Daimler Y | B29R |
| WD 9, 10 | Daimler Y | B32? |

### CHARS-A-BANC

| WS 12, 13 | Daimler Y | 28 seats |
|---|---|---|

The B had been second-hand from the War Department in 1921, the Daimlers were the reconditioned War Department type sold off after the war and the Straker Squires had been new or almost new to H&B in 1922 and 1923. The Strakers were not to the taste of the LGOC, nor apparently to Walter Iden, and he was charged with the task of disposing of them as quickly as possible at the best price, but not to operators in the London area. Iden had difficulty finding a buyer at the price being asked, although a deal with Barton which would have brought £750 a vehicle came close to completion. As there were no NSs immediately available because

of a temporary lull in production, it was agreed instead that the Strakers should be kept to cover the needs of the summer programme in 1925. As things turned out, they were not withdrawn until 1928. However, Iden put considerable pressure on Pick to let him have some new NSs as he claimed to be 'getting it in the neck' from the local authorities and the public over the condition of the buses. Fearful of opening the way to more competition, Pick instructed George Shave to find some buses for National and six were offered near the end of October for delivery in fourteen days but Iden had apparently asked for PS, which caused Pick some concern. Iden was beginning to show the stubborn persistence in influencing the choice of buses he should operate which was to lead to some disenchantment by Pick a few years later. In fact, National had been operating the new NS type since January 1924, when seven were allocated, and had built up a total of 23 by the end of the year. Four had replaced Bs, six were those just mentioned and the rest had been used to build up services.

By this time the number of buses operating in the Watford area had begun to outgrow the capacity of the small premises in Leavesden Road, Watford but it had been built on a confined site and there was no scope for enlarging the building. The LGOC Board therefore decided to build a new garage and gave approval to the expenditure of £25,490 and for the contract to be placed with Messrs Jarvis & Son. The new garage was erected on the western side of Lower High Street, opposite the gas works, and opened for business in about July 1925, when Leavesden Road closed.

The introduction of the Route Approval provisions of the London Traffic Act on 1st December 1924 entailed wholesale renumbering of services, those from the north being allocated numbers from 301 upwards. The complete list of routes then being operated by National on behalf of General was as follows, those taken over from H&B earlier in the year being annotated accordingly.

| 301 | (N2) | Bushey Station–Northchurch |
|---|---|---|
| 302 | (N3) | Bushey Station–Hemel Hempstead |
| 303 | (N7) | New Barnet–Hatfield Station |
| 304 | (N8A) | Borehamwood Station–St Albans |
| * | | |
| 306A | (N13) | Watford Junction–Waltham Cross |
| 306B | (N30 ex H&B) | Waltham Cross–Epping Forest |
| 307 | (N16) | Watford–Harrow via Rickmansworth, Northwood. |
| 308 | (N20) | Havering–Aveley |
| 309 | (N22) | Watford–Harefield |
| 310 | (N25 ex H&B) | Hertford–Waltham Cross |
| N1 | | Rickmansworth–Fleetville |
| N4 | | Dunstable–St Albans |
| N5 | | St Albans–Hitchin via Stevenage or Codicote |
| N6 | | Watford–Berkhamsted via Amersham |
| N8 | | St Albans–Kimpton |
| N9 | | Bishops Stortford–Brentwood via Epping, Ongar |
| N10 | | St Albans–Hertford via Cole Green |
| N10A | | St Albans–Hertford via Essendon Corner |
| N11 | | Hertford–Bishops Stortford via Widford |
| N14 | | Hemel Hempstead–St Albans |
| N15 | | Watford–Bedmond |
| N17 | | Watford–Great Gaddesden |
| N18 | | Chipperfield–Abbots Langley |
| N24 | | Watford–West Hyde |
| N26 | | Waltham Cross–Watton via Hertford Heath |
| N27 | | Rye House–Stevenage via Hertford Heath |
| N28 (ex H&B) | | Ware–Bengeo |
| N29 (ex H&B) | | Ware–Woolmer Green |
| N31 (ex H&B) | | Hertford–Royston via Buntingford or Barkway |

* The number 305 was reserved for the N12 shorts between Watford and Bushey Heath, but these were withdrawn on 29th November 1924.

A few more gaps in the network were filled during 1925, in both urban and highly rural areas. Another Watford route came on the scene in February working from Harebreaks to West Watford station numbered N19, the second route to bear the number. There were two developments in Hertford the same month when former H&B route N28 was modified to operate from Hertford Post Office to Hertford North or Bengeo, and a new route N33 linked Hertford to Dane End. A service to Hertford North from Ware, numbered N32, had been notified for operation in August 1924 but it almost certainly did not run and was eventually covered by the N28. Another service was added in September 1925 between the county town and Wareside (N22) and in November the Lea Valley services were strengthened by a new 312 working Ware to Waltham Cross. Co-incidentally with the 312, the 306 was extended to Epping from Waltham Cross. Having acquired H&B, the LGOC was taking Hertford and the Lea Valley seriously, for reasons explained below. The competition provided by the 306 between Enfield and Waltham Abbey ultimately led to the withdrawal of Charles Waymann from the scene on 1st July 1926. His premises in High Bridge Street Waltham Abbey were taken over on lease by National in September 1926, adding another small garage to its LGOC portfolio.

Some new types of bus appeared in the National fleet during 1925 to operate these additional services. Four Lancia single-deckers and two Chevrolet 14-seaters no doubt represented Iden's influence but there were also three of the new single-deck Ks which had just gone into production, the LGOC's first with pneumatic tyres. The Lancias had been bought for operation in Watford to meet local competition and had been favoured over the alternative Talbot because, although more expensive at £1035 a bus, they had a longer wheelbase and four-wheel brakes. They had Dodson bodies and this raised Pick's eyebrows because the LGOC had 'quarrelled' with Charles Dodson and no longer bought bodywork from him. George Shave was not impressed by the Lancias and thought they would be unlikely to pass the Metropolitan Police's stringent demands. He conceded that they gave a comfortable ride but noted that the windows rattled and would be draughty in winter. They were somewhat costly, had only 24 seats but had to carry a conductor and had a fuel consumption of 8 mpg at best. The seats over the wheel arch were very uncomfortable and had knee room sufficient only for children, according to Shave.

*Left* The last S-type buses to be built were thirteen single-deckers (S 915-927) for National, delivered in February 1927, which had pneumatic tyres and the improved body styling already introduced in the K-type. The three different styles of fleet name on the side, the dash and the radiator header tank are noteworthy. S 927 is at Watford Junction on route 311 which started as Watford to Radlett via Aldenham in October 1926 and had a leg added via Borehamwood and Shenley in August 1928. (Alan B. Cross)

The Ks had been despatched to National at short notice to combat competition in the Lea Valley. Competition in the northern Country Area was beginning to worry Pick who believed that Redburn and Birds were preparing to move into the area and in October 1925 he suggested that twelve converted K with single-deck bodies should be sent to NOTC. Iden was told that he was required to hold the roads to the north of London in greater strength, particularly on the east side and that further roads which might be tempting to independent proprietors should be occupied as a matter of urgency. 'Days count', said Pick and instructed that B-types, by now well into their dotage, should be used if need be.

In April 1926 both Watford and Hertford got new routes but both were withdrawn in October. The N16 ran from Watford (Met) Station to the Market Place and the N20 from Hertford to Roydon. A longer-lasting innovation came in July with the introduction of route 313 between St Albans and Enfield, a direct ancestor of the London Buses route under that number running in 2003. By October, the 301 and 302 were extended southward from Bushey Station to Watford Heath and a new route 311 started running between Watford and Radlett via Aldenham.

Despite the tough words of October 1925, the number of buses dedicated to National did not increase during 1926. Eight additional K single-deckers were supplied, as were two S-type and three NS but the General Strike in May seriously interrupted the supply of new buses and not all plans could be fulfilled. A little help came from the transfer of responsibility for route 307 to the LGOC in March but a serious blow was dealt by the Metropolitan Police who refused to license any more B-type for operation on route 308. The stock of Bs therefore shrank by eleven, including the ex-H&B example and three of the Daimler Ys also had to go.

In 1927 the LGOC widened its sphere of influence to include the area south of Luton, not by introducing new routes but by the transfer of routes from National's Bedford Area, most of which were former Road Motors services. National had bought the entire business of Road Motors Ltd, including its operations in the Weymouth area, in 1925 for £64,000. This was a joint deal with the LGOC who contributed some of the capital for the purchase of the Luton area part of the business. The Luton services came under the control of the Bedford Area at first but were transferred to the Watford area, realising LGOC's interest in the transaction, on 1st January 1927. Another business which had succumbed to the blandishments of the LGOC/National combination was the F.C.H. Motor Haulage and Engineering Company, of Ashburnham Garage, Luton. Their licences were transferred to National on 8th March 1926 who then operated the routes (which became the N52A and N64) as part of its Bedford Area until January 1927.

The exact date of some of the transfers is uncertain but former Road Motors route N51 (Luton to St Albans) appears to have been a pioneer of these changes as it appeared in the April 1926 Watford Area timetable. The routes believed to have transferred to Watford Area control in January 1927 were: former F.C.H. N52A (Luton to Hitchin via Ley Green or Whitehall) and N64 (Luton to Tea Green via Cockernhoe); and former Road Motors N55 (Luton to Markyate), N60 (Luton to Caddington), N61 (Luton to Wheathampstead), and N66 (circular route: Luton, Batford, Harpenden, Redbourne, Markyate, Caddington, Luton). The N60 did not appear in the April 1927 timetable but was listed in October 1927, so this route may have transferred later than the others. Another route that was transferred from Bedford to Watford control was the N16B (Luton to Studham via Dunstable) which switched allegiance in April 1927 but then went back to National in October. (Much later, in October 1931, it again returned to Watford Area control.) These services were operated from the former Road Motors garage in Langley Street, Luton but this was replaced by premises in Castle Street in 1928. A new route 55A was added in November 1927, running between Luton and Kensworth and this became the N55A in April 1928.

There was also some more growth in Essex in April 1927 when route 308 was extended from Havering to Stapleford Abbots and a new route N50 was inaugurated running from Ongar to Romford via Brentwood and Harold Wood. In June, National's route 34 from Grays to Romford via Aveley and Rainham was transferred to the Watford Area and became N34 but was renumbered N36 in July. In the border country between north-west Essex and Hertfordshire, route 315, ran for the summer of 1927 between Waltham Cross and High Beach starting on 31st July 1927. In November 1927 it was cut back to Waltham Abbey with journeys to Epping Forest and extended to start from Hertford. It was again extended to High Beach in April 1928 but withdrawn between Hertford and Waltham Cross in that October, becoming Hertford to Epping Forest in February 1929.

The Luton transfers sparked off a prolonged correspondence between Walter Iden, Frank Pick and other LGOC officers about vehicle policy, which eventually strayed far beyond the immediate cause of the debate. General's original plan, submitted on 2nd April 1927 was to supply nine double-deck PS and six single-deckers, also described as PS. This was apparently not acceptable to Iden and the proposal was modified in June to be nine NS and six ADC 32-seat single-deckers. These were in addition to the vehicles already ordered for National, which comprised thirteen S single-deckers, four S double-deck, four NS and five coaches. The buses were intended as replacements for three B-type, two Daimler Y and two Straker Squire double-deckers and four B-type, five Daimler Y, two Chevrolet, two C-type one-man buses and one N, a total of twenty-one.

Iden was still not satisfied because the NS was 'not capable of operating the service because of the hills' and the ADC had a poor performance on the road. He preferred to have fifteen single-deckers on pneumatic tyres for the Luton area because speed was essential if the competition was to be challenged successfully, the point being that the speed limit for solid tyres was 12 mph whereas for pneumatics it was 20 mph. He told Pick that it would be advantageous to get some into service on the St Albans road as soon as possible to check the growing competition there. There was certainly something for the two companies to worry about as the road southward from Luton through Harpenden had already attracted Blowers (Express) and Comfy Cars and the road from Dunstable also saw Blowers, as well as Cobb's Albanian, St Albans & District and, later, Swatman. Pick was also concerned about the delays because he felt the opportunity to acquire licences in Luton might be lost and suggested that some of the LGOC's own Dennises might be sent to Luton. In the meantime he offered immediate delivery of nine Leylands which had been acquired with some of the London Independents who were then being taken over in large numbers (two from Atlas, four from Invicta and one each from Empress, Vivid and Alberta). The Leylands, which Iden greeted with some enthusiasm at first, were delivered between 16th and 25th July and a K was added at the end of the month. Subsequent scavenging produced two Guy BB 24-seaters (G 1 and 2, formerly owned by Uneedus) in September and four Dennis 2½ ton 25-seaters (D 53, 55-57) in November. The delay in sending the Dennises was because Iden had refused to take them at first.

In the meantime, Pick had been trying to find out why Iden was not happy with the ADC. This was, after all, the main single-deck bus model offered by the fellow Underground Group company Associated Daimler and if it was not up to scratch, he wanted to have it improved. In fact the ADC 416 was a very successful model with a strong order book but it was a stolid stroller rather than a sprightly sprinter, so Iden had a point. Norman Hardie, General Manager of the Associated Daimler Company claimed that there was an ADC available which was comparable to the Dennis E in performance providing an appropriate rear-axle ratio was specified but this had the Daimler sleeve valve engine which Iden described as an experimental design. He preferred the poppet valve type and was not alone in being wary of the sleeve-valve engine which was notoriously unreliable. Another problem was that six-cylinder engines were not at the time acceptable to the Metropolitan Police and there was some doubt whether they could be used on through cross-boundary services. A lighter version of the ADC for the 1928 season had an improved specification including Ricardo cylinder heads, a new type camshaft and Duralumin connecting rods, and the LGOC's Chiswick experts thought this would 'do the job'. Iden's response to this was to repeat that the Leyland or Dennis could 'make rings around the ADC'. He even tried a little blackmail on ADC by

Nine Leylands which had been acquired from London Independents were sent north to National in July 1927 in an attempt to calm Walter Iden's vociferous dissatisfaction with the fleet he had on loan. XT8752, numbered L 2 in the NOTC fleet, was a Leyland LB4 with Dodson bodywork which had been bought by Alberta in May 1924. The N31 was the former Harvey & Burrows route from Hertford to Puckeridge which retained its 'N' number because it did not penetrate the Metropolitan Area. (Alan B. Cross)

saying he knew what he wanted and if ADC could supply it he would consider the company in future as supplier of his own (non-LGOC) needs. He went on to complain that the vehicles supplied to him in the past had arrived in disgraceful condition which did not merit much confidence. Writing separately to Pick he said that 'your people will have to get more up to the mark' if he wanted to continue to enjoy good favour with the operating companies. Pick's response was a terse acknowledgement.

In July 1929, route 310 was extended from Hertford to Stevenage over the route established by Harvey & Burrows between Hertford and Watton in March 1921 and on to Stevenage in May 1922, later numbered N27. Starting handles were always a curse for photographers as they often obscured the registration number, as here, but this is known to be UC2205, one of the Hall Lewis-bodied 29-seat ADC416s delivered to National in 1928. The photograph was taken in September 1929, soon after the extension, which may explain why the destination was on a separate board and not included in the blind display. (Alan B. Cross)

The new bus was to be on display at the Olympia show and, with great reluctance, Iden was persuaded to inspect it and later to road test it. By this time he was either getting impatient at the delays or, as some of the content of the correspondence could imply, had been given an ultimatum by Pick but, either way, he decided to cut his losses and go for fifteen ADCs. In his report on the road test Iden referred to the 416's poor performance on hills when heavily laden. The new engines were expected to be a bit more powerful but the Police had already said they would not approve the 423 and 424 type, so it was important to ensure that they would be accepted before becoming too committed.

The prolonged debate about competition made Pick realise that the time had come to make the buses more attractive, particularly where they were to be used on competitive services in the country area. He gave instructions to George Shave to do what was necessary, including the need to ensure that the seating was really comfortable.

In September 1927, the National/LGOC fleet comprised:

| DOUBLE-DECK | | SINGLE-DECK | |
|---|---|---|---|
| 3 B-type | 34-seat | 4 B-type | 26-seat |
| 13 PS | 54-seat | 26 S | 30-seat |
| 2 PS | 50-seat | 1 S | 32-seat |
| 4 S | 54-seat | 2 C | 20-seat |
| 15 NS | 52-seat | 2 CH | 14-seat |
| 14 NS | 50-seat | 4 L (Lancia) | 24-seat |
| 1 WD | 40-seat | 4 WD | 26-seat |
| 1 WD | 44-seat | 1 WD | 32-seat |
| 1 WD | 47-seat | 2 Guy | 24-seat |
| 9 L | | 5 AW | c-a-b |
| (Leyland) | 48-seat | 4 Daimler | c-a-b |
| 2 WS | 44-seat | 1 Daimler | c-a-b |
| 2 WS | 46-seat | | chassis |
| 1 WS | 48-seat | | |
| 2 WS | 52-seat | | |

The revised order for 1928 was for two NS, 39 ADC 416D single-deckers and four ADC coaches. The twenty-seven single-deck S were also to be fitted with pneumatic tyres. The vehicles to be withdrawn and scrapped were three B double-deck, two Daimler double-deck, six Strakers, nine Leylands, three B single-deck, two C, six Daimler single-deck and four Daimler chars-a-banc. Others to be withdrawn and sold were the four Lancias and two Chevrolets. This gave a net increase of four vehicles for expansion.

Almost as soon as this episode was over, Iden was again asking Pick for help, this time at Ware. He had five Daimler 26-seaters which were in a bad state of repair and needed expensive remedial work to make them fit to pass the Metropolitan Police test. He asked for five Dennises to cover until the new rolling stock arrived. Pick's reaction is important in illustrating the very different relationship he had with Iden compared with Hawkins at East Surrey, which surely must have been an influence on the eventual decision to expand the Reigate company's activities to include the northern area. Writing to his Commercial Manager, Pick complained that NOTC 'took advantage of our facilities' but were unwilling to hold and use buses until they were life expired if they needed work done to them. He had never been content that National should refuse to take and work for two or three years some of General's Dennis buses for their own fleet in Ware yet now Iden was asking to borrow them in place of their existing vehicles.

What may have prompted Iden's action was the appearance on the Hertford scene of a new operator, People's Motor Services, who started two new services between Hertford and Bishops Stortford in October 1927. One of these went into direct competition with National on the N11, the other went by a new route through Stanstead Abbots and Sawbridgeworth. This was followed by a route from Ware to Baldock via Walkern and Stevenage and the company soon built up a substantial network. Its most serious attack on National/LGOC was on the old battleground of the main Hertford Road down to Wormley, which it began to serve with a route running via St Margaret's and Rye House in March 1928. National/LGOC made

no significant alterations to their own routes to counter the competition but when People's arrived in Wormley, National responded by running extra buses ahead of the newcomer's timings. They were warned off this action by Hertford Borough Council who threatened not to renew their licences if it persisted, a threat National could not ignore. The 'spoilers' were taken off, leaving People's to compete until 1933.

In other parts of the area, 1928 was a year of consolidation and concentration on warding off the competition with a couple of bits of organisational housekeeping thrown in. There were a few minor extensions, mainly over roads already served and one important revision in April which linked the 303 with the northern end of the N5 to create a major trunk route from New Barnet to Hitchin. The 'housekeeping' was in Essex, where, in May, the N50 was transferred from National to the LGOC, who numbered it G2 in the special series they had created for routes running wholly outside the Metropolitan Police District. In November National's Chelmsford Area route 40 (Grays to Upminster) was extended to Romford, transferred to Watford Area control and became N40, running jointly with the LGOC's G40 between Romford, Upminster and Grays. This was a unique joint operation between the two sides of the fence, which paved the way for a similarly unusual, but short-lived, arrangement when the LPTB took over, at which time route 40 had been back under Chelmsford's control since July 1929.

A new garage was opened in South Street Bishops Stortford in 1928, which operated both LGOC agreement routes and NOTC Chelmsford Area services which until then had been run from outstations. There was a curious episode there in September 1928, which is strictly not part of this story but superficially appears to be. The two National Chelmsford Area routes from Bishops Stortford to Saffron Walden (13) and Henham (13A), were operated by 'General crews' from that date and renumbered into the LGOC series as N13 and N13A. They were not, and never became, routes run on behalf of the LGOC, did not pass to LGCS in 1932 nor to the LPTB in 1933 but became part of the Eastern National network. The renumbering created an anomaly which was presumably a device to make a distinction between routes on which staff were employed on 'London Country Area' conditions of service and those covered by NOTC agreements.

The famous blue triangle symbol of the Associated Equipment Company appeared in 1929, at first attached to the Daimler-designed radiator shell on the new Reliance chassis. YW8048 was numbered R 5 by LGOC but later took the number R 49 in its final years with the LPTB. It was one of fourteen delivered to National in 1929 and is seen on the stand at the Clarendon Hotel, Watford Junction on route 306, alongside S 343 on route 142A and another S on route 158. (Alan B. Cross)

A similar pattern was followed in 1929 with no major route developments. It is of interest to note that by February 1929, the intense competition on the Watford to Aylesbury road had been tamed, in the sense that routes 301 and 302 were now formally operated jointly with C. Aston of Watford, the Aylesbury Bus Co (301 only), the Chiltern Omnibus Service and West Herts. The former Road Motors route N51 between Luton and St Albans was similarly operated as a joint service with Comfy Cars and Blowers (Express). This year's housekeeping took the form of routes N36 (Grays to Romford via Aveley) and the Waltham Cross to Epping Forest section of the 315 being released to the control of LGOC. The 315 was absorbed into the 306 group as the 306B.

Iden's vehicle requirements for 1929 again caused irritation at 55 Broadway. He had let Shave know that, at the very least, fourteen single-deck Ss should be equipped with four-wheel brakes but left Shave in little doubt that he really wanted something new, either Reliances or (what he really wanted) from some other manufacturer. Pick's reaction was to say that 'we have already spent too much money on this undertaking which is unprofitable' and told Shave to get on with converting the S-types to give them another three years life and to do so as cheaply as possible. However Shave pointed out that this would be a complicated and expensive job, at the end of which they would still be running a vehicle with an out-of-date specification. He had calculated that the real cost of converting the S-types would be £1,010 a vehicle, whereas a new Reliance with a completely up-to-date specification could be bought for 1,175. Pick was convinced by Shave's arguments and it was agreed to replace the fourteen S with a like number of new Reliances, which were delivered to Watford in June and July 1929.

At the end of 1929 National was operating 139 vehicles on behalf of the LGOC from garages at Bishops Stortford, Hatfield, Hemel Hempstead, Luton, Ware and Watford. The fleet comprised six Guys, 32 S, 31 NS, one Morris, four Lancia, three Dennis, 39 ADC 416, fourteen R and nine chars-a-banc.

An army of National staff and some attendant schoolboys pause to pose while clearing a path through the snow ahead of S 920. It is not clear whether the bus is stranded or is the snow clearers' own transport but the scene is one that would have been repeated all over the operating area in the deepest winter months. (Alan B. Cross)

The K single-decker entered the National fleet in 1925, K 1053 being one of the second batch of twenty-five which were mounted on overhauled older chassis from double-deckers. It is on route 313 which ran from St Albans to Enfield via Potters Bar and Botany Bay starting on 7th July 1926, and is a direct ancestor of the route still running in 2003. (Alan B. Cross)

## CHAPTER SIX

# General Spreads Its Wings: The West

Compared with the extensive operations undertaken in co-operation with East Surrey and The National Omnibus and Transport Company, those on General's western flank were trifling. LGOC buses had been running out as far as Slough since 1912 but otherwise, apart from summer extensions, got no further than such as Ealing, Twickenham or Kingston until the early post-war years when daily services reached Egham from Hounslow (117) and Chertsey from Kingston via Addlestone. Apart from a brief venture to Maidenhead during the summer of 1921, General showed no great ambition to extend its sphere of influence as far out west as it was to go north and south. Nevertheless it had given the appearance of just such ambition in March 1921 when it put on a new route 95 from Uxbridge, which it had not yet reached from the London direction, along the main Oxford road to High Wycombe, fourteen miles distant. The route was further extended in June to West Wycombe. In July route 93 arrived in Uxbridge from Hounslow.

For a year before these events, the LGOC had been negotiating with the Thames Valley Traction Co to establish agreed spheres of operation and operating rights along and around the boundary between them. When these were close to reaching a conclusion, the General Board decided to offer Thames Valley the opportunity to become its operating agents in the western area, starting with the Uxbridge routes. Frank Pick reported the successful conclusion of such an agreement to his Board on 9th February 1922 and it was formally ratified on 20th April. It followed the same broad principles as those with ESTC and NOTC but contained the important difference that Thames Valley was to supply its own vehicles. The 'Area Agreement' boundary ran to the west of Egham, Old Windsor, Windsor, and the Slough to Beaconsfield road, and then south of the Oxford road to High Wycombe, eastward to Amersham and then north-east of the Amersham–Aylesbury road. The 'Uxbridge Special Area' was between that and the Metropolitan Police boundary.

Thames Valley retained running rights between Staines Bridge and Windsor and General invited the company to extend the route over the bridge into the town but this was not approved by the Metropolitan Police.

*Above* High Wycombe, a centre for furniture making and paper manufacture and then still an elegant town with much seventeenth and eighteenth century architecture, was reached by LGOC buses on route 95 in March 1921. The subsequent hand-over to Thames Valley brought double-deckers to the Traction Company's fleet in the form of Thornycroft J9s, which were replaced on the Uxbridge Area services in 1926 by Thornycroft JBs such as this, bought from the LGOC who, in turn, had acquired them from Independents. Dodson-bodied 124 (XP5985), seen in High Wycombe High Street, came from Cambrian who had bought it in November 1923. (Ken Glazier collection)

On 14th June 1922 Thames Valley took over the newly-built Uxbridge garage and the two routes it was by then operating, which were renumbered during July to W20 (93) and W21 (95). The buses allocated by the Berkshire company were all refurbished former War Department 6.2 litre-engined Thornycroft Js, six Birch-bodied and one Brush-bodied single-deckers and seven with LGOC B-type double-deck bodies. The particular combinations had been chosen because they conformed to the rigid London specification, but the Metropolitan Police licensed them with some reluctance and warned the company that no more converted vehicles of this kind would be licensed by them. The double-deckers were the first to be operated by Thames Valley.

Two more routes were soon added, the W22 on 7th July between Uxbridge and Windsor via Iver, Langley and Slough and the W23 on 28th July between Uxbridge and Great Missenden via Denham, The Chalfonts and Amersham. The W23 was rerouted to run via Gerrards Cross and Gold Hill from 19th August to serve Gerrards Cross station but the northern end of the route proved to be a poor earner and it was cut back to Amersham on 1st January 1923. The W24, which started on 13th August 1922, has already been mentioned in chapter five as it was a joint operation with National's N24 from Uxbridge to Watford via Denham and Rickmansworth. When National cut its operation back to West Hyde on 7th October, Thames Valley continued to operate the W24 right through but it did not prosper. This was not very productive territory in the early 1920s and the route ran for the last time on 31st December 1922.

The tentacles of the London Traffic Act reached out to these routes which were renumbered in the western series of Bassom numbers from 1st December 1924, the W20 and W21 getting their third number in two years:

501 (W20)  Uxbridge to Hounslow via Cowley, West Drayton and Bath Road.
502 (W21)  Uxbridge to West Wycombe via Gerrards Cross, Beaconsfield and High Wycombe.
503 (W22)  Uxbridge to Windsor via Cowley, Iver, Langley and Slough.
504 (W23)  Uxbridge to Amersham Old Town via Gerrards Cross, Gold Hill and The Chalfonts.

Apart from one more to come in High Wycombe, under rather special circumstances, that was the sum total of Thames Valley's contribution to the LGOC network.

When Thames Valley had taken over Uxbridge garage in 1922, they had found themselves in charge of a building that Frank Pick, writing internally to his Commercial Manager in November 1925, described as 'cheap and shoddy'. Perhaps it was significant that it had been built by the Group's own Building Department under the supervision of the Chief Engineer (Railways). Thames Valley had complained from

One of the J9Bs in trouble in the snow. The destination board of 116 (XP9831) has been turned upside down which implies that the journey has been abandoned but what has happened to the passengers? However, the driver has not given up and is ready with his spade to clear a path. (D.A. Ruddom collection)

the start about the high cost of repairs and had objected to them being charged to the Joint Services account, especially as those services yielded no profit. Pick's comment was made in the aftermath of the latest dispute concerning the cost of repairing the garage gates, which the LGOC agreed to bear but only after first insisting that it was Thames Valley's responsibility. Pick thought that even after the repairs had been done the garage would still be unsatisfactory and issued instructions for a set of standards to be drawn up for use by the Building Department on future projects. In August 1926, Pick's blood pressure was again sent soaring when complaints were received from local residents about the condition of the drainage, which was accepted by LGOC officers as unsatisfactory, one remarking that 'very little attention was paid to the building in the first place'. An outlay of £500 was needed to install a proper septic drainage system but this was a considerable sum of money in 1926 and, before anything was spent, Pick asked for a report on just how suitable the building was for continued use as a bus garage. Most significantly, in view of later events, he commented that most of the trouble came about because of divided responsibility. The work was done but when

the garage was about to be handed back to the LGOC in 1928, repair and maintenance work costing £370 had to be carried out before it was in a condition acceptable to the LGOC.

In 1926 Thames Valley set about improving the fleet at Uxbridge by replacing the Thornycroft Js, with the later JB, a more powerful machine with a 7 litre 50hp 4-cylinder BB4 engine. The buses, all of which were fitted with Dodson 50-seat bodywork, were bought from General, who had acquired all but two of them when they took over the Cambrian business, the odd two coming from Olympic and Ubique. All were therefore fully up to the standards demanded by the Metropolitan Police and seven of the sixteen purchased were allocated to Uxbridge during April and May 1926. Consideration of the needs of the single-deck fleet was deferred for a year but in May 1927 the LGOC agreed that Thames Valley should seek approval from the Metropolitan Police for the replacement of the old Thornycroft Js with some of its new Tilling Stevens B9As. The likelihood that approval would be given was quite high but this enterprise did not get very far before the two companies were in discussion about the future of the operating agreement.

The Uxbridge Area routes returned to LGOC control on 1st January 1929 and the Thames Valley buses, both single- and double-deck, were replaced by standard S-type single-deckers. S 890 was photographed in Uxbridge on 2nd September 1929, having arrived from Windsor on route 503. (Alan B. Cross)

Amersham & District 18, a 32-seat Strachan-bodied Dennis E, was one of the buses purchased by the LGOC as equity in the company. It is working on the High Wycombe–Gerrards Cross route. (J.F. Higham)

At the end of 1926 the two companies and the other major operator in High Wycombe, City of Oxford Motor Services Ltd, were confronted with a proposal by Chepping Wycombe Council, to seek bus operating powers, which all three agreed to oppose jointly. Negotiations with the Council led to them agreeing to withdraw their application for powers if LGOC and Thames Valley would agree to operate a local service between Wycombe Marsh and Desborough Park Road with fares of a penny for two stages. The agreement which emerged was intended to remain in force for fourteen years, subject to review after the first year and to arbitration of any disputes by the

Minister of Transport. The service was required to start on 1st July 1927, which it did, running without a route number for some reason and operated by Thames Valley from its Wycombe Marsh garage. It eventually became the 26 and, as 326, was to be a rare example of joint operation between London Transport and another operator after 1933. Associated with this agreement, the Council also introduced restrictions on buses operating in the town, including maximum layover times and fixed bus stops.

On 19th November 1927, the LGOC gave notice that it did not intend to renew its agreement with the company for operation of services in the Uxbridge area. Neither side

had been particularly happy with the way things had worked out, Thames Valley because it did not feel that it was making enough money from the enterprise and the LGOC because it was unable to persuade the Traction Company to expand and run more mileage. The divorce was therefore a cordial one, even though Thames Valley then began to worry about the effect on its own development on the eastern side of its area. The LGOC took back control of Uxbridge garage and routes 501-504 on 1st January 1929.

Pick's scouts had found a more promising potential collaborator in the form of the Amersham & District Motor Bus and

Small Strachan-bodied Dennises were typical of the Amersham & District fleet at the time the LGOC began to take an interest in the company. No.2 (PP7251) was a 2½-tonner with a 26-seat saloon body and is seen in High Wycombe on the Hazlemere route.
(The Omnibus Society)

Another vehicle in the Amersham & District fleet when LGOC came on the scene was this Gilford 1660T 30-seat coach with the inevitable Strachan body. It is standing outside the company's garage at Amersham, a building which survives at the time of writing, unlike its younger and grander sibling built by the LPTB, which has disappeared under a supermarket.
(The Omnibus Society)

Haulage Company, a small company which had been registered in October 1919 and had since established a network of services around its home town. At the end of June 1928, the LGOC wrote to the Managing Director inviting him to a meeting at 55 Broadway to discuss 'certain matters'. The meeting between the Commercial Manager of LGOC and the Chairman and Managing Director of A&D took place on 9th July, when the 'certain matters' emerged as a proposed agreement to work together on agreed routes, on terms similar to those included in the other joint operating agreements. Further negotiations took place, culminating in Frank Pick's attending the Amersham &

District Board meeting on 2nd September to settle the financial details.

There followed the usual drawn-out negotiations with correspondence being exchanged or meetings held almost weekly. While these were in progress the LGOC provided the funds for ten new buses, nine Dennis Es and a Gilford and this expenditure was to form the basis of General's stake in the smaller company. The Amersham & District Board sealed the agreement on 26th August 1929, at which time General was allotted 5,578 ordinary shares and 6,663 6 per cent preference shares, the latter being in consideration of the balance of the cost of new buses (£1,663) and £5,000 as an advance

commitment for a new garage at High Wycombe, the contract for which was about to be let. The agreement was completed on 9th October 1929.

Most of the developments by Amersham & District were carried out between 1930 and 1933 but the LGOC had been in discussion with Thames Valley since early 1929 about services in the Wycombe area which culminated in the purchase of the operating rights to routes 28 (High Wycombe to Amersham via Hazlemere and Penn) and 35 (Chalfont St Peter to Windsor). Together with the half interest in route 26, these were handed over to Amersham & District to operate from 1st March 1929.

## CHAPTER SEVEN

# Vehicle Developments

At the LGOC Board meeting on 6th July 1922 there was a discussion on bus design, during which Lord Ashfield announced that work was in hand with AEC to design the new type of bus that was needed. He issued instructions that there should be no more orders for existing types. What Ashfield and his Board were looking for was a bus which could have a covered top deck to increase revenue during wet weather when open top buses became virtual single-deckers because people were unwilling to risk being drenched on the upper deck. Buses had fallen behind in this respect compared to trams, most of which had top covers by that time.

In London, as ever, the biggest hurdle that would have to be surmounted was the attitude of the Metropolitan Police, who were concerned about the stability of such a vehicle. The solution is believed to have been the brainchild of the Chief Draughtsman of AEC, Charles Edwards, who had been study-ing developments in north America where the Fifth Avenue Coach Company of New York had produced some buses with lower floor levels. He saw this as a way of reducing the overall height of the bus and lowering its centre of gravity, thereby increasing its stability. These principles led to the new design, which was given the type letters NS by the LGOC. There has been much written and debated about the use of this code, the first of General's to have two letters, and the meaning of the letters. The most popular explanation is that it meant 'Nulli Secundus' (second to none) and this was certainly used by General's publicity department. Evidence that no name of any sort was attached to the bus when the letters were chosen is contained in a Traffic Circular item dated 19th May 1923, after the first NSs had gone into service, which lightheartedly invites staff to submit ideas for a name. The text suggests that 'None Superior' sounds good and so, it says, does 'Nulli Secundus', but *'we like English'* (author's italics). The text also describes the NS as a 'one-step' bus, which seems to eliminate another favourite theory that NS stood for 'No Step'. The most likely explanation is more mundane, that it simply meant 'new S', the sort of working name which might have been attached to the project in its early development period and then just stuck.

*Above* Things to come – eventually. This official photograph shows NS 1 as it was first presented to the police, with a removable upper deck top cover. Comparison with other photographs of the final design show a number of differences, notably that the upper saloon windows are much shallower and the roof, which looks flatter, does not overhang the front and rear ends. The front mudguards also differ from standard, continuing forward over the top half of the front of the wheels and giving a rather matronly impression to the finished product. (Capital Transport collection)

The NS as it went into production, without top cover. NS 53 was one of the first twenty-two to enter service on 10th May 1923, allocated to Hammersmith garage for route 11. The NS was clearly a relative of S 496 just visible behind it on route 15, its main attribute being a lower floor line. (Arthur Ingram)

The new chassis was essentially a modified version of the S-type whose mechanical specification and proportions it shared, although it was fractionally longer with a wheelbase of 15ft 6ins instead of 14ft 11ins and an overall length of 25ft instead of 24ft 8¼ins. The early examples of the type had a new constant mesh gearbox, but this was soon replaced by the chain gear of earlier types. What made the NS a landmark bus was the design of the chassis behind the front axle. This was cranked down between the axles so that the main frame was lower than on the S, while behind the rear axle, the extension of the frame which supported the platform was cranked even lower. To achieve this it was necessary to abandon the traditional flitched timber frame and use pressed steel instead. The rear axle, which had an underslung worm drive as on previous types, was a double-reduction unit which enabled the centre section, where the gangway passed over, to be lowered. Taken together these features enabled the lower deck floor and the overall height of the complete bus to be lowered by nearly a foot. The

platform was even lower, low enough for it to be reached by one step from the kerb, with one more step to reach the lower saloon. This general arrangement was to remain the standard on rear-entrance double-deckers for over forty years and the step heights were not bettered, nor always even matched, on production buses, until the advent of the Bristol Lodekka a quarter of a century later which eliminated the step into the lower saloon.

NS 1 was completed on 23rd November 1922 and was ready for inspection by the Board at the beginning of December but it was not licensed for service until 8th May 1923. Its body had been fitted with a removable covered top and the complete vehicle was submitted to the Metropolitan Police for approval but this was not forthcoming and the top cover, prudently not part of the main structure, was removed. Despite this major disappointment, which was perhaps expected, the LGOC shrugged its collective shoulders and bided its time. Approval to the open top version was given subsequently to NS 5, the second completed bus whose chas-

sis was first received on 29th January 1923, although the chassis of NS 2 had been in stock for a few days, mounted with a lorry body. NS 3 and 4 did not arrive until August.

The General Board obviously had great faith in the model as they approved the purchase of 500 NS buses, for early delivery, at their meeting on 8th February, and another 350 were added on 8th March when the formal expenditure requisition was submitted. Further orders added another 750 which, with the pre-production batch of five, brought the total ordered for delivery by September 1924 to 1,605. The bodywork for the production buses was to be supplied by Short Bros of Rochester (875, including 25 spares for the overhaul float), Brush Electrical Engineering, Derby (265), Ransomes Sims and Jefferies of Ipswich (100) and the LGOC itself (390). The overall design of the bodywork of the NS was similar to that of the S-type but there was a number of detailed differences, quite apart from the obvious one that it was 8½ inches lower. Because of the few inches of extra length and the extended wheelbase, there was a short

window at the front end of the saloon, matching a modified one at the back. The position of the upper deck relative to the lower was again altered to give a smaller overhang over the front canopy while at the rear being extended further than on the S to cover the front half of the platform. The corners of the upper deck were curved, rather than forming a right-angle as on earlier types and the driver's canopy was more slender and also more curvaceous. The underframe lifeguards on the side of the bus were reduced from five to three slats, with a correspondingly beneficial effect on the appearance of the bus. The extra weight of the more complicated chassis of the NS, 5 tons 17 cwt compared with the 4 tons 10 cwt of the S, meant that the seating capacity had to be limited to 50 (26/24) to keep the axle loadings within the maximum allowed.

The arrival of the chassis for NS 6 at Chiswick on 31st March 1923 marked the beginning of the regular flow which was to continue until NS 1603 was licensed on 24th October 1924 (NS 1605 had an experimental engine and had been delivered three months earlier). The first twenty-two were licensed at Hammersmith garage on 10th May 1923 and went into service on route 11, to much acclaim. Between then and early July, after the completion of route 11, they were allocated to Mortlake, Tottenham, Palmers

Green, Battersea, Chalk Farm and Seven Kings for operation on trunk central area routes 9, 73, 29, 25 and 25A, by which time nearly 400 were in service. The buses replaced were mostly of the S-type but also some K-type, and the usual game of 'pass the parcel' ensued, with S-types replacing Ks which replaced Bs, all designed to put the largest available buses onto the busiest routes. Included in these movements were the transfer of twelve S-type to National, in place of Bs, and ten K and twenty S to East Surrey, partly to replace Bs and partly for expansion. Of the first 1,605, seventeen NS had been leased to the National Omnibus and Transport Co for its London Country Area operations. By the end of October 1924, the number of Bs licensed for service with LGOC and its associated companies had been reduced by 644 to 522 and the licensed fleet had grown by 1,163 buses.

At the same time as the first production NSs were arriving at Chiswick, a more powerful version of the S-type was being produced for National, who needed it for its more arduous routes. This was the AEC 502, known by the metropolitan-minded LGOC engineers as the 'Provincial S' (PS), which had the larger 6.8 litre engine with a quoted output of 45 bhp and a longer wheelbase. A prototype, classified 403 at the time, was delivered to LGOC on 8th January 1923,

fitted with a 54-seat body and operated experimentally at Hammersmith on route 11 from 29th March until 18th May when it was sent to National. The twelve production models allocated to National at this time were 43-seaters, the first three going to Watford on 5th May, the remainder between 29th June and 12th July. Two more were sent to NOTC in 1926, bringing the total to fifteen (PS 1-15). These all had bodywork of the same style as the S-type but could be recognised by their longer bonnet, which projected some way in front of the dash. East Surrey became a bigger operator of the PS type, taking a total of forty-four for both LGOC agreement routes and for its own fleet, between May 1924 and March 1927. The first thirty went to the Reigate company between May and July 1924 and had 48-seat bodywork by Ransomes Sims and Jefferies.

*Above* The nearside view of NS 588, one of 42 received by Chalk Farm garage for its first allocation, shows some minor changes in detail compared to the lower deck of NS 1, including the reversion to a shorter type of front mudguard. The single step up to the platform can be seen on the bus in front to the left of the photograph. At this time route 68 ran from West Norwood (Rosendale), where the photograph was taken, on Sundays or Tulse Hill Hotel on Mondays to Saturdays, to Kilburn Park. (Ken Glazier collection)

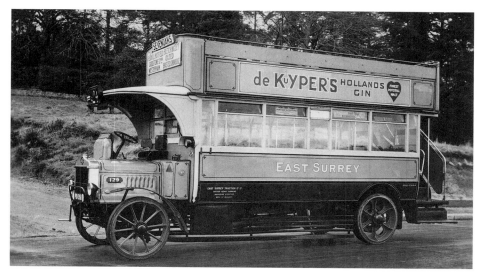

The AEC 502 (PS-type), a more powerful version of the S, was introduced in 1923 for operation in the 'London Country Area'. The first fourteen, with bodywork of the S-type design, went to National but most of the production models went to East Surrey, who ended with a total of 44. These had Ransomes, Sims and Jefferies bodywork similar to the NS design, with rounded corner panels on the upper deck. Apart from that, a PS could be distinguished from an S by its longer bonnet, as shown here on 129, one of those owned by East Surrey that went into service on 15th July 1924. (Snook & Son/ Ken Glazier collection)

These were similar in style to the NS with the same lower deck window layout, rounded upper deck front corner panels and a curved driver's canopy but with two steps up to the platform as on the standard S. They were unique to East Surrey. Six more were delivered in January 1926 and eight in March 1927, this time with LGOC 48-seat bodywork of the S-type design. These last eight had AEC 507 chassis, a steel-framed version of the 502 with improved and simplified mechanical design, which had been introduced by AEC in October 1925. At this time AEC had started to apply model names to its chassis and this model was known as the 'Ramillies'. The East Surrey PSs (although they did not give them class letters) were used on the hilly trunk routes across the North Downs, the S6 (406), S9 (409) and S10 (410) as well as on their own routes.

Concurrently with these events, things were happening in the fleet of Thomas Tilling which were directly related to General's activities. The two companies had entered into an operating agreement in 1912 which restricted Tilling's London fleet to about 5 per cent of the total, then about 150 buses, and by 1923 it was 166. These were all Tilling-Stevens TS3A-type petrol-electrics with 48-seat bodies by Thomas Tilling and had been built in 1921 and 1922. The LGOC became aware in 1923 of the interest of Tilling-Stevens Ltd and British Allied Investments in threatened competitive action in London and sought to forestall this. It did so by entering into a supplemental agreement with Thomas Tilling, signed on 10th April 1923, under which the LGOC would purchase 166 buses which Tilling would then work on its behalf on particular routes to agreed schedules, thus doubling the size of the Tilling fleet. The 166 buses purchased under this agreement were the latest Tilling-Stevens petrol-electric model, the TS7 and all again had Thomas Tilling-built 48-seat bodies assembled at the company's Lewisham and Lee works. They were known as the O-type by LGOC. The first five were allocated to the enlarged Catford garage and entered service on 25th July 1923 on route 21A, replacing General workings from Old Kent Road garage. Later deliveries completed the 21 Group of routes and the remainder were used either to replace LGOC workings on the agreed routes or to strengthen services already run by Tilling. The last went into service on 11th November 1924.

Thomas Tilling Ltd had renewed its fleet in 1921/1922 with 166 Tilling Stevens Petrol-electric normal-control TS3A type, with bodies built by the company. Their distinctive heavily rounded radiators, mimicked by the curved panels of the lower deck, could not be mistaken for anything else and neither could the mixture of electrical and mechanical sounds that they emitted. Tilling 189 was photographed in Peckham Road on route 12C during the General Strike in 1926, which is why the policeman is acting as an escort. (Ken Glazier collection)

*Left* The 166 additional buses bought by Tilling to meet the requirements of the new agreement with the LGOC in 1923 were a forward-control version of the Tilling-Stevens petrol-electric, classified TS7 and known as the O-type by General. The styling of the bodywork, again Tilling's own handiwork, differed only in detail from that on the TS3As and the move to a forward-control layout did not increase the seating capacity above 48. O 29 is in Rennell Street Lewisham, the southern terminus of the 1C from Willesden, where Wally's Refreshments proclaims itself a 'good pull up for carmen', in the well-worn phrase, and claims that busmen and all motormen are specially catered for. Further along is a Royal Blue coach booking office. (Ken Glazier collection)

*Centre* Whereas the double-deckers in the O class were licensed to Tilling and carried 'Thomas Tilling' fleet names, the twelve single-deckers bought for route 109 (O 168–179) carried 'General' fleet names and legal lettering for the first five years or so of their operation. The Tilling-built bodies comprised the lower deck part of the double-deck design, mounted on identical chassis. (Ken Glazier collection)

*Bottom* The series of manoeuvres following the acquisition of Timpsons in March 1926 led to six of these Tilling Stevens TS3s entering the fleet in February 1927. They remained in the silver livery of Timpsons until that company was absorbed by Tilling on 1st January 1928, after which they were repainted into Tilling red, as seen on 1217 (formerly Timpson 55) in Rushey Green, Catford. These buses had started with Cambrian Landray as chars-a-bancs in 1920 but had been fitted with Hickman 48-seat double-deck bodies in 1924/1925. (Ken Glazier collection)

Another agreement was signed on 20th October 1925 under which Tillings were to operate twelve buses on single-deck route 109 (the ancestor of route 227). The operation had in fact started on 7th May 1924 when, as a temporary measure, General lent Tilling twelve of the B-type single-deckers which had been created in 1921/1922 from double-deck chassis and new LGOC 26-seat bodies. The twelve buses ordered for long-term operation were single-deck versions of the TS7 and had 30-seat bodies built by Tilling. Unlike the double-deckers, which were in Tilling livery, they were painted in LGOC livery and carried the GENERAL fleet name until 1930 when they were licensed in Tilling's name and repainted accordingly.

While on the subject of Thomas Tilling, it is appropriate to note that the bus business of A. Timpson & Son was acquired by General on 25th March 1926 who sold it immediately to Tilling, bringing eighteen Straker-Squires and two Frost Smith petrol-electrics into the fleet. Five of the Strakers remained in the ownership of LGOC, although operated by Tilling, to maintain the correct balance of workings under the agreements. All twenty buses were allocated to Bromley garage but continued to operate as Timpson until 31st December 1927, after which they were absorbed into the Tilling company. The two Frost Smiths were not in good condition and were soon withdrawn by Tilling, who transferred their bodies to two Straker Squire chassis, formerly chars-a-banc, obtained from Timpson. Six of the Strakers were exchanged in February 1927

K 1066 was one of the chassis made up from spare parts at Chiswick in 1924, mounted at first with a spare double-deck body and then with one of the new 24-seat single-deck bodies. The styling of these bodies represented quite an advance on what had gone before, with an altogether smoother finish and less austere look, helped by the inward curve of the lower panels. Solid tyres were necessary on buses allocated to hilly routes as they required sprag gear, which was incompatible with pneumatics. The countrified look of the background to the bus is a snare as this is the Finsbury Park terminus, where the railway goods yard is shielded by this row of poplar trees. (Ken Glazier collection)

Had things worked out differently, the single-deck K may never have been built because in 1925 AEC introduced a new model 411 named the Renown, the first AEC chassis to be given a model name. It was designed to be fitted with pneumatic tyres from the outset and had an unladen weight within the new limit which allowed speeds of up to 20 mph, instead of the 12 mph limit for solids. The LGOC took delivery of five (R 1-5) between 20th June and 3rd July 1925 but all were returned to AEC on 21st July and nothing more was heard of the project. The bodies, of the same design as the Ks, were presumably used on five of those chassis. R 1 was the only one of the five to be licensed but it did not enter service as far as is known.

The initial batch of K single-deckers were the first LGOC buses to be fitted with pneumatic tyres. K 859 was a 24-seater from one of the later batches mounted on former double-deck chassis and was first allotted to National before returning to General. It is seen at Grove Park station in LGOC service, probably on route 136D (Lewisham–Bromley Common), judging by the destination blind, but no route number is displayed. (The Omnibus Society)

for a like number of Tilling-Stevens TS3A petrol-electrics by then owned by LGOC who had acquired them when they took over Cambrian Landray. The bodies of the remaining Straker Squires were mounted on a variety of Tilling-Stevens chassis scavenged from other sources in the Tilling fleet, mainly vans and chars-a-banc, restoring the total dominance of the petrol-electrics.

An unexpected happening in May and June 1924 was the appearance of fifteen apparently new K-type 46-seaters at Cricklewood garage (K 1063–1077). These had been made up at Chiswick using parts already in stock and were mounted with spare bodies taken from store. This did not herald a rebirth of the double-deck K, but the type did have one more surprise to spring a

year later when, in September 1925, a single-deck version appeared. Twenty-four (K 1078–1101) were built on new chassis which, like their NS contemporaries, were made up at Chiswick. They were the first LGOC buses to be fitted with pneumatic tyres and had bodywork of markedly more modern appearance than the B-types they were destined to displace. The lower half of the side panelling

The twenty 20-seat Ks assigned to the feeder services to the newly extended City & South London Railway at Morden had their main body panels painted silver, which had the effect of giving the metal bonnet number a ghostly appearance. The fleet name on K 533 is also less conspicuous than usual. (Ken Glazier collection)

The rear view of K 388 shows how the body styling was moving towards the designs immortalised in the T, ST and LT classes a few years later. The poster pasted ahead of the rear wheel announces that the bus runs to and from the new Underground station at Morden. (Ken Glazier collection)

was curved inwards and the large saloon windows were made deeper than on their B-type predecessors by replacing the inward opening vents at the top, by full-depth horizontally sliding glasses. Internally, they had upholstered seats, as provided on the NS, rather than the wooden seats of the K double-deckers so far built. All but two were 24-seaters, the exceptions being 20-seaters for use on the weight-restricted route 111 at Muswell Hill. The first five were licensed on 10th August 1925 at Hounslow, followed five days later by a sixth, and were used on route 162B (Slough to Leatherhead). Three (K 1096–1098) were allotted to the National Omnibus and Transport Company and the remainder of the LGOC vehicles went to Kingston to work on the routes radiating southward from that town and to Sutton for the 113.

Another 25 were ordered at the beginning of 1926 and should have been numbered K 1102-1126 but their bodies were ready before the chassis and they went instead onto overhauled chassis from double-deckers randomly numbered between K 45 and 1053. Two further orders for 79 bodies, completed between June 1926 and April 1927, and eleven in 1928, all mounted on old former double-deck chassis, brought the total of K single-deckers to 139. The 104, delivered in 1926 and 1927, were a mixture of types. Seventy-five, intended for use on hilly routes, retained solid tyres as they had to be fitted with Sprag gear which was not readily compatible with pneumatic tyres. Of these, fifty were 20-seaters for routes 41 and 111, which had weight restrictions to contend with, and the remainder 24-seaters. Nine of the pneumatics were 24-seaters, like the first batch

but the remaining twenty were 22-seaters which were painted in a special silver livery for operation on feeder routes to the Underground when the City & South London Railway was extended to Morden in September 1926. The eleven delivered in 1928 were 26ft long (3ft 6ins longer than the others) with an additional window bay and seated 30. They displaced some of the smaller vehicles at Hounslow and Kingston.

The contrast in styling between the K and S-type single-deckers is well illustrated in this scene inside Kingston bus station, where K 126 is flanked by two of the original S-type, S 371 and S 424, after they had been fitted with pneumatic tyres. K 126 was a 22-seater from one of the later batches which were mounted on former double-deck chassis. (Mike Sutcliffe collection)

The new chassis intended for the second batch of single-deckers received instead double-deck bodies which were either overhauled, rebuilt or new and became K 1102–1126. By this time, many of the earlier K bodies were in need of replacement or major rebuilding and this need was fulfilled by building 100 new bodies and rebuilding 100 more. Ninety others had their double-deck bodies replaced by the new single-deckers just described. The new or rebuilt bodies were easily recognised because they had inward curving lower side panels, as used on the NS, and a fully glazed front bulkhead, instead of the upper part being a blank panel. The lower saloon seating was also of the latest, upholstered, type. Some of the new bodies had longitudinal seating on the lower deck, which reduced the total seating capacity to 44.

Even then, the K was not quite finished as six were bought from Devon General in 1926. K 1126-1132 had been bought by the Torquay Tramways Company in 1921 and their Devon registrations in the TA series made them stand out from the rest.

The S-type also had a final burst in December 1926 when the LGOC built-up the first of another twelve double-deckers, four of which were allocated to National for operation on route 308 (Romford to Aveley) and eight to Cricklewood garage. These were followed in May by thirteen single-deckers (S 915-927), all of which were for National who sent them to Watford to work on routes 306 and 311. These had the improved style of body similar to the K single-deckers being built at the time.

The important ground-breaking developments in the single-deck field were taking place elsewhere while General was continuing to churn out what were basically four or five year old designs. In November 1925, Sir Raymond Dennis, Managing Director of Dennis Bros of Guildford, had sent a blueprint of a new single-deck design, the E, to the Metropolitan Police for their consideration. The big step forward in the proposed vehicle for London was the adoption of four-wheel brakes, which operators hoped would be accepted by the Police as a substitute for Sprag gear. The Metropolitan Police took a lot of trouble to canvass opinion from operators outside London, including Walsall, Dublin, Rochdale, Leeds, Lincoln municipalities, Yorkshire Woollen District and Chas. W. Dawson of Stoke-on-Trent. Almost without exception their experience with four-wheel brakes had been favourable. Tests on Muswell Hill drew a complimentary report from Supt Claro who remarked that they were the best brakes so far submitted to the Public Carriage Office and of a high standard 'similar to that used on a Rolls-Royce car'! Tests undertaken at the same time with an LGOC NS specially equipped with four-wheel brakes were not so favourably received. Claro's report on those tests concluded that, although the safety of the NS was generally high, attention needed to be paid to the front axle and steering.

The test of the Dennis E had been undertaken with the assistance of A.T. Bennett of the Admiral bus company and he was granted seven of the ten experimental licences for operation on route 529 (Winchmore Hill to Victoria) issued on 9th November 1926. On 24th February 1927, the Met Police announced that they would accept the Dennis E for licensing as motor buses. This was the type which Walter Iden of National favoured so strongly, as described in chapter five. The use of four-wheel brakes on an LGOC double-decker had to await the new Regent and Renown models in 1929 but the London Independents were again ahead on this because the Leyland Titan, which came onto the road in 1928, had them as standard.

Returning to the story of the NS, the LGOC Board gave authority in October and November 1924 for two more batches totalling 132 to be built, including three for National and ten for East Surrey (NS 1606–1737). In the event, National received nine, the extra six being replacements for part of the Harvey & Burrows fleet at Hertford, the background to which is described in chapter five. These were not built by AEC at its Walthamstow works. Whether by chance or design, the opening of the new Chiswick overhaul works in 1921 had created a potential rival to AEC as the builder of LGOC's buses, despite the fact that both were subsidiary companies of the Underground Group and shared the same Chairman, Lord Ashfield. This later developed into a serious battle when Chiswick was authorised to design its own chassis as a possible rival to the new range introduced by AEC in 1929. The transfer of overhaul work away from Walthamstow to Chiswick had already hit the finances of AEC who had sought, and obtained, changes to the agreement with LGOC which enabled it to sell more freely on the open market. Chiswick Works had already assembled 235 of the 895 S-types and they were about to embark on a more ambitious programme in which the NSs delivered between October 1924 and early June 1928 were built up at Chiswick.

Just over three weeks elapsed between the delivery of the last chassis from AEC and the completion of the first built-up chassis and the bodywork continued to be the same open top 50-seat type. Short Bros of Rochester supplied the bodies but some went onto overhauled chassis and earlier bodies built by others took their place on the new chassis. National's needs were urgent and the delivery of their first six was made between 31st October and 12th December (NS 1606-1608, 1612, 1613, 1616). The first of the batch licensed for LGOC use was NS 1609 on 24th October and deliveries continued until 27th May 1925 when NS 1733 went into service at Chalk Farm.

In the meantime, the corridors of power had been buzzing with activity. On 30th October 1924 the Ministry of Transport wrote to the Metropolitan Police to tell them that a departmental committee of the ministry had decided that the time had been reached when a test of covered top buses should be undertaken. The Metropolitan Police area had been suggested as the place for such a trial as it could then be supervised more closely. The MoT expressed the hope that the Met Police would license such

Although the majority of buses for the 109 were supplied by Thomas Tilling, the LGOC operated three from Sidcup garage. Two were Ks but the third was 26-seat B 925 which was photographed in Widmore Road, Bromley on the morning of 3rd May 1927, a matter of days before it was withdrawn.
(Mike Sutcliffe collection)

vehicles for the test. Even the Metropolitan Police could not deny a 'request' from a Minister and a letter went from them to LGOC on 7th November inviting an application for a test of four covered top NS-type. Although this was what General had been waiting for, Pick was wary of the motives of the Police and foresaw the possibility of some abortive expenditure. He sought an assurance therefore that, even if the experiment should prove unsuccessful, the LGOC should be allowed to continue to operate the four buses for at least six months and preferably a year, providing only that their operation was not unsafe. This was not well received by the Police who pointed out that all their tests were fair and would not give such an undertaking. This appears to have been accepted without comment by Pick and George Shave wrote to the Police on 13th August suggesting that the experiment should be carried out on route 21 between Wood Green and Farningham, starting on 26th August 1925. This was not approved because of overhanging lamp standards and trees on the Eltham to Farningham section. Shave then wrote suggesting the 88 but, for reasons not recorded, he cancelled this in a telephone call. The reason could have been that the 88 did not have a sufficient variety of operating conditions for the test to be conclusive, as route 21 and the route chosen in the end, the 100 (Elephant & Castle to Epping), both had a good mixture of city, inner London, suburban and country running.

The four buses were the last of the Short Bros-bodied batch, NS 1734–1737, and they had fifty-two seats, the 28 on the upper deck being upholstered for the first time. Continuation of plentiful supplies of fresh air for those addicted to the open top deck was assured by giving every side window (five on each side) a horizontally sliding section which could be opened to half the width of the frame. The extra structure added about 8cwt to the unladen weight of a complete bus. NS 1734 had been completed by 7th July and, once this had been inspected and approved, the other three were finished in time for the original starting date of 26th August. They were first licensed at Loughton on 1st October 1925 and went into service immediately. A Police report dated 9th November stated that there had been no adverse criticism and the consensus was that they were satisfactory. However, the author suggested that in these early days the drivers may have been on their best behaviour and recommended that the trial should be extended, the fear still being that because of the extra weight on top, a sudden swerve by the bus might cause it to overturn. Lord Ashfield, with powerful support from Sir Henry Maybury, advisor to the Ministry and chairman of the London & Home Counties Traffic Advisory Committee, proposed on 16th November that a more extensive trial should take place to get better coverage of public reaction. Pick put flesh on this five days later by seeking authority to operate

another fifty buses, suggesting these should go on routes 11, 17 or 29. A physical test of route 11 proved satisfactory, subject to some restrictions, and this emboldened George Shave to increase the bid to 100 buses. This was agreed by the Metropolitan Police on 11th December 1925, a red letter day in the development of the London bus.

On 5th November, before the trials had been completed, the LGOC Board approved expenditure of £70,000 on the purchase of 50 covered-top NSs. At £1,400 a bus, this was £200 more than the last batch of open toppers. At the same meeting fourteen open toppers were authorised, eleven for East Surrey (two of which were for its own fleet) and three for National. Another 150 covered top buses were authorised on 7th January 1926 and by 1st July 1926, it was possible for

*Above* NS 1734, the first London double-decker to be fitted with a covered top for service use, crosses London Bridge on route 100 from Epping. It is fitted with headlamps for operation on country roads. The four prototypes had their route number and destination displays at the front arranged in the same layout as on the open-toppers but otherwise the chosen design was adopted for the immediate production runs. Evidence of the continuing widespread use of horse haulage is present in the form of several horse-drawn carts and the malodorous deposit of another. (Alan B. Cross)

the Board to agree to spend £139,000 on fitting all existing open top NS with top covers while ordering yet another 100 new, bringing the total to 300. By June 1928 NS fleet numbers had reached 2296.

The first of the new buses went into service at Hammersmith garage on route 11 on 10th March 1926 and there then followed a continuous flow of deliveries, apart from the interruption of supplies by the General Strike in May 1926, spreading gradually to the more important trunk routes. The programme of fitting top covers to the earlier NSs ran alongside these deliveries so that by February 1927 more than half of the 1,812 scheduled for service (977) were covered top and during the next twelve months the total rose to 1,684 covered and 460 open.

*Above* The first route to receive closed top NSs was the 11E between Shepherd's Bush and Liverpool Street, which was in the eye of politicians in Whitehall and journalists in Fleet Street. NS 1539, seen passing the National Gallery, was one of the existing open-toppers given top covers once approval had been given by the police. On these, the centre third of the front window was used for the route number, which moved up from the canopy, with the destination laid flat, rather than sloping forward, beneath it. There was also a prominent lamp attached to the canopy, which illuminated the display at night. (T. Cooper)

NS 42 at Finsbury Park on summer Sunday route 72 to Rye House, after being fitted with a top cover. Passengers craving for the fresh air of a ride on an open-topper were not overlooked as every upstairs window could be opened by sliding it horizontally. Another feature new to these buses was the valance shield projecting down from the canopy which gave the driver some protection from glare. (W Noel Jackson)

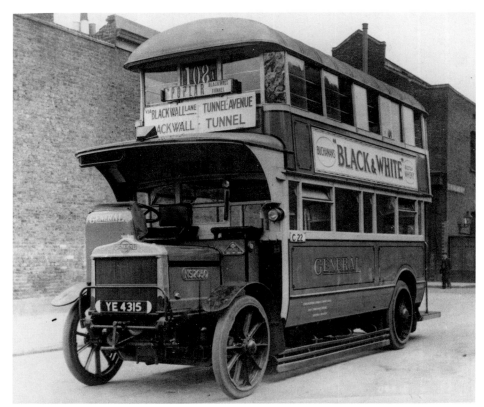

The only significant variation from the standard NS specification was in a group of vehicles specially designed to operate through Blackwall Tunnel, where the heavily used 108 was confined to single-deck operation. In theory it was possible to operate a standard covered top double-decker through the tunnel but the clearances were tight. In the eyes of the Metropolitan Police, at least, there was a risk that the bus roof might collide with the tunnel as it bumped and swerved over the uneven granite-sett road surface. The acute bends, which can still be observed in the northbound bore of the tunnel, were also seen as a hazard because the back end of a bus might hit the wall as it swept the curve. A special body was therefore designed which was narrower and lower than standard, incorporated a domed roof to match the tunnel profile, and had a rounded back with enclosed staircase, the upper deck section of which resembled a modern tramcar of the period. The seating (24 up, 22 down) was all longitudinal, that on the lower deck in conventional fashion facing inwards along the sides, but that on the upper deck being arranged in two back-to-back benches down the middle, knifeboard style. The upper deck gangways on each side of the saloon were sunken, and the area under the seats provided the required headroom in the lower deck gangway. The upper deck arrangement led Chiswick to name them 'clerestory', a description which survived in Chiswick circles into and throughout the STL era.

The experimental body was mounted on NS 2050 on 5th April 1927 and the bus went into service at Athol Street on route 108A four days later, the first London bus with an enclosed staircase. It was a success and a production batch of 24 was put in hand in September 1927 taking numbers in the series NS 2210–2239. These went into service between 17th October 1927 and 3rd January 1928. In preparation for this the 108 was split to operate in two sections as the route north of Bow was not suitable for double-deckers: Clapton to Bromley-by-Bow (108D, single-deck) and Bromley-by-Bow to Forest Hill (108B, double-deck). The first seventeen of the tunnel buses were the same as NS 2050 but the remainder, built between 15th and 22nd November (NS 2233–2239) had a different arrangement of seating on the upper deck which reduced the capacity to 22 passengers. The seats were still in the same position but were now individual so-called 'bucket' chairs set at an angle facing forward. The others were later altered to conform. When the need arose for additional buses on route 108, the six buses which were added to the tunnel fleet had open staircase bodies and a conventional arrangement of seating. These bodies were mounted on overhauled chassis and therefore took numbers scattered randomly.

The upper deck of the first eighteen 'clerestory' NSs had long bench seats for 24 passengers back-to-back along the centre of the saloon, with depressed sloping gangways on each side. On the last seven these were replaced by twenty-two individual 'bucket' seats and the rest were later brought into line. The pronounced dome of the roof is brought out strongly in this photograph by the shape of the front bulkhead. (London's Transport Museum)

The appearance of the rear end of the tunnel buses must have caused quite a stir at a time when nothing so bold and modern had been seen before. The strong curvature was needed to prevent the bus hitting the walls or opposing traffic on the sharp tunnel bends and the enclosure of the back inspired the use of roller blind displays for the first time on a double-decker. The handle for changing the blind can be seen hanging down above the platform of this unidentifiable NS on the stand at Bromley-by-Bow. (The Omnibus Society)

Tilling & British Automobile Traction replaced their fleet of pre-war Daimlers with 33 of these AEC 509s bodied at Chiswick by the LGOC. The contrast in size and relative modernity between the 48-seat NS (BAT 518) and the 34-seat Daimler, with its overtones of the B-type, is brought out well in this view of the two sharing the stand at South End Green, Hampstead Heath. An LCC tram on route 5 to Moorgate can be glimpsed on the other side of the green. (Clive O. Cheeseman)

*Right* British Daimler 479 was a CC, designed by Frank Searle, former Chief Motor Engineer of the LGOC and the man behind the B-type, with which it shared a number of design features. The engine was a 30hp 5.7 litre sleeve-valve unit. (Ken Glazier collection)

Another important group of NSs which were not owned by the LGOC but were operated as part of the London Pool, were 33 operated from its Camden Town garage by Tilling & British Automobile Traction on route 24. This company had one of those symptomatic agreements with the LGOC, dating from January 1913, which limited them to the operation of no more than thirty buses in London (plus spares). They had been operating elderly 34-seat Daimlers and, in 1923, had become entangled in a dispute with LGOC about the interpretation of the agreement in respect of BAT's share of the Pool now that its Daimlers were so much smaller than the average LGOC bus. The dispute widened into one about the size of the fleet, which Sidney Garcke of BAT considered too small to be efficient. Frank Pick even went so far as to suggest that Garcke should try to persuade the Board of Tramways (MET) Omnibus Company to transfer 70 of its entitlement so that a more efficient operation with 100 'modern type' buses in a new garage could be established. Pick wrote in exasperation to Lord Ashfield in August 1923 that he found Garcke 'entirely unaccommodating' in negotiation and the dispute had been 'left over'. It had been left open for Garcke to approach Ashfield directly but, Pick warned, 'he is a tiresome and obstinate person'. If there were any subsequent discussions between Ashfield and Garcke, the record is not available but the BAT clearly did not get its way because the number of buses remained the same. The 'modern fleet', when it arrived, took the form of 33 covered top, solid tyred AEC 409s, the classification used by AEC for the 'provincial' NS. They were 48-seaters, bodied at Chiswick, and went into service between 31st May and 17th November 1927. When these eventually fell into the hands of London Transport in 1933 they were numbered NS 2379–2411.

There were four NSs which were not part of this story. NS 1738 was not even a double-decker but a coach which was a prototype for the AW class. NS 2051-2053, although given numbers in the LGOC series, were sold to Greyhound Motors of Bristol.

The NS had been in production for four years when what might have been seen as its successor, the LS, made its spectacular appearance in June 1927. Although designed in the AEC drawing office at Walthamstow, it was a product of Associated Daimler a company jointly owned by AEC and Daimler which had been formed in June 1926. An interest in the potential of six-wheelers as high capacity city buses had begun to develop among many operators in the mid-1920s and Guy Motors of Wolverhampton had been among the first to take up the challenge, introducing a normal control model in 1926. A forward control version, the FCX model was to follow in 1927 and the LGOC was aware that the London Public Omnibus Company planned to put a number of them into service. Consequently, the development of AEC's rival model, which was to be the first LGOC double-decker built new with pneumatic tyres, was done with great urgency and much working into the small hours. The result was that chassis number 802001 was delivered to Chiswick on 23rd May 1927 and fitted with its new body in time to be licensed at Cricklewood on 3rd June, three months before LPOC fielded its Guy. It was classified LS, and came to be known as the 'London Six', but this could well have been the same kind of afterthought as 'Nulli Secundus' for the NS, as the conservatively minded Chiswick engineers are just as likely to have called it the 'long S'.

*Top* The 'London Six' in its original form, with enclosed staircase and seats for 72 passengers. The body design shows no advance on the NS, apart from the small extension of the upper deck over part of the cab and bonnet and the enclosed rear end. The lamps carried on brackets on each side of the bonnet were not kept. (London's Transport Museum)

*Centre* An advertisement for sardines may have been more appropriate on one of the ADC works transport buses into which 102 or 104 were crammed but LS 4 was more spaciously laid out for its fare payers. The front end had this strikingly different radiator and bonnet design which enclosed the nearside front bulkhead fully below the saloon window. In the original design, there was a door on the driver's cab which gave the offside a sleeker appearance but this has been removed by order of the Metropolitan Police, with this untidy result, which contrasts with the neat and modern-looking rear end. LS 4 is at Chiswick Works apparently being prepared for operation at Palmers Green on route 29A. (Arthur Ingram)

*Right* The Crown Hotel at Cricklewood had witnessed many developments from the earliest days of motor bus operation in London and it is fitting that it was to be served by the latest 'last word' for the full ten years of operation of the LS class. LS 3 was one of those built with open staircases and one of only three which received the intended AEC A121 engine, so can stand as representative of the class as it finally became. (Ken Glazier collection)

The wheelbase of 18ft 10½ ins enabled bodywork of up to 30 feet in length to be fitted and LS 1 had an overall length of 29ft 8¼ ins, 4ft 8¼ins longer than the NS. It seated 72 passengers, fourteen more than the maximum so far achieved on a London double-decker, and was the largest bus so far built in the United Kingdom. It looked even more massive because although the driver's seat was still exposed to the capricious British climate, the staircase was fully enclosed and, as built, there was a door on the driver's cab which helped make the bonnet look much longer and sleeker. Neither the cab door nor the enclosed staircase were to survive long as the dead hand of the Metropolitan Police soon descended and they had to be removed. Otherwise, the body design was similar to the NS but the upper deck again crept a little way further forward over part of the cab and the bonnet and radiator were a new design also used on some single-deck ADC chassis. The nearside sloped outward towards the back so that it enclosed the lower part of the front bulkhead, and the radiator was more rounded and slightly bulbous. The power unit for the new model was intended to be AEC's first 6-cylinder engine, the A121, which had a swept volume of 7.6 litres, but the A121 was not ready in time and LS 1 went into service with the Daimler CV35 5.7 litre sleeve-valve engine instead. Transmission was through a single-plate clutch and four-speed crash gearbox, both rear axles were driven and only the rear wheels were braked. As things turned out, the A121 engine was fitted only to three of the type (LS 2, 3 and 12), the rest following the lead given by LS 1. The single-decker, LS 6, had a 34-seat rear entrance body and was unique in having a form of petrol-electric transmission but this was removed and replaced by conventional transmission in 1929.

The LGOC took a total of eleven double-deckers and one single-decker but this modest sample took eighteen months to be delivered and put into service. Of the double-deckers, seven were built with enclosed staircases and seated 72 (LS 1, 2, 4, 8, 9 and 11) and the rest with 70-seat open staircase bodies. It is not clear what determined whether they were open-backed or not as delivery of both types alternated, which at least suggests that there was no sudden change of policy. Whatever governed this, all the enclosed staircase examples were altered to open-back and the seating capacity reduced to 66 soon afterwards. The last five double-deckers had an improved body style which was being used on NSs at the time. They had better seating and the windows on both decks were of the vertically sliding type, operated by a catch. At the front of the upper saloon the untidy three-window arrangement was replaced by two and the route number stencil was moved down to the canopy.

LS 2 joined LS 1 at Cricklewood on 29th July 1927 but LS 3 did not appear until February 1928. After that, five went to Mortlake to operate on route 33A, one to Palmers Green for route 29A, and two to Tottenham for route 69B, the last to go into service being LS 12 on 3rd January 1929 at Mortlake. They were generally very well received by the Press and public but when Lord Ashfield took a ride on one he was appalled by the 'fearful grinding of gears', although he was impressed with the smooth ride it gave. The introduction of such a revolutionary bus did not go through without some problems with the staff, however, caused mainly by misunderstandings. One of the conditions imposed by the Metropolitan Police was that a list of drivers who had been specially trained to operate the LS had to be lodged at New Scotland Yard. This meant that there

had to be a separate duty schedule for the work covered by the LS-type but the buses themselves had to be operated as part of the standard schedule because the company claimed that it could not afford to run them as extras. As a concession to staff operating the larger bus, the duties transferred to the LS schedule were the shorter ones, which had the unpopular effect that staff working the main schedule had to work longer hours. Matters were made worse by Traffic Superintendent H. Lansdowne's having a meeting with the chosen staff where he gave undertakings about possible compensation payments for working the larger bus. Staff at other garages accused the Cricklewood branch of the Union of having sold out to the management and various rumours ran around the fleet. It became such an inflamed issue that the dispute had to be resolved at a meeting between Frank Pick and Ernest Bevin, then General Secretary of the Transport & General Workers' Union. Other issues raised at that meeting were the ventilation of the driver's cab, which needed improving, the sloping section of floor at the rear of the lower saloon, which they wanted removed or at least adjusted, and the mixture of open and closed staircase buses. On the latter point, all they asked was that all buses should be one or the other; they did not express a preference either way. All was eventually settled by agreeing a variable bonus payment of £5 for the first six crews on the rota and £3 for the rest.

*Above* The single-deck LS 6 spent its entire working life on route 104 and its successor 240 and was therefore a frequent visitor to Golders Green, where it is seen crossing Finchley Road in front of a Metropolitan Electric type A tram on route 40 to Whetstone. The notice attached to the traction standard on the right reads: 'EXTRA CARS FROM NEXT STOP DURING RUSH HOURS'. (London's Transport Museum)

The LS proved to be one of the byways of history. Only eight were built apart from the LGOC batch and two of those were for use by ADC to transport workers from their Walthamstow homes to the new AEC factory at Southall which opened in 1927. These were perhaps even more famous than the LGOC buses as they were not restricted by the regulations covering service buses and were built to carry 104 and 102 passengers respectively. These remarkable totals were achieved by having tip-up seats in the gangways, rearward-facing benches at the front of each deck and even seats under the stairs.

Five went as demonstrators to Westcliff-on-Sea Motor Services, Maidstone & District, Southdown, Birmingham Corporation and Sheffield and one (chassis 802009) did not even receive a body before it was broken up by the LGOC in August 1929. That was where the story of the 802 ended but one of the demonstrators (802006) later found its way into General ownership by the back door. It had operated for Southdown but was returned in 1928 when it was converted to open top, with sixty seats, and sent to East Surrey who numbered it 45 and ran it on local route 21 (Reigate to South Merstham).

The approval of the Metropolitan Police to the use of pneumatic tyres on the LS was a sign that they were prepared to accept them more generally on double-deckers. The LGOC wanted to fit them to the NS-type also but were unable to do so because when fitted to the large rear wheels, the tyres increased the overall width of the bus beyond the regulation limit of 7ft 2ins. The Police finally relaxed this regulation in July 1928, after which London buses could be built up to a maximum width of 7ft 5ins. The LGOC immediately ordered 75 of the new ADC 422 model the last twenty-five of which

The approval by the Metropolitan Police to the use of pneumatic tyres on the NS class prompted the LGOC to order 56 of the new ADC422 chassis. Apart from being three inches wider, changes to the body design included the removal of the route number stencil back to the canopy roof to allow two front windows to replace the earlier three-piece arrangement. These and all the other windows opened vertically, rather than horizontally, which in the case of the side windows gave greater ventilation. The other notable difference that smartened the appearance of the bus, was the new Associated Daimler radiator shell which was based on the Daimler design. Cricklewood's NS 2311 is at Hendon Central at the northern end of route 121A to Peckham Rye. (W. Noel Jackson)

A programme to fit the extant NS fleet with pneumatic tyres ran in parallel with the delivery of the new 422s. These could always be distinguished from the latest vehicles by the arrangement of the front upper deck, the use of horizontally sliding windows and the way the rear wheels projected outside the line of the body. The exchange of bodies between chassis over the years confused the distinction between the radiator designs but NS 347, on route 89 from Wallington to Charing Cross, is here fitted correctly with the traditional type. (W. Noel Jackson)

were to have been fitted with a new 6-cylinder engine but this got no further than the experimental stage and that part of the order was cancelled. An additional six were ordered in 1929 and these 56 buses, the last of the class to be purchased by the LGOC, were numbered NS 2297-2346 and 2372-2377, the missing numbers being the cancelled order. The LGOC embarked simultaneously on a programme of fitting pneumatic tyres to the earlier NSs, including the entire fleet operated by National and East Surrey.

When the chassis for NS 2299 arrived at Chiswick from Southall on 7th June 1928, it was the first to be built by AEC for four years. The Chiswick-built bodies for these buses were wider than earlier types, allowing a more spacious layout of the passenger saloons and incorporating the changes already noted on the later LS-type vehicles. The 422 chassis had a slightly more powerful engine, the A128, still with 5.1 litre swept volume but developing 57bhp. They also had the more modern and neater looking ADC radiator, embossed with 'GENERAL'. The first of this batch was licensed at Mortlake garage on 3rd July 1928 while the very last of the type, NS 2377, was received on 19th April 1929 and went into service at Cricklewood on 1st June.

The delivery of new double-deckers had slowed down considerably by 1928 and became a mere trickle in the second half of that year and for most of 1929 but there was more activity in the single-deck fleet. In June 1926 General had taken into stock six 'all-weather' coaches numbered AW 1-8 which broke away from the reliance on derivatives of the B-type. Their chassis were built up at Chiswick using NS parts but they were powered by Daimler sleeve-valve six-cylinder engines. Chiswick also built the 24-seat bodies which had canvas roofs that could be rolled back to leave the saloon fully open They ran for only three years before being sold. Thirty-nine coaches of similar specification but built at Southall by Associated Daimler who classified them 419D, were delivered to the LGOC in April 1927. Six were also taken by East Surrey Traction. All forty-five had Short Bros 28-seat bodywork and had a bonnet and radiator design similar to that on the LS-type, already described. These coaches were unlike anything supplied to any other operator and were to remain a unique group in the LGOC and East Surrey fleets. The main needs of General and its associated companies were to be met by the 416, ADC's most successful single-deck model with strong sales in the 'provincial' market. The 416 was introduced by ADC in 1927 and was the first AEC or ADC single-decker to have a cranked frame, as pioneered on the NS, giving it a lower level saloon. ADC offered a choice of AEC or Daimler engine, the AEC being the A119 5.1 litre which developed a meagre 45bhp at 1,500rpm, and the Daimler the CV25 6-cylinder 3.6 litre sleeve-valve engine which, despite its size, developed 70bhp at 3,000rpm. This was the model about which Walter Iden was so chary, as recorded in chapter five.

*Below* The entire fleet of ADC419D Short Brothers-bodied coaches delivered in April 1927 seems to have been lined up for this official photograph which captures the arresting bull-nose bonnet and radiator design to fine effect. This design was used otherwise only on the LS type. The canvas roofs have been rolled back to demonstrate the open-tourer character of the vehicles. (London's Transport Museum)

The first ADC416s to pass through Chiswick's hands were fourteen 30-seaters destined for East Surrey. Nine were owned by General and five by ESTC. The LGOC bought a total of 53 ADC416s, 43 of which were to meet the needs of National. They were never given official fleet numbers but their record cards were marked informally with the numbers AD 1-53. These were never carried on the vehicles. The first six 32-seat buses were delivered to National in November 1927 and these were followed by the balance of 33 between February and April 1928. The remaining fourteen were 28-seat coaches, four for National and ten for General and were taken into stock in March and April 1928. General also bought two ADC427 eighteen-seater coaches (unofficially AD 53/54) and one 423 twenty-seater, described as a 'parlour coach' which was not numbered, even informally. The 427 was a normal-control chassis, mechanically similar to the 417, the bonneted version of the 416, but with some design improvements which showed Daimler influence, including a new style bonnet and radiator and curved aluminium castings covering the dumbirons. The 423 was a Daimler-built version of the 416. The forward-control companion to the 427 was the 426, of which East Surrey bought three with Chiswick-built 28-seat bus bodies in June 1928. National's small bus needs in 1928 were met with a batch of six Guy BA 20-seaters, which were delivered at the end of May 1928 (UC2267–2272).

At the end of 1928, the change of allegiance in the north-west Country Area became apparent when the LGOC bought ten buses for the Amersham & District Motor Bus and Haulage Company. These comprised one Gilford 16660T with a 32-seat Wycombe body, which later became GF 161 with London Transport, and nine Strachan-bodied Dennis E 32-seaters (KX1645, 1924–1928, 2219, 2793 and 2794). Dennis E KX1645 was delivered to Amersham in December 1928 and the rest in February and March 1929.

Dennis products suddenly began to feature at this time, albeit in a small way but made the more prominent by the absence of new vehicles for the LGOC at the end of 1928. Perhaps the most unexpected was the purchase of three Dennis H double-deckers which, even more surprisingly, had open-top bodywork by Hall Lewis. The H had been in production since 1927 and had been bought by a few London Independents but by the time General bought its trio, was about to be superseded by an improved model. It was powered by a Dennis 4-cylinder 6.24 litre petrol engine with an output of 70 bhp and had a conventional four-speed crash gearbox. DH 1-3 were delivered on 29th January 1929 and licensed at Putney on 13th February.

The other Dennises which appeared on the scene on 12th and 15th March 1929 were six Dennis 2½ ton DS-type single-deckers which were taken on loan from the London Public Omnibus Company. They were allocated to Tottenham garage for route 263, formerly operated by Public and were joined by another four on 1st May. They kept their

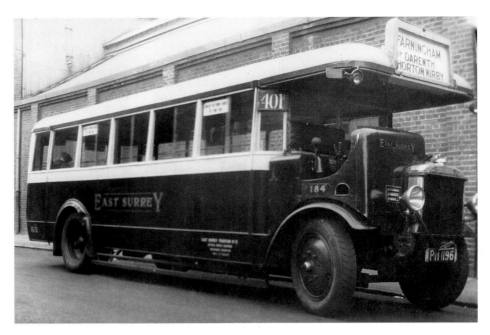

East Surrey 184 was one of twelve ADC416A buses with 32-seat rear entrance Short Bros bodywork which joined the fleet in 1927 and 1928 for operation on behalf of General. It is in Dartford on route 401B to Farningham. (Ken Glazier collection)

Public numbers (DS 6, 9, 10, 13, 19, 25, 26, 31, 33 and 47) and also their blue colour scheme but had boards fixed to the side panels bearing the 'GENERAL' fleet name. By this time, General had a controlling interest in the LPOC and by the end of 1929 the whole of the Public fleet had come under the wing of the LGOC, adding 177 Dennis, 28 Leyland and the fourteen Guy FCX six-wheelers to the fleet.

The absorption of the London Public fleet brought the Guy FCX competitor of the LS into the LGOC fleet, though briefly as most found their way into the City Motor Omnibus fleet within three years. Their home while with Public and General was on the 529 between Winchmore Hill and Pimlico, for which GS 7 is dressed here. (Alan B. Cross)

YW8015 was one of the twenty 'semi-saloon' coaches on AEC Reliance 660 chassis, delivered in May 1929, painted in this version of General's red and white colour scheme. They had 'all-weather' bodies built at Chiswick, with an opening section in the centre of the saloon roof which can be identified by the slight slackness in the canvas and by the fixing studs above the windows. The 32 seats were well upholstered, as can be seen through the saloon windows. (London's Transport Museum)

The last new buses to be delivered to LGOC before AEC launched its revolutionary new series of models in the summer of 1929, were 34 AEC Reliances. The Reliance was something of a hybrid, being a holding arrangement while the new Regal was being developed by John Rackham, who had joined AEC as Chief Engineer in July 1928. He had given priority to the design of a new six-cylinder engine for the new chassis range but the project was accomplished so quickly that it was ready to go into production at the end of the same year and AEC decided to use the engine in a modified 426 chassis. In its new guise the chassis started a new 6 series for

AEC with the classification 660 and was given the name Reliance. The new engine was the A130, a 6.1 litre unit with a power output of 95 bhp but in most other respects the chassis was the same as the 426, one important exception being that it had Marles steering. One of the prototypes (chassis number 660003) was delivered to East Surrey in November 1928, becoming number 48 (PK4243), and this was probably the first Reliance to go into service. It had a Hall Lewis two-door body and the only noticeable external difference between it and a 426 was that the bonnet was longer because the engine was bigger (photograph on page 54).

The LGOC took a total of 34 production models, fourteen buses for National with 29-seat Chiswick-built bodywork, which were numbered R 1–14 and twenty 'semi-saloon' coaches with 32-seat bodywork, also built at Chiswick, which at this time were not numbered. Although not within the scope of this book, in the interests of clarity it is worth pointing out that R 1–14 later became R 45-49, 26–34 in the London Transport numbering, and the unnumbered ones R 6-25. The coaches went into service at a variety of LGOC garages between 1st and 13th May 1929 and the fourteen buses were delivered to National in June and July.

By now, General had taken delivery of the first Renown six-wheeled chassis (UU6611) which became LT 1 (on 24th June), the prototype Regent (UU6610), on 2nd July, and a Regent for experimental service with Thomas Tilling (UU9161) on 10th July, all of which had versions of the new engine. The LGOC had been considering bringing their LS fleet more up to date with a new design of body on a shortened chassis but the arrival of the Renown caused a change of plan and the body was mounted on LT 1 instead. In this form it went into service on route 16A from Cricklewood garage on 2nd August 1929. The prototype Regent had an open staircase 51-seat body by Short Bros and was sent for trial running to East Surrey and its subsidiary Autocar on 4th July. The Tilling Regent was one of three experimental vehicles run on the company's London services in 1929 to determine what type to adopt to replace its open-top fleet. The other two were Tilling-Stevens TS17A petrol-electrics with Tilling 52-seat open staircase bodywork (GU6483 and 7750). Tilling-Stevens GU7750 went into service on 18th May, the Regent on 28th July and the other Tilling-Stevens on 11th October. The first Regent chassis for LGOC's own fleet arrived on 7th October and the completed bus went into service on 27th November. The year ended with the delivery of the first of the new generation AECs to go into service in quantity, the AEC Regals which LGOC classified T. The first to be licensed was T 4, at Romford (RD) garage on 3rd December and by the end of the year 38 were in service.

That completes the story of vehicle developments by the LGOC in the 1920s but it would be wrong to close the chapter without considering the contribution made by the London Independents to the bus scene of the period. At its peak this amounted to nearly 680 buses, fifteen per cent of the total.

*Top* The prototype AEC Regent 661 as originally built, in Autocar livery and fitted up with clips for destination boards and a lamp to light them, although the blanked panel of an aperture for a roller blind display is clearly visible. The Short Bros body seated 51 and it was the only open-staircase Regent owned directly by the Combine. It eventually became ST 1139 in the LPTB fleet. (Ken Glazier collection)

*Centre* Before placing orders for new buses to replace the Tilling-Stevens TS3As, Thomas Tilling ran three experimental buses, one of which was this AEC Regent UU9161, with a Short Bros body similar to UU6610. Although the Regent won the competition, this bus was returned to AEC after five months service in London and another seven in Brighton. (Capital Transport collection)

*Right* The two Tilling-Stevens TS17As were fitted with Tilling 52-seat bodywork in a style that was to become familiar in the modified form adopted for the company's STs delivered the following year. (Capital Transport collection)

Although most of the Independents did not have fleets large enough to create their own standards, the buses they used did conform to a pattern which was unique to London because of the conditions imposed by the Public Carriage Office on their design and maintenance. Under long-standing powers held by the Metropolitan Police, every type of bus had to be approved and certified by them and once in operation had to be overhauled and repainted once a year and submitted for inspection. The regulations imposed stricter rules about dimensions, axle loadings and overall weights than was general in the rest of the country. All this applied in equal measure to the LGOC but they had their own manufacturing facilities which could standardise production on London designs. Other chassis manufacturers produced special models for the London market and a group of body manufacturers grew up specialising in London conditions.

The first Independent bus of all in this period was a Leyland designed for London, the normal control LB1, which was built for the Chocolate Express in 1922. This started a new series which was improved gradually and had reached LB5 before being superseded by the Titan in 1927. The LB was a lighter version of Leyland's standard G7 with a four-cylinder 40hp side-valve engine and, to comply with London regulations, had a constant mesh gearbox whose quiet operation met Metropolitan noise standards. It also had three independent brakes and its frame had a tapered front end to meet the turning circle limit of 55ft but this proved inadequate and the type was not allowed to use some important terminal workings where clearances were tight. The improved LB4 appeared in 1923 but was soon replaced by the LB5, on which the turning circle inadequacies were rectified, and this became the most popular first generation Leyland among London Independents. LBs in service reached a maximum of 174 in 1925.

Leyland's main rival in London was Dennis Bros of Guildford who presented its 4-ton chassis for approval in 1923. This had a 36hp side-valve engine built by Dennis at its White & Poppe factory and a four-speed crash gearbox. The first, with Dodson body-work, was licensed on 3rd August 1923 by A1 who operated from a garage in Hackford Road Brixton, and the number in service reached a maximum of 250 in 1926. Dennis was also the only significant supplier of single-deckers to the London market, which was never very large. The single-deck equivalent of the 4-ton was the 2½ ton chassis, of which Dennis managed to sell 48 by 1926. This model was the first to be approved for pneumatic tyres by the Police, the vehicles concerned being in A.T. Bennett's Admiral fleet, which contained seventeen of the type. Bennett was an enterprising man and he was also instrumental in getting approval for four-wheel brakes, this time on a Dennis E, as described earlier. The E, which was the next most popular chassis for single-deckers, had a 4-cylinder 6.24 litre engine capable of producing 70 bhp and was a high-performing reliable and highly regarded bus.

Arthur Partridge was instrumental in introducing the Leyland LB to London and he remained loyal to the model until the Titan became available in 1927. XT4951 was an LB4 with Dodson 48-seat bodywork, new in May 1924 and is seen in Strand, passing the only section of Bush House built at the time, the empty space behind it being the site of Australia House. (Capital Transport collection)

*Centre* Pioneer's immaculate Dennis 4-tonner with Dodson bodywork was first licensed on 28th June 1928, a very late date for this model and therefore rather outdated compared to the Titans of other Independents and the latest pneumatic-tyred NSs of the Combine. It is at the King's Cross terminus of route 218E, one of those numbers which could equally well have been a variant of another route, in this case the 18. (W. Noel Jackson)

*Below* Most of the buses which survived for any length of time beyond 1928 were fitted with pneumatic tyres by their owners. Reliance's Dennis 4-tonner XX5800 was one of these and it survived to become D 200 in the LPTB fleet. It is in Leytonstone having arrived on route 366 from Brentwood. (J.F. Higham)

Another model which sold well for a time was the Straker Squire A, powered by a 54hp overhead-valve engine. It was built in the company's well-equipped modern factory in Edmonton, and was usually supplied with the company's own bodywork. It was significantly cheaper than the Leyland but it proved unreliable in service and fell out of favour within two years, none being sold after 1924. There were 119 in service in 1925 but this had sunk to only two in 1927, partly because many of them were owned by companies acquired by the LGOC who replaced them with standard types.

The first forward-control model available to Independents was the model J from Thornycroft of Basingstoke, the first of which was put into service by Pioneer in July 1923. Four years had elapsed since the K had been launched by AEC but the Walthamstow company, as part of the Underground Group, was forbidden to supply vehicles to Independents. The performance of the J was plodding and lacked the sparkle of other types and it failed to catch on in London. Only thirty-four were sold to London operators and all had short careers in the capital, most having been withdrawn by 1926 and all having gone by 1929.

Apart from a few rebuilt chars-a-banc in the early days. the only other chassis used by Independents in the period before 1927 for double-deckers were rebuilt Daimler Y-types, the work of Josiah Roberts of Shepherd's Bush, some Frost Smith petrol-electrics and twenty similarly powered Tilling-Stevens bought by Timpson. Single-deckers included small numbers of Crossley, Fiat, Maudslay and Guy.

The Chocolate Express LB had 48-seat bodywork by Christopher Dodson of Willesden, a name that was to recur repeatedly during the Independent era as his products came to dominate the London scene. He became a champion of the Independents' cause, offered favourable credit terms for the purchase of new vehicles and was often known to guide budding entrepreneurs in the arts of bus operation. Dodson had supplied quite a lot of bodywork to the LGOC in earlier years but refused to do so after October 1922, a significant date just two months after Partridge started running his Chocolate Express. Other important suppliers of bodywork to the Independent sector, with designs not far removed from those of Christopher Dodson, were Birch Bros, the Wilton Carriage Company, Strachan & Brown and Hickman. All supplied bodies for the Dennis, all but Hickman for the Leyland, Dodson and Strachan & Brown for the Thornycroft, Hickman and Strachan & Brown for the Daimler, Dodson for the Frost Smiths and some of the Straker Squires and Hickman for the Timpson Tilling-Stevens.

After 1927, when Leyland introduced its new Titan TD1, the tables were turned and the Titan became the most popular model by a considerable margin. The new Dennis H, HV and HS were completely outshone by the new competitor and managed sales of only sixteen between them. The best selling vehicle apart from these was the six-wheeled Guy

The Dennis 2½-ton chassis was a popular model for single-deckers and dominated the small London market between 1925 and 1928. All but one of the seven single-deckers owned by The Orange Service were this model and all passed into LGOC ownership in May 1927. This Dodson-bodied 25-seater operating on the Islington–Finsbury Park route 550, still in orange and black livery and with Orange fleet name, is now under LGOC stewardship, with the number D 58 and Chalk Farm garage codes. It was one of the four later sent to National to pacify Walter Iden. (Ken Glazier collection)

*Above* The Dennis E had a special place in the history of the London bus as being the first to secure Metropolitan Police approval to the use of four-wheel brakes. Unlike its 2½-ton predecessor, it had a formidable rival in the Leyland Lion and never reached such heights of popularity. The Westminster Omnibus Company had this solitary example, new in April 1927 with Dodson 30-seat body painted in a dark red and cream livery. Although dressed for route 73, it ran at first on the 26D (Ilford–Chigwell Row) and later on the 203 (Belsize Park–Kensal Rise) (W. Noel Jackson)

*Left* The Thornycroft J was the first forward control model available to Independents in London and Pioneer, true to its name, put the first one into service, MF1001, on 3rd July 1923. Painted crimson and white, the body was by Christopher Dodson. It is seen at King's Cross on route 247A, the number given to the Sudbury route before it was redesignated 218E. (W. Noel Jackson)

This Leyland LB4 has a Strachan & Brown 48-seat body, with a distinctive outward bulge at the waistline. It was bought by Carswool in February 1924 and remained the company's only bus, surviving until being acquired by the LPTB as the last Independent bus with solid tyres still running. At first it was in this all-red livery but it was later repainted red and white. It is seen at The Wellington stand, Wood Green, on route 21 where it spent most of its operational life. (J.F Higham)

The Leyland Titan, many with these handsome Dodson covered top bodies, became the most popular marque for Independents after 1927. The Westminster Omnibus Company bought nine TD1s, this example, which appears to be taking part in a publicity event for R.O.P motor oils, being licensed for the first time on 28th October 1929. Westminster was one of the successful operators, starting in April 1924 and growing to a fleet of thirteen vehicles by the time it was taken over by the LPTB.

The Leyland Lion PLSC was a popular alternative to the Dennis E in the late 1920s. This Dodson-bodied PLSC3 is in the chocolate and cream colours of the Prince Omnibus Company, which was later to achieve fame by being the last London Independent to be acquired by the LPTB. (J. Higham)

FCX, launched at a time when the idea of a high capacity six-wheeler for city service was enjoying a brief vogue. Only sixteen came onto London's roads and fourteen of these were owned by one concern, the London Public Omnibus Company, who may have been as much as anything concerned to make a splash with a sensational-looking vehicle to implant the company's name in people's minds. The other two went to City and Chas. H Pickup. Among single-deckers in the late 1920s, there were really only two contenders, the almost legendary Leyland Lion PLSC and the Dennis E but there were a few Beans, Guys and Karriers. The supply of bodywork in these later years was again dominated by Dodson, with Birch also claiming a prominent place.

The 1920s had been a remarkable ten years which had started with the mechanically primitive, if reliable, chassis and horse-bus derived body of the B-type and finished as the heralds of the modern generation had just gone into production.

CHAPTER EIGHT

# Controlled Competition

Chief Constable Bassom showed himself to be a man with a considerable streak of reforming zeal in his makeup when it came to applying the provisions of the London Traffic Act. He had strong views about reducing the number of Approved Routes and was also suspicious of the purpose of short workings, which he wanted to limit severely. For these reasons his first draft list was, like that of a budding poet, an extremely slender volume. His forceful views also extended to route numbering and it was with this aspect of the operation of the Act that his name was to become synonymous.

He believed that each short working should have its own distinguishing mark because the use of the same number for buses going to different terminals was 'bad and needed to be rectified'. Frank Pick went to see Bassom on 27th September 1924, only nine weeks before the new schedules were due to start, primarily to discuss how schedules could be produced in a form acceptable to the Met Police but he took the opportunity to suggest a method of numbering which could meet the points made by Bassom. At this stage of preparation, Bassom had yet to decide on the rest of his numbering strategy

and Pick therefore assumed that suffix letters would still be used for bifurcations from main routes, or 'forks' as Pick described them. His proposal for distinguishing short workings was to use suffix letters starting at Z and working backwards up the alphabet, leaving the letters from A upwards for variations from the main route. Quite how a short working on a bifurcated service would have been numbered does not seem to be on record but it could have led to such monstrosities as 12CW, for example, so the method eventually adopted, although justifiably maligned, was at least better than that.

In his internal note about his meeting with Pick, Bassom showed himself more sympathetic to the needs of the small proprietors than he has usually been credited. The schedule form proposed by Pick was based on the one used internally by General and contained a considerable amount of detail, which Bassom thought would be too heavy handed for the smaller operators. He designed a simplified version which showed the name of the proprietor, the route identity, the days on which it was to be worked, the schedule between the hours 'a to b' and the maximum number of buses to be worked. There was also a similar form showing fares. For variations of service in bad weather, such as on Sundays to Dorking, Pick wanted the schedule simply to specify the maximum and minimum number of journeys and for the operator to be left to decide the appropriate level of service within that range. Again Bassom thought this would work unfairly against small operators, particularly those with only one bus, who would not have the flexibility of the Combine in determining levels of service. He preferred the preparation of separate schedules leaving it for agreement between the operator and the Licensing Authority to decide what should be operated at any given time. Even the matter of spare buses was covered in these plans. A proposal to allow ten over the number scheduled was said by Bassom to be meaningless to small operators and he proposed instead one in every ten working buses, so that a one-bus operators could carry one spare. Pick had suggested that for services in excess of a given headway, the individual

departure times should be shown on the schedule but Bassom pointed out that this would work against small operators who might run a bus every hour on a given route, on which General were running every three minutes. He did however concede that where the service was not better than half-hourly in total, definite timings should be shown, although he was unsure of the Commissioner's powers in this respect.

*Below* This is an example of an Independent working on a route in the 'LGOC' series, and of a number which follows the 'plus 100' rule for services that previously carried suffix letters. The 73A (Stoke Newington–Kingston) became 173 under Bassom, the weekday operation being on 173A (to Roehampton). Leyland LB2 MF399 was Prince's first bus and is actually working on route 173D, for which it had a schedule, despite the number carried, an error which perhaps illustrates the degree of care applied by operators to operating the Bassom system. (Ken Glazier collection)

It is clear from Metropolitan Police files that Bassom underestimated the volume of work involved and how much time operators would need to prepare schedules for routes, once they were notified of what services they would be authorised to run. Some Independents found themselves at sea trying to understand the technicalities of scheduling and were slow to submit their schedules but the LGOC also had a vast amount of work to do. To add to their problems, the first set of 'Bassom' schedules had to be produced without full knowledge of exactly what routes would be approved, what short workings would be allowed and what numbers would be allocated to many of the short workings. The result was that many of the numbers used by the LGOC between 1st December 1924 and April 1925 differed from those approved by the police. The first official list of Approved Routes was issued on 9th October 1924 and was remarkably thin on short workings. For example the 25-odd mile long route 59 had only two, the 59A and 59B Camden Town to Coulsdon and Streatham Common respectively. Route 11 had only

one. Following protests from operators the list was expanded on 12th December, eleven days after the new system started, to include a lot more, with the 59 now extending up to 59N. This was only a temporary arrangement and all but twenty-two were supposed to be withdrawn by 31st December.

This was a hopelessly ambitious timetable and Pick had to seek an extension on 30th December when he asked for another month. A revised deadline of 31st January was granted but all operators continued to have problems and as late as 29th January, Pick was having to ask for another extension because the lists sent to the police were still being analysed. Publicly, Bassom was unsympathetic and claimed that General had only themselves to blame as they had been notified clearly about what was required. A note by Bassom dated 3rd February on the Met Police file showed that privately he recognised that General had a genuine problem. He was worried about the legal position as certain provisions of the Act had not yet been enforced and he therefore 'told off' the Chief Inspector to go to 55 Broadway and sit

'for a whole day if necessary and until 10 pm' to clear off the LGOC's shorts. In fact Bassom was more concerned about the number of short workings for which the Independents had applied. More than 900 had been extracted from schedules where there were many duplications but 79 operators had applied for a total of 305 to be approved. Independent proprietors were told in a letter dated 4th February that the list was still being examined and that there was no guarantee that they would become Approved Routes. The revised list was not published until 6th April 1925. General applied the changes which this required in that year's summer schedules which started on Good Friday. The system was finally established.

*Above left* One of the more famous examples of a route allocated to services offered by the Metropolitan Police to Independents was the 284, whose full extent was Hatfield to Pimlico but normal all-year daily operation was on the 284A which went no further north than Hadley Highstone. Its principal operators were the Dangerfield companies and it therefore fell into the hands of the Combine but was never operated by the LGOC. XO3160 was licensed on 21st June 1923 and was Dangerfield Ltd (Carlton)'s fourth Dodson-bodied Leyland LB2. (Ken Glazier collection)

*Above right* Route 291 (Hounslow Heath–Liverpool Street) was a Cambrian route but after the fall of that company it became an LGOC operation, being one of many that spoilt Bassom's neat and tidy arrangements. Strachan & Brown-bodied Dennis 4-tonner D 7 is on short working route 291A at Kew Green 'Coach & Horses' during the period when the company continued to trade but was wholly owned by the LGOC, as the garage code (CA) and running number plates attest. This bus retained the number D 7 in the LGOC fleet. (W. Noel Jackson)

*Left* The 369 superficially conformed to Bassom principles, as it was a variant of the 69 (the numbers 169 and 269 already having been used), and crossed the Metropolitan Police boundary, but it was an anomaly because it was in the series reserved for Independents in the northern area. It was never operated by an Independent and in its final form ran only as a peak hour service between Edmonton and Herne Hill, entirely within the Metropolitan Police area, numbered 369B. Buses owned by the Tramways (MET) Omnibus Company were spread around a number of LGOC garages, Camberwell being the home of K 644 seen on route 369B at Edmonton. (W. Noel Jackson)

Bassom's route numbering system was a cumbersome arrangement which met his overriding requirement that every individual route should have its own distinct identity and that the same should apply to every short working journey. The numbers were also sorted into the following blocks:

1–199    LGOC routes, including those also operated by Independents.
201–299  Reserved for routes offered by the Police to Independent operators.
301–350  Routes entering the Metropolitan Police Area from the north. (See chapter five.)
351–399  Reserved for small Independents in the northern Metropolitan area.
401–499  Routes entering the Metropolitan Police Area from the south. (See chapter four.)
501–508  Routes entering the Metropolitan Police Area from the west. (See chapter six.)
509–599  Routes submitted by Independent operators and approved, which were not covered by the 2xx series.
601–699  Introduced in 1927 for new LGOC routes.

*Top* Although not in the same league as some others, the 525 attracted twelve operators onto its tortuous cross-suburban run from Enfield Town to Cubitt Town. The Batson brothers chose the fleet name 'Direct' for their only bus, this Strachan & Brown-bodied Dennis, which they bought new and registered on 1st April 1925. Cyril Batson was the driver and is seen in the driver's seat in this photograph, probably posed shortly before the company was acquired by the LGOC. Brother Reginald was the conductor but he is lost among the interlopers. The trilby-hatted gentleman leaning on the offside mudguard is believed to be F.F. Downes of Horseshoe, who used the same premises in Culross Road, West Green, where the photograph was taken. (Ken Glazier collection)

*Centre* The 612 was one of the less noted of the routes in the series introduced at the end of 1927 for new Combine services. It ran between Kew Gardens and East Dulwich on summer Sundays from 1928. Although the Tramways (MET) Omnibus Company did run buses on the 612 from time to time from Hammersmith garage, none of its buses was allocated to Shepherd's Bush so presumably K 1012 is on loan. (Ken Glazier collection)

*Right* An example of how Bassom's system was not foolproof can be seen in the sequence 33, 133, 233. The 133 (Liverpool Street–South Croydon) had no connection with either the 33 (Waterloo–Hampton Court) or the 233 but the latter was an obvious relative of the 33 as it followed the same route from Hampton Court to Aldwych before continuing to East Ham. Even this had been numbered 295 until January 1928, as the number 233 was originally allocated to a route from Muswell Hill Broadway to Hammersmith which did not operate. This Dodson-bodied Dennis at Hampton Court was owned by Premier who shared the route with Renown. (J.F. Higham Collection)

*Above* The bus business of the South Metropolitan Tramways and Electric Lighting Company was wound up and absorbed by the Tramways (MET) company on 1st January 1928. K 426, parked on the stand at Addiscombe (Black Horse), was one of three allocated to the company in August 1923 to replace Bs.

*Above right* Renown had one schedule on route 15 which continued the operation started in October 1924, before the London Traffic Act came into effect, and also ran on route 15A on Sundays when restrictions did not apply. Dodson-bodied Leyland LB5 HM7440 was Renown's third bus, bought in April 1927, and was still in the fleet when the company was acquired by the LPTB, becoming L 67, then L 47. It was photographed in Duncannon Street some time after being fitted with pneumatic tyres. (Ken Glazier collection)

The neat division between wholly Independent routes and mainly LGOC was not to survive for long as General was soon running buses on routes in the 200s and 500s when they began to acquire Independent companies. Routes operated by or on behalf of the LGOC wholly outside the Metropolitan area were numbered in the N, S or W series which have been covered in earlier chapters, but General's own routes in the Romford area were numbered in the G series.

The method used to distinguish short workings was to allocate a suffix letter to the main route number, for example in the list for 1st December 1924, route 8 ran from Kingsbury (Blackbird Cross) to Old Ford, 8A Willesden to Old Ford, 8B Willesden (White Hart) to Tottenham Court Road Station, 8C Bank to Old Ford, 8D Tottenham Court Road Station to Old Ford, 8E Kingsbury to Tottenham Court Road Station and 8F Marble Arch to Old Ford. This was one of the routes on which Bassom decided to cull the short workings from 28th February 1925, when the 8B, 8D, 8E and 8F disappeared from the list. In the revised list of Approved Routes dated 6th April 1925 there were further changes which illustrate how unstable the system was. The idea of allocating a separate number to each variation might imply a unique and distinct identity but in practice it was often nothing of the kind in the longer term, as the changes to the 8 group showed. They provided for the extension from Kingsbury to Wembley for

the British Empire Exhibition, to which the number 8 was then allocated. The Kingsbury service, which had been 8, became 8B and the 8D was a new short working between Wembley and Oxford Circus. This example also shows how the system frequently allocated suffix-lettered numbers to the main operation when the full extent of the route was a Sunday only, summer only or some other special operation. Sometimes the plain number was allotted to a route which was formally approved but was never taken up by anybody. A famous example of a route where the plain route was rarely used is the 11, where the Wembley service usurped the main number, forcing the regular operation between Shepherds Bush and Liverpool Street to take the demeaning number 11E.

At first no limit was set on the number of suffixes that could be applied to any given number and in the first flush of operation, routes 11, 23, 29 and 35 reached G and the 33 got to H. The record was held by the 59 which stretched right up to N. This seems to have offended Bassom who decided to set the limit at F, any short workings still required beyond that being given a fresh number. It is not clear why he thought this was necessary, unless he feared that the system was at risk of being made to look ridiculous.

In allocating new numbers to bifurcations which had been identified under the old system by a suffix letter, Bassom tried to maintain some affinity with the main route, preferably by adding 100 to the number, the 23B (Marylebone Station to Becontree Chittys Lane) becoming 123 for example. Where this was not possible the adjacent number could be used (59B became 58) or perhaps one that looked similar but did not follow any of these rules such as the 10A (Elephant & Castle to Epping) which became 100. There were also examples of suffixed spur workings being given a distinctly different number. The Waterloo to Hackney Wick morning peak journeys on route 6, which had not been separately identified under the old system, became 64, which might be said to look like a deformed 6A! The restriction on short working suffixes was often helped out by these routes, one example being the 122C (Poplar to Dagenham), used as a short working on Monday–Saturday route 23

(Marylebone to Rainham) which had used up its allowance of suffixes. The main 122 was a Sunday only version of the 23 which diverted at Selfridges to run to Wormwood Scrubs.

Despite Bassom's determination to have a well-ordered and logical system, it was larded with anomalies right from the outset. The biggest departure from the basic plan was the case of 'when working' journeys to and from garages, some of which were extremely long. These were allowed to run in service for up to five miles showing the number for the route on which the bus was scheduled to work, any mileage in excess of that being run 'light' but a strict interpretation of the Bassom rules would surely have required such journeys to carry the number of the route along which the garage runs were made. It was, of course, open to the operator to obtain a schedule on the linking route and this is what the LGOC did for route 166 (London Bridge to Waterloo) during the time it was run by Middle Row garage. Buses operated to and from London Bridge as 107s, an arrangement that continued for some time after the main 107 service was withdrawn and until the 166 was reallocated to Dalston.

The 'when working' concession could be worked in favour of the enterprising operator. The Renown Omnibus Company operated buses on the 202 (New Cross to Rotherhithe) from their garage in East Ham with garage runs via Barking Road and Rotherhithe Tunnel. George W King, secretary and manager of Renown who later became a senior manager with London Transport, told how Barking Road was a much more fruitful source of traffic than the 202 itself but additional schedules on that road could not be obtained. In the absence of formally approved schedules the company maximised its income by designing its schedules with an abundance of when working journeys, covering almost as much mileage as was operated on the 202! No doubt other operators took advantage of similar opportunities over the years.

Bassom also showed some flexibility in the case of short workings which departed from the main route to reach a stand. Perhaps the most extreme example was on route 76 where the Victoria and Waterloo to Liverpool Street spur services were deemed to be short workings and were allocated the numbers 76A and 76B, despite its being a long deviation from the main route. This makes an interesting comparison with the treatment of the Waterloo journeys on route 6. Others were journeys to and from Brook Green Hammersmith and Kilburn Park Station on routes which by-passed these points, but in those cases the deviation was solely to reach a stand and was comparatively short. In contrast, the journeys to Aerator Works in Angel Road Edmonton previously part of the 76; were numbered 167, even though the distance involved can have been little different from the Liverpool Street deviation. Some years later, when route 194 ran through Croydon to Wallington and beyond, the short workings to Croydon were numbered 494 simply because they ran around the loop from George Street via Katherine Street and Park Lane. A curiosity among all this was route 18. The Police List for 6th April 1925 assigned the number to a new Approved Route from Wembley to London Bridge which, in the event, never operated. This was actually a substantial bifurcation from the main route which continued to run from Willesden to London Bridge via Harlesden but renumbered 18B.

The impact of these changes on the travelling public was considerable. Before Bassom a journey from Poplar to Plaistow could have made, depending on the day of the week, on one of five bus routes the 5, 9, 15, 23 or 40 (plus the trams which were outwith the scheme). From 1st December, without any change to the routes themselves, there were twenty-four to choose from, the 5, 5A, 15, 15A, 15C, 15F, 23, 23A, 23B, 23C, 23E, 40, 40A, 40C, 92, 92A, 105A, 122, 122A, 122C, 122D, 123, 123A, 124. It is hard to discern any real value in this to the ordinary passenger who, as ever, had no say in the matter, but the system managed to survive for ten years and outlived its inventor, who sadly died at an early age in January 1926. Had he lived he might have moderated some of these excesses but, at least until the LPTB was on the horizon in 1932, his successors continued to apply his methods diligently, perhaps out of a misplaced sense of loyalty.

The Police powers to approve routes and schedules were underpinned by the other important provision of the Act, the power granted to the Minister of Transport, on the advice of the London & Home Counties Traffic Advisory Committee, to impose Restricted Streets Orders. One of the main aims of these orders was to reduce the number of buses using the same roads as trams. These were to prove a serious impediment to all operators but came as a particularly powerful blow to the Independents who had often chosen tram routes as their target. The first Order, which covered roads in inner London and the City, was announced on 13th January 1925 and published on 17th February but to the dismay of operators it was backdated to 1st January. This meant that many buses put into service during those six weeks

One of the associations set up following the imposition of Restricted Street orders was the West London Association, operating route 526 with twelve members at its height, three of whom are represented in this panorama at the Swan & Pyramids, North Finchley. The Cornwall Motor Omnibus Company's Strachan & Brown-bodied Dennis is on the left, one of Robert Thackray's Dodson-bodied Dennisses is on the right and Birch's B 3, a Birch-bodied Leyland LB5 is between them. (Ken Glazier collection)

would have to be withdrawn, even though the proprietors had deposited their schedules as required and received approval to operate them. Some of the companies affected were brought close to bankruptcy by this action. A special 'Hard Cases' committee set up by the L&HCTAC which heard appeals from operators, rarely granted any concessions but did concede that the date of operation of this order should be altered to the date of its publication, 17th February. This was announced on 18th June, after which the operators were able to restore the withdrawn buses.

The second Order, foreshadowed in an announcement on 17th April 1925 was dated 5th June 1925 but had come into effect two days earlier. It covered nearly every tram route and Bassom went further by announcing that he would be imposing service cuts on established routes using the same roads as trams. At the same time he supplied a list of routes using unrestricted roads on which he suggested the Independents might consider operating services. This sparked off one of the beneficial side-effects of the Act. Some

of the operators displaced by the Orders did move onto these routes and several were built up into major services, notably the 511 (Chingford to Stratford), 525 (Enfield to Cubitt Town), 526 (North Finchley to Wandsworth Bridge) and 536 (Archway to Brockley originally but extending to West Wickham at its fullest extent). In some cases the proprietors formed Associations, a name handed down from horse bus days, with joint administration and management and a common livery. The most successful of these was probably the West London Association which operated route 526 and which attracted twelve proprietors at its zenith. The East London Association had sixteen members working route 511 and the North London Association, on route 284A, had eleven. The West and North London Associations eventually broke up but the 511 remained a bastion of Independent operation until the last. Other significant routes started and developed by Independents were the 263 (five operators) and the 551 (Whetstone to Edmonton; ten operators).

The East London Association operated route 511, which attracted no fewer than sixteen operators, usually on the 511A or 511B (Chingford Mount/Chingford–Stratford Broadway). Two are represented here at the Chingford Mount terminus, a Pro Bono Publico brown and cream Dodson-bodied Dennis 4-tonner, followed by a similar but red and white Gordon Dennis. (Ken Glazier collection)

Into the unpromising landscape of early 1925 stepped the Birch family. This venerable name had first been associated with bus operation in 1847, eight years before the LGOC appeared on the scene, but had last operated buses in the capital in 1912. Ten LB-type chassis had been ordered from Leyland in September 1924 with the intention of developing services in London. After abandoning the idea of joining forces with Dangerfield on various routes, Birch received an approach from City suggesting they might become the third partner in the joint operation of the Archway to Brockley route. City and United had been working on the 517 (Archway to Peckham Rye via Tottenham Court Road and Oxford Street) since 5th December 1924, as described in chapter three, but from 21st January 1925 the two companies moved their entire operation onto the 536 (Archway to Brockley) which ran via Great Portland Street instead of Tottenham Court Road. The longer route needed more buses and these were provided by Birch whose first two Leylands went into service on that route, but this was one of those caught by the retrospective Restricted Streets Order and the extra buses had to be withdrawn. They went instead onto route 526D (North Finchley to Wandsworth Bridge), and became the nucleus of the Birch contribution to the West London Association when it was formed on 31st August 1925. This was the most successful of the associations, its members being Alma, Clarence, Favourite, Glandfield, Paragon, The Royal, Tally Ho!, J.D. Thackray and Varsity, each contributing one bus, Birch (3 buses), Cornwall (5) and Robert Thackray (4). The scheduling, administration and supervision was carried out by Birch on behalf of the Association members and a common red and white livery, embellished with a gold star symbol, was adopted. The Association closed down when the London Public Omnibus Company acquired most of its members in 1927 but the route survived, as did the Birch association with it.

*Top* The crew of Leyland LB5 A 26, in their smart summer uniforms, stand ready in the Queen's Road Peckham yard to start a day's stint on the 536 while the man on the right gives the bus a final polish for the benefit of the camera. A 26 was new in March 1927, shortly before the route was extended as 536 from Southend Village to 'Beckenham, Elmers End' on 14th April 1927. (Ken Glazier collection)

*Centre* The third Leyland LB5 delivered to Birch was intended for route 536 and its Birch-built body was painted in the livery of two shades of brown and cream used by the three participants in that operation. The fleet name 'ARCHWAY' was used by the company at first. LB 3, unable at first to work on the 536, went into service on the 526 instead. (Ken Glazier collection)

*Right* The United Omnibus Company was the third partner in route 536, supplying six buses and a spare which they kept at Toler's garage in Lothian Road Camberwell. The company started in June 1923 and was still in business in 1933 when the LPTB took over, by which time seven Leyland Titan TD1s had replaced the original fleet of LBs, six of which had Dodson bodies and one a Wilton. (Ken Glazier collection)

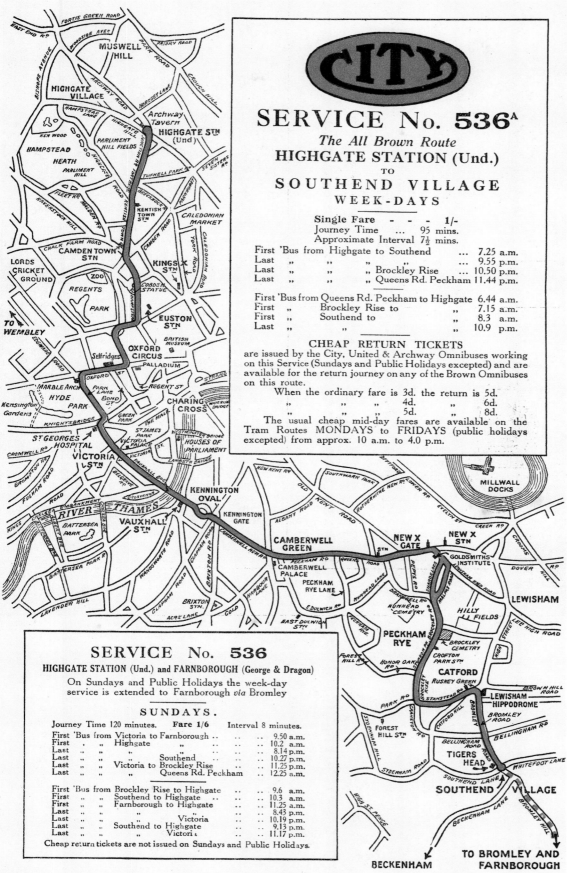

# CITY

## SERVICE No. 536ᴬ
### *The All Brown Route*
### HIGHGATE STATION (Und.)
### TO
### SOUTHEND VILLAGE
#### WEEK-DAYS

Single Fare - - - 1/-
Journey Time ... 95 mins.
Approximate Interval 7½ mins.

| First 'Bus from Highgate to Southend | ... | 7.25 a.m. |
| Last " " " ... | | 9.55 p.m. |
| Last " " " Brockley Rise | | 10.50 p.m. |
| Last " " " Queens Rd. Peckham | | 11.44 p.m. |

First 'Bus from Queens Rd. Peckham to Highgate 6.44 a.m.
First " Brockley Rise to " 7.15 a.m.
First " Southend to " 8.3 a.m.
Last " " 10.9 p.m.

#### CHEAP RETURN TICKETS

are issued by the City, United & Archway Omnibuses working
on this Service (Sundays and Public Holidays excepted) and are
available for the return journey on any of the Brown Omnibuses
on this route.

When the ordinary fare is 3d. the return is 5d.
" " " 4d. " 6d.
" " " 5d. " 8d.

The usual cheap mid-day fares are available on the
Tram Routes MONDAYS to FRIDAYS (public holidays
excepted) from approx. 10 a.m. to 4.0 p.m.

## SERVICE No. 536

### HIGHGATE STATION (Und.) and FARNBOROUGH (George & Dragon)

On Sundays and Public Holidays the week-day
service is extended to Farnborough *via* Bromley

#### SUNDAYS.

Journey Time 120 minutes. Fare 1/6 Interval 8 minutes.

| First 'Bus from Victoria to Farnborough .. | .. | .. | 9.50 a.m. |
| First " " Highgate " | .. | .. | 10.2 a.m. |
| Last " " " | .. | .. | 8.14 p.m. |
| Last " " Southend .. | .. | .. | 10.27 p.m. |
| Last " " Victoria to Brockley Rise | .. | .. | 11.25 p.m. |
| Last " " " Queens Rd. Peckham | .. | .. | 12.25 a.m. |

| First 'Bus from Brockley Rise to Highgate .. | .. | 9.6 a.m. |
| First " " Southend to Highgate .. | .. | 10.3 a.m. |
| First " " Farnborough to Highgate | .. | 11.25 a.m. |
| Last " " " | .. | 8.43 p.m. |
| Last " " " Victoria | .. | 10.19 p.m. |
| Last " " Southend to Highgate | .. | 9.13 p.m. |
| Last " " " Victoria | .. | 11.17 p.m. |

Cheap return tickets are not issued on Sundays and Public Holidays.

*by S.M. WARREN.*

An example of the high
quality publicity leaflets
produced by City
advertising the 'All Brown
Route', with a clear map
and timetable information.
It dates from 1925 when
the Sunday service ran to
Farnborough and includes
advice on the back on
getting to Wembley
Exhibition, by changing at
Marble Arch on to a 'Direct
Wembley Bus', without
mentioning who might be
the operator!

The alteration to the date of operation of the Restricted Streets Order enabled Birch to restore their two buses to the 536 but they were again forced off the route on 11th April by the second retrospective Restricted Streets Order. They were able to return on 1st August when the operational date of the restrictions was amended, finally establishing an association with City and United that was to last until they were acquired compulsorily by the LPTB. Meanwhile, the route had been extended beyond Brockley via Catford to Southend Village (Tigers Head) on 15th April, with a summer Sunday only extension to Farnborough (536). The route reached its maximum on 14th April 1927 when it was extended, as 536, to Elmers End via Beckenham by which time it needed thirty-six buses, three Birch, six United and twenty-seven City. The buses for the 536 were painted in a common brown and cream livery and this was an important selling point, as Birch discovered by the adverse reaction to its occasional use of red buses from the 526 pool. The 536 was a powerful example of Independent operation at its best and stood as living proof that companies who were prepared to work within the limitations of the 1924 Act could nevertheless carve out a distinct and successful enterprise of their own.

Birch was to expand considerably over the next few years, partly by its own enterprise and partly by the acquisition of three smaller operators in 1929. The fleet had built up to a total of twenty-eight by the end of 1929 but this was some way below the company's ambitions which were constantly thwarted by the police and the L&HCTAC as the company sought new areas in which to expand. Examples of proposed services that were opposed by the traffic authorities include a new route between Hampstead Heath and Pimlico, jointly with Thackray, which was refused and Ealing to Greenford where the police claimed that the roads were unsuitable. The company's appeal to the Minister was rendered pointless when he declared Haven Green, Castlebar Hill and Cleveland Road Restricted Streets while he was considering the appeal. The buses intended for the Ealing service were used instead on routes 26D and 26E at Ilford which were at that time unrestricted but far distant from base and therefore expensive to operate. One famous enterprise which was finally successful was route 231, which eventually ran from Hampstead Heath (South End Green) to Harlesden (231A), with a Sunday extension to Park Royal, but only after a long battle which started with a very different proposal. Birch had wanted a route from

Hampstead to Hammersmith running via Bayswater, whose local traders wanted a link from Maida Vale to Queensway to serve, among other things, the famous Whiteley's department store. The application was rejected and Birch made do with a service numbered 203 from Belsize Park to Kensal Rise using a series of local roads where the presence of overhanging trees and protruding street lamps enforced the use of single-deckers. The natural objective at the eastern end was Hampstead Heath (South End Green) where it could connect with the trams and other bus services but this was prevented on Mondays to Saturdays by the existence of a Restricted Streets Order on South End Green (a tiny but vital part of the proposed extension). Birch continued to battle for permission to run over this essential section and for a westward extension to Harlesden and beyond but it was not until 1930 that these were finally granted. This brief summary of one operator's struggle to establish a profitable portfolio of routes may serve to illustrate the circumstances in which all proprietors found themselves after December 1924 and which many found too hard to handle.

*Top left* Birch took refuge on routes 26E and 26D (Ilford–Chigwell Row/Barkingside) when its attempt to start an Ealing–Greenford service in 1927 was thwarted. Another refugee already operating on the service was Empress Motors Ltd, whose Dodson-bodied Leyland Lion PLSC3 this is. (J.F. Higham)

*Top right* Birch had a long battle to get approval to route 231, which they were able to run only on Sundays when Restricted Street Orders did not apply, but the fullest extent achieved before 1930 on Mondays–Saturdays came in November 1928 when route 203 was extended to Hampstead Town Hall and renumbered 231A to bring it into line with the Sunday operation. Dennis E B 14 is at the other end of the route, Kensal Rise Station, in the standard brown and cream livery and with the new fleet name 'BIRCH'. (W. Noel Jackson)

*Left* There were five other participants in route 231A, which caused the route to be so overbussed that receipts were meagre and the operators did not always run their full schedules. This Dodson-bodied Leyland PLSC3 at Kensal Rise station was owned by Albert Ewer who had a schedule for one bus. Ewer sold his bus business to LGOC in September 1929 but continued to operate coaches until May 1934 when he sold them to Grey Green. (W. Noel Jackson)

The Independents always believed that the Act was used to stunt their growth while allowing the Combine a much freer rein and nothing was to provide more flammable fuel for that belief than the decision announced by the Minister in June 1925 to cut the number of buses running over tram routes. Two sections of road were specified, Uxbridge Road from Shepherd's Bush to Uxbridge and Romford Road from Stratford to Ilford. The number of buses decreed to be cut was the number that had been put on the two roads since 1st April 1923, which came to 27 LGOC and 32 Independents. The first road chosen was Uxbridge Road, where the main presence of the Combine was the frequent service of trams on the Shepherd's Bush to Uxbridge route, as well as some other local operations, but where the majority of bus operators were independents. The proposals, announced in January 1926, were like a thunderbolt. On route 526 alone, which the L&HCTAC wanted to reduce to a risible 30-minute headway, fourteen of the twenty-one buses would have been removed. Cuts of a similar order were proposed for other routes. The effect would have been catastrophic, particularly for the small operators of one or two buses who were in no position to make proportionate reductions. The proprietors were acutely resentful of what they saw as grossly unfair treatment and the public also condemned the proposals, so the owners prepared a petition to Parliament. When the Minister wrote on 6th March suggesting that the operators should decide among themselves how to apportion the cuts, the reaction of the West London Association (route 526) was to tell him they had no intention of making any cuts. They were particularly incensed that it broke the assurance given by Chief Constable Bassom in April 1925 that schedules would be secure, provided operators deposited them in good time. What Bassom may or may not have thought about the proposals or how he might have defended his integrity will never be known as he had already died by this time. The proprietors' tempers were hardly improved by a suggestion from the L&HCTAC that they should set up a voluntary fund to compensate those who may suffer as a result of the workings of the Act. Such insensitive behaviour continued to inform the activities of the various parties lined up against the Independents, many of whom were in despair that everyone in authority opposed them. Two operators (Dominion and T & W) did withdraw but did not take up the offer of alternative schedules elsewhere, preferring to cut their losses and sell to the LGOC who were always willing to acquire schedules, even those in abeyance as in this case. The Police issued a summons against various Independents and the LGOC and a test case against one proprietor, Cornelius Beattie, was heard at Ealing Magistrates Court. The magistrates dismissed the summons for two reasons. When the regulations were made, the authorities took into account the economic position of the tramways, which the Act did not empower them to; and the two 'additional' members

of the Traffic Advisory Committee were not present when the Regulations were considered. Although this was a victory of sorts, it was ultimately overturned on appeal and many small proprietors now saw the writing on the wall.

Despite the difficulties imposed by the 1924 Act, Independent proprietors continued to enter the London bus scene, although at a markedly reduced rate after April 1925. Twenty-four new operators started work between January and April 1925 but there were then no more during that year, there were five in 1926, only one in 1927, four in 1928 and one in 1929. A number of the operators who started in these later years did so to take advantage of new suburban housing developments, notably the Becontree Estate in east London. Some made a great success of it but by the second half of the decade, the fortunes of the existing operators had taken a sharp downward turn and the market was no longer so welcoming, except for the most hardy. Five of the twenty-four who started

The section of Romford Road between Stratford and Ilford was mentioned alongside Uxbridge Road in the Minister's statement of June 1925, announcing the policy of reducing bus services along tram routes. Victory operated on both route 25 and, to a lesser extent, the 86, both of which were caught up in the proposals. TW3167 was a Dodson-bodied Leyland LB5 bought in May 1926 to replace its original Daimler, whose poor mechanical performance had brought the company close to bankruptcy. Victory survived to be taken over by the LPTB in 1934. (D.W.K. Jones)

Lyle Newstead, one of the early participants in the Admiral enterprise, had three phases of bus operation in London, this chocolate and white Strachan & Brown-bodied Leyland LB5, named 'Empire', being his third attempt. Empire operated on routes 294 (Pimlico–Lower Edmonton) and 529 but this photograph was taken just after the business was sold to London Public in November 1927 when the bus was already carrying its LPOC fleet number (L 33) and had been transferred to west London. It is at Uxbridge Road Station (just west of today's West Cross Route roundabout) on route 17, one of those entangled in the Uxbridge Road dispute. (Alan Cross, JB Atkinson Collection)

during 1925 became successful enough to stay in business right through the remainder of the Independent era, although one was Romford District Motor Services which was free of the restrictions imposed by the London Traffic Act.

The first of the four metropolitan newcomers, Robert Hawkins, started with a Wilton bodied Dennis on 1st January 1925, which he ran on the 3A and 59A. Later he acquired a Leyland PLSC Lion, which he ran for a time on route 551 before settling onto route 202, nearer his Peckham base. Frank Miller started in February 1925 with one Leyland on the 15A and 101B and later expanded into the newly developing Becontree and Dagenham areas with a second Leyland, a Dennis 4-ton and a Leyland PLSC single-decker which were used on routes 292 (Poplar to Becontree Heath) and 266 (Leytonstone to Chadwell Heath). What eventually became the Essex Omnibus Company started on 2nd February with a Dodson-bodied LB5, operating mainly on the 23 group, which was joined in 1929 by a Leyland Titan. The last of these 'stayers' was also the largest. Martin started with a single LB5 on 21st April 1925 and accumulated a fleet of eleven by the end of 1929, partly by the acquisition of the Paterson and Gretna companies. Martin started on the 23 and 86 but, when further expansion was thwarted by restriction orders, pioneered route 292. Both Martin and Miller continued to expand in the early 1930s and reached a maximum of thirteen and seven buses respectively by the time they were acquired by the LPTB.

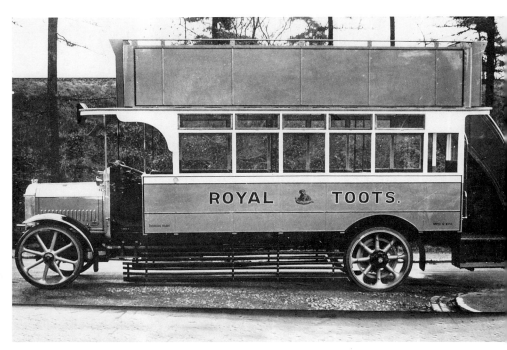

*Above* One of the more fanciful names chosen by an Independent was Royal Toots, a company formed in November 1924, just before the London Traffic Act took effect. Its owners, Mary and Theodore Hoare, obviously had a sense of humour, the bus being painted in a bright yellow and cream livery and carrying a 'coat of arms' illustrating a puppy sitting on a regal cushion. It was housed at Page Street under the care of S.H. Hole but was not a success. The Dodson-bodied Dennis was sold to J. Thomson ('Regal') of Croydon, in April 1925.

*Below* The Comfort Omnibus Company Ltd of Enfield Wash was registered on 25th January 1925, a latecomer to London bus operation, its GWL fleet name being the initials of the father and two sons George, Wilfred and Leslie Lewington. It is believed that George's loyalty to his home town of Basingstoke was behind the choice of a Thornycroft. MH4646, bodied by Dodson and painted red and white, ran on route 525 (Enfield–Cubitt Town) but for barely two years, as the Lewingtons sold out to London Public in June 1927. (Ken Glazier collection)

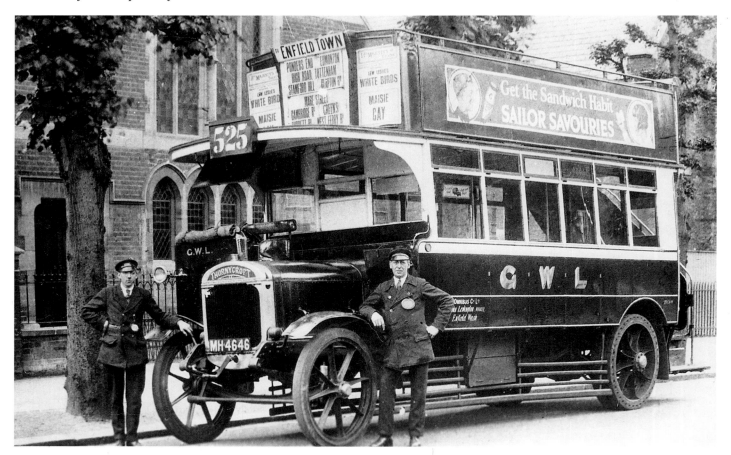

The harsh realities of bus operation in a controlled regime came home to many operators during 1926 and that year proved to be a turning point. It was also the year of the General Strike and the conduct of the Independents during those crucial nine days introduced a new bitterness into the already strained relationships between their staff and those of the Combine. The strike was called by the Trades Union Congress in support of the miners who had been in dispute with their employers about imposed cuts in wages. It started at midnight on 3rd May 1926 and on the following day, the Combine suffered a complete withdrawal of labour, as did the main line railway companies and the municipal tramways. Overnight 214 licensed Bs were transferred into Chiswick Works where they were garaged under the protection of the army, additional buses being added on subsequent days, some of which were K, S and NS types. These were to be used to run emergency services driven and conducted by volunteers and carrying a policeman or special constable on each bus as a protection from attack by strikers. The volunteers were described as mainly people normally employed but available for service during the strike, and a small number were unemployed people glad of a chance to earn some money. Despite the gloss put on the subject by the government-controlled press and subsequent reports, only about one-fifth were students or people of independent means. No buses were run on the Sunday, which was designated as a rest day.

The first 86 buses went into service on 5th May on a special circular route (numbered 1) from Ealing via Shepherd's Bush, Notting Hill Gate, Oxford Circus, Holborn, Aldwych, Piccadilly, Kensington, Hammersmith, Chiswick, Brentford and South Ealing. Route 5 followed on 6th May, circling from Hendon via route 13 to Trafalgar Square, Victoria and route 16 (84 buses). The third circular route (3), using 64 buses, started on 7th May and ran from Chelsea via route 31 to Camden Town, Bloomsbury, Aldwych, Charing Cross and route 11. The last was route 4, starting on 8th May and running from Harlesden via route 18 to King's Cross,

Islington, Bank, Holborn, Marble Arch, Shepherd's Bush and Scrubs Lane. Cricklewood garage reopened under police protection on 10th May and volunteers were used to operate a mixture of K, S and NS on routes 2, 13, 16 and 60 (220 buses). Emergency routes 1, 4 and 5 ran for the last time on 10th May and the following day Chiswick began to run buses on routes 11, 18, 27, 33 and 184 (266 buses) followed by routes 14, 49 and 73 next day (160 buses). The remaining circular route 3 ran for the last time on 11th May and on the 12th May sixteen buses were sent to Regents Park to operate on route 31 for one day only, by which time there were

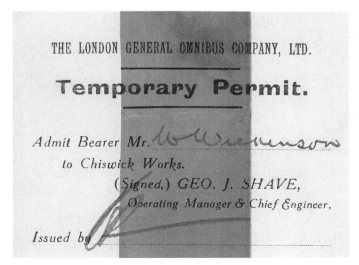

*Above* Armed and steel-helmeted soldiers guard the buses lined up for action at Chiswick Works, while a group of what appears to be volunteers looks on with some apprehension.

*Left* Volunteers were issued with these Temporary Permits to allow them into Chiswick Works. (Ken Glazier collection)

It is not clear what is going on in this photograph which is full of volunteers milling around and many crammed into the buses in the line on the left. It must have been taken on 11th, 12th or 13th May when Chiswick was running buses on normal routes 11 and 18 but the scene has a valedictory air about it and may have been on the last day of the strike. By this time the Bs had been joined by NSs (as here) as well as K and S-types. The sinister looking armoured car on the left is standing alongside notices which have been erected for the period of the special operation. (Ken Glazier collection)

662 buses in service. Thomas Tilling was also able to keep a service going from 6th May, concentrating on route 12C between Dulwich and Oxford Circus. After bus No. 849 was set alight in Walworth Road by striking busmen, the route was diverted through Kennington instead. The buses were kept at their Bull Yard, Peckham premises and were manned by a mixture of their own office staff and volunteers from the general public. Later it was found possible to increase the total in service to the surprisingly high figure of 318, which enabled the operation of a number of normal routes.

In the Independent sector, it was a different story. Few staff were members of a Trade Union and nearly all continued to work throughout the stoppage. The inflamed feelings of LGOC staff led to some nasty incidents involving Independent buses and the situation was so serious along the Hertford Road from Tottenham down to Kingsland Road that Redburn stopped running there more or less immediately. Similarly, Admiral withdrew from the 29 on 6th May because there had been so many stone-throwing incidents at Camden Town. It soon became apparent that the buses were most at risk overnight in their own garages and arrangements were made for them to be kept in a compound in Regents Park, where they were protected by an army guard. The strike even led to a new operator appearing for a few days when a vehicle builder at Shepherd's Bush, J.M. Roberts, took advantage of the relaxation of route licensing during the emergency to run some buses he had in stock. They ran from 6th May to 12th May.

E Gray and Son's LB4, one of nine Leylands owned by the company, would normally have worked on routes 6, 8, 38 or 69 but the relaxation of the licensing rules during the General Strike brought it onto route 129 (North Finchley–Victoria via Wood Green). The properly signwritten destination board on MF9645 would have been borrowed from the route 38 stock but the company has had to resort to inelegant and less-than-clear chalk lettering for the other information. The boarding over the saloon windows and the wire netting across the front of the driver was a protection against stones or other missiles. Gray survived until 1930 but then was acquired by the LGOC.

The Independent crews at Regents Park were camped out with their buses and had to accept the minimum of comfort and separation from their families for the duration of the emergency. Those working for the LGOC were luckier as they could take advantage of the canteen and recreational facilities provided for the permanent staff. Each volunteer was given a pass authorising them to enter the premises, and a crudely printed 'Ration Book' with small tear-off vouchers which could be exchanged for various meals and drinks. The company also produced a 'roneoed' newspaper called the Gazette. Out on the road, of course, they were just as vulnerable to attack from strikers and their sympathisers. The strike was called off on 13th May but normal services did not resume until 15th May.

At a joint meeting of all the Common Fund Boards on 20th May, Lord Ashfield expressed appreciation for the work of the volunteers 'especially the undergraduates from Oxford and Cambridge' and suggested that there should be some permanent record. He also drew attention to the freedom from accidents which reflected great credit on the volunteers. There was a formal vote of thanks in recognition of 'the courage displayed by the large number of officers and staff who stayed loyal'. There was a celebration dinner for directors and officers at Hotel Victoria on 31st May. Ashfield also reported that he had met the leaders of the various

It seems unlikely that the driver or the owners of the bus were parties to the demonstration in support of the miners taking place on the upper deck of K 672, running under Cambrian colours on route 185B. K 672 replaced a Straker Squire in the Cambrian fleet on 21st December 1926, which indicates that the miners' march was taking place after their humiliating return to work empty-handed in November, six months later than the other participants in the General Strike (Capital Transport collection)

Albert Ewer's Dodson-bodied LB5 has abandoned the 38 group, the 266 or the 525 to operate a section of route 11 in central London, where it was obviously badly needed. The volunteer conductor, wearing a flat cap and standing on the platform leaning against the staircase rail, has either given up trying or hopes to collect fares as people board or alight. (London's Transport Museum)

# EVENING NEWS

Largest Evening Net Sale in the World.

Thursday: May 6th, 1926.                    One Penny.

LONDON WEATHER FORECAST:- Occasional showers, cold. Further outlook; cold, changeable.

THE SITUATION:- The third day of the General Strike found the public as determined as ever in its backing of the Government.   There is as yet no obvious move towards a settlement.   No Cabinet meeting was held to-day: Ministers are all occupied in supervising the public services.   Trade Union Council Strike Committee met privately. Traffic news to-day is good.   All the Underground lines will, it it is expected be open to-night.   2,000 trained men, it is hoped, will be running the L.G.O.C. buses to-night.   200 buses are working on No. 1 circular route. It is stated officially to-day that 70 or 80 L.G.O.C. buses were damaged in various parts of London yesterday. Magistrates are dealing with many offenders.

A section of the emergency typewritten Evening News for Thursday 6th May, the third day of the strike, records details of transport services which appear to refer to the previous day's as additional route 5 was introduced on 6th May. The large number of buses damaged by strikers was not recorded in the LGOC's official Board minutes, perhaps because it was considered a security issue. (Capital Transport Collection)

DAILY SKETCH, SATURDAY, MAY 15, 1926.

## CABINET'S BIG EFFORT TO BRING PEACE TO THE COALFIELDS

# DAILY SKETCH

ONE PENNY

EMERGENCY EDITION Telephones {London—Museum 9841.  Manchester—City 6501.}  LONDON, SATURDAY, MAY 15, 1926.  [Registered as a Newspaper.]

## WE'RE ON THE MOVE AGAIN---BY TRAIN, TRAM AND BUS

London will see most of its Tube, tram and bus services operating to-day.  An official announcement of a " satisfactory settlement " between the companies and the unions concerned is welcome news to City workers. This picture of Regent's Park as a bus depot shows volunteers going on duty for the last time.

The front page of the Daily Sketch for 15th May 1926 announcing the end of the strike has a picture of the LGOC buses sent to Regent's Park on 12th May for operation on route 31. (Capital Transport collection)

Trades Unions on 13th May. They had called for a negotiated settlement and for the re-instatement of staff and, according to Ashfield, had admitted doing the companies a great wrong by calling the strike. They hoped that future relations would be on a more satisfactory footing. This must have sounded a tall order in the overheated emotional climate of the time but the Combine, no doubt under Ashfield's guidance, adopted a conciliatory approach. This was shown in a decision of that same meeting when it was agreed that the wages which had been earned before the strike but withheld from staff for breaking their contracts with the company, should now be paid. Formal negotiations with the Unions started immediately and by August 1926 an agreement had been signed under which the Trade Unions were given official recognition by the companies, and there was also a revised agreement on pay and conditions which led to substantial improvements in working conditions for LGOC staff.

The reactions among Independent proprietors were mixed. Some Union members had always been employed by the Independents and some others had joined the Transport & General Workers' Union during the strike. Once the strike was over, some proprietors sacked staff who were Union members, others just those who had joined during the strike but none went as far as the Combine in their attitude to the Unions. Inevitably old antagonisms between the staffs of the two sectors, which had been in decline, rose again and there was an increase in cases of harassment on the road or physical attack by Combine staff, who would never find it in their hearts to forgive these 'blacklegs'.

Ironically, many of these were to find themselves working alongside each other as colleagues in the next few years, during which most of the smaller operators took flight and sold their assets, the most valuable of which were the schedules they held. This movement had already started before the General Strike and was not necessarily stimulated by that event. Bernard Cosgrove's Edmonton Bus Company had sold out to Earl on 14th January 1926 but all others in this period were direct sales to the Combine. The first was Cambrian, the largest of all, whose fifty-two buses (eight Dennis, thirty Straker Squires, fourteen Thornycrofts) came under the control of the LGOC on 23rd January 1926. Although it was an ailing business, this was a major coup for the LGOC as Cambrian was the biggest of the Independents at the time, its buses being part of a large and successful coach and haulage fleet. Like Birch and City, it set high standards of service with well turned out staff in smart uniforms and a well-presented and maintained fleet, at least until it went into its final decline. An unwise decision in June 1925 to replace its operating bases at Brixton and Mount Pleasant, which were well placed to operate its services, and concentrate its activities on new premises in North Acton, led to a sharp decline in standards, an increase in costs and eventual financial failure.

Cambrian Straker Squire S 66 working a Sunday schedule on route 549 at Stoke Newington, after the company's acquisition by the LGOC. The buses had been moved into General's Hanwell (HW) garage on 23rd February 1926, but operated as a separate entity until the company was absorbed fully by General on 30th April 1928, using the garage code CA. The name of the Receiver's special manager, William George Darvill, appears on the side of the bus which also has a General style fleet name. S 66 and sibling S 52 were replaced on 17th September 1926 by K 610 and 844 which had been repainted into Cambrian livery. The chassis of S 66 was scrapped and its body used as a replacement on a chassis acquired from another Independent. (W. Noel Jackson)

Although in normal circumstances it would have been a poor bargain, the LGOC nevertheless acquired a controlling interest in the Cambrian Coaching and Goods Transport Company Ltd on 11th January 1926, by purchasing the shares held by its founder Athol Murray Kemp-Gee. By arrangement, Kemp-Gee purchased the vehicles used for the coach and haulage activities and moved back to his Bloomsbury offices. The L&HCTAC gave authority for thirty-four of the acquired buses to be overhauled and operated on thirty schedules, the other twenty-two being held in abeyance as part of the expected reduction in service along Uxbridge Road. General eventually acquired the remaining shares in the company and one of the transactions brought with it the Central Omnibus Company, a subsidiary of Commercial Hires Ltd, a Cambrian shareholder. Owing to the complex nature of Cambrian's finances General applied for the company to be put into receivership. The main routes operated on Mondays–Fridays at the time of the acquisition were the 286 (Liverpool Street to Southall, 29 buses) and 291 (Liverpool Street to Hounslow Heath, 18 buses). Cambrian also had schedules on

Two Ks were repainted into Cambrian livery and delivered to Southall on 14th April 1926, to start the replacement of the Thornycrofts for despatch to Thames Valley. One of them was K 296, seen here on route 291E at Hammersmith Underground station with an LGOC S on route 127A to Teddington following. By the end of April 1928, there were 31 Ks in the Cambrian fleet, the balance comprising eight Dennis 4-tonners. (Ken Glazier collection)

*Above* One of the changes made under LGOC management was to transfer the schedules on route 286 (Liverpool Street–Southall) to route 185, which was just a change of terminal in Southall. Thornycroft T 108 is at one of the LGOC's new 'domed' Bus Stops attached to a Birmingham Guild cast iron post at Shepherd's Bush on the revised working. All fourteen Thornycrofts were sold to Thames Valley, T 108 becoming 120 in that fleet (see chapter 6). (London's Transport Museum)

*Left* The business of Alexander Timpson & Son was acquired on 25th March 1926 by the LGOC who passed the operation on to Thomas Tilling. Among the fleet changes made during this period was the transfer of former Cambrian Landray Tilling Stevens petrol-electrics to Timpson, including XB9888 (56) whose chassis had been a char-a-banc, its body coming from one of the former Frost-Smith petrol-electrics. No. 56 is at Plumstead Common (The Old Mill). (Ken Glazier collection)

*Above* Timpson's Straker Squire 47, photographed on 16th July 1926, was one of eighteen taken over by General and sold on to Tilling. They were soon withdrawn and sold, mostly as lorries, but 47 was scrapped. (Alan Cross/W Noel Jackson Collection)

*Above right* Olympic had started as the Diamond Omnibus Company in 1924 and its bus ran on routes 15A/C/E Mondays to Fridays and 25/C/D on Saturdays and Sundays. The Olympic Traction Company Ltd was formed on 18th March 1926 in preparation for its acquisition by the LGOC on 10th April, when the operation was transferred to Athol Street garage. The solitary Thornycroft JB was whisked off to Chiswick for overhaul and sale to Thames Valley and was replaced on 27th April by K 89, whose dual allegiance is evident in the conflict between cab dash and radiator. (W. Noel Jackson)

routes 34C (Liverpool Street to Thornton Heath), 38A (Victoria to Walthamstow), 59B (Camden Town to South Croydon), 88A (Acton Green to Mitcham), 268 (Liverpool Street to Uxbridge) and 290A (Aldwych to Windsor). These were later tidied up by General to be concentrated on the 185 group and 291 with journeys on the 59F, 184, 268, 286 and 290A. The services continued to be run from the North Acton base until 23rd February 1926, after which they were transferred to Hanwell but continued to carry CA garage codes.

The acquisition of Cambrian brought with

it the company's holding in Cambrian Landray and it was not long before General offered to acquire that company too. Operational control passed to the LGOC on 1st January 1927 but full ownership had to wait until 2nd March, when control of the Brixton Omnibus Company also passed to General. Five Tilling-Stevens buses and one Daimler changed hands, along with seven coaches. The coaches were disposed of quickly and the Tilling-Stevens were exchanged for a like number of ex-Timpson Strakers from Thomas Tilling. They and later the Daimler were replaced in the Cambrian Landray fleet by Ks. Also acquired was the garage at Waterworks Road, Brixton, which was retained as a Private Hire garage (BX) by the LGOC and later LPTB.

Fourteen more companies came under the control of General between 8th March, when Fleet and Paul capitulated, and 20th April when Direct and Royal Blue came into the fold. The acquisition of Dominion and T&W by General during the Uxbridge Road proceedings has already been noted but between then and the end of 1927 another seventy-six followed their lead. The operators concerned were generally those whose finances were in a delicate state and who would almost certainly have failed eventually and in some cases their state was such that selling out saved them from collapse by a mere whisker.

Contrarily, it was the very existence of the 1924 Act which gave the LGOC the opportunity to make these acquisitions. When competition was uncontrolled the purchase of a competitor was no guarantee that another would not appear in its place but under the terms of the Act, the schedules were the valuable commodity, rather than the companies themselves as once a schedule had been acquired, nobody else could have it.

Nevertheless, there were many who would not sell out to the LGOC, to whom they remained implacably hostile but the reality was that there was nowhere else to go. The LGOC was well aware of this attitude and was considering other ways to deal with the matter. A hand-written note from Lord Ashfield to Frank Pick on 12th May 1925, when the effectiveness of the 1924 Act was beginning to be apparent, shows the direction their thinking was taking. It referred to a conversation between them the previous day when Pick had apparently mentioned the possibility of 'some outside person' purchasing 'pirates' on behalf of the LGOC. The purpose of the note was to question the legal position regarding the transfer of schedules, which was not allowed by the regulations, and appears to have been the occasion on which the idea was formulated of keeping the companies as subsidiaries but operating LGOC buses.

It is not known who Pick had in mind but it is probably no co-incidence that the company was approached during May 1925 by Charles W. Batten with a scheme for a working agreement between his Atlas and East Ham companies and the LGOC. In truth, he was in financial trouble and his proposal amounted to the sale of the two companies but on the basis that they would retain their separate identities and continue to be managed by Batten. The proposal was agreed and the exchange of shares took place in April 1926. This unusual arrangement seems to have been acceptable to the LGOC because they intended to employ Batten as an agent to acquire companies who would not sell directly to General. The companies purchased in this way became part of the 'Batten Group', discreetly owned by the LGOC but operated under Batten's control. Two groups of companies were placed under his management, one based at premises in Claremont Street, Edmonton acquired from Howard Barrett, another cog in the General's acquisition wheel, and the other from two garages in East Ham formerly owned by Atlas (Tilbury Road) and Invicta (Wellington Road). There were five companies at Edmonton: Cosgrove, Loveland, Tottenham Hotspur, W & P and White Star; and six at East Ham, Atlas, Britannia, the East Ham Omnibus Company (an associated company of Atlas), Grangewood, Invicta and Vivid. The fleets were standardised on Leylands which were gradually exchanged for the incumbent buses as they were acquired from others, and they also had their own livery of brown and cream. Those at Edmonton also carried the fleet name V.C.N., which apparently stood for 'Vul-cold-Nize', a tyre repair product in which Howard Charles Merrett, the Batten Group's financial and business affairs manager, had an interest.

Batten's reign came to an abrupt end on 31st December 1926 when the LGOC took the group under its own direct control. This may have been precipitated by Batten's decision to set up another company, the Aro Omnibus Company, on 26th April 1926, running seven buses on the 263. Pick may have been glad of a reason for terminating the agreement because, as will be seen, the LGOC now had bigger fish in their fryer. The Edmonton Claremont Street base was given the garage code UE (Upper Edmonton) and continued to operate under the supervision of Tottenham garage until it closed after traffic on 8th February 1927, its buses being transferred to Tottenham. At East Ham, both garages continued to function and were coded E (Wellington Road, known officially by LGOC as 'Invicta') and EH (Tilbury Road). The Invicta garage closed on 17th October 1928 but East Ham remained in use until the enlarged and rebuilt Upton Park Garage absorbed its work in December 1931.

Another personality who helped find companies for General to acquire was S.H. Hole who had set up Samuelson's New Transport in the early days of Independent competition, as described in chapter three. He had continued to be involved in bus operation on behalf of companies who used his garage at Page Street, Westminster and through part ownership of the A1 bus. He sold out to General in March 1926 and part of his agreement with Frank Pick was that he should be found work for his garage. The result was that the A1 and Marathon buses were placed under his direct control at Page Street until 17th August 1926, when they were exchanged for the thirteen Straker Squires of the EP fleet. Hole was responsible for every aspect of the business, except the sale of advertising space which was reserved to the LGOC and, in effect, he continued to work as though the proprietor of the business. Other companies which had used Page Street and which were acquired by LGOC through Hole's good offices were Florence, District, T & W and Dominion, the last two being the dormant victims of the Uxbridge Road restrictions. Hole was not happy with the EP Strakers which were difficult to keep on the road but he had to keep them going until the contract expired on 16th March 1927, when the whole operation was transferred into LGOC garages and the Strakers replaced by Ks.

At this time the L&HCTAC was considering the whole question of co-ordination and common management and had highlighted as a particular obstacle the existence of a large number of smaller operators who would not fit into any grand scheme. One suggestion made by a leading member of the Committee was that the salvation for the small proprietors was to amalgamate themselves into larger businesses so that they could be represented effectively in any co-ordinated structure. Was it then knowledge of this opinion or chance that led to the creation of a new company to do just that, or was there something more sinister afoot? However prompted, in the spring of 1927, A.T. Bennett sent letters to all the Independents announcing the formation of a new company which he said would amalgamate and combine small bus businesses, the proprietors of which were invited to sell them for cash or shares. They were assured that the company would remain completely independent and would be large enough to compete with the might of the Combine. He managed to remove one major obstacle by negotiating successfully with the Metropolitan Police and the Minister of Transport to have the regulations regarding transfer of licences relaxed, to allow the schedules of the selling companies to be transferred to the new concern.

George Pauncefoot and Violet McReadie's Legion Omnibus Company had started in March 1924 and ran on a number of west London-oriented routes from Goldhawk Garage, Brackenbury Road Shepherd's Bush. It was acquired by General on 4th October 1926 and the Thornycroft was sold to Thames Valley and replaced by K 903, operating from Hammersmith garage. (Alan Cross/J.B. Atkinson collection)

The man standing with a proprietorial hand on this Dodson-bodied Dennis is a former cinema projectionist John MacDonald Potter who started the Cardinal business in July 1924, first running between Archway and Victoria and later, under the London Traffic Act, on route 284A. The words 'North London Association', the short-lived operators' association on the route, appear above the route number. Potter would not sell to General or Dangerfield but sold his bus and schedule to Claremont in January 1927. (R.G. Westgate)

The London Public Omnibus Company was incorporated on 8th July 1927 with a share capital of £600,000 and some people immediately asked questions about the source of the company's funds. Suspicions were aroused also by the size of the sum being offered for the purchase of each bus, £3,000, which was twice what the LGOC would normally pay. Nevertheless Bennett's credentials as a successful Independent operator in his own right and friend of the Independent sector seemed to be unassailable and his name bought the trust of a large number of proprietors who needed to sell but would not do so to General. Bennett's partner in the enterprise was the Marquis of Winchester and there were some who thought that he was the architect of the idea. The suspicions were well founded. At its Board meeting on 29th July 1927 the LGOC approved the advance of £300,000 by M. Samuel and Company to the London Public Omnibus Company, and this was followed up with a further advance of £50,000, ratified on 6th October.

In blissful ignorance of these clandestine activities, the first seven companies sold out to Public, the pioneers being The Carlton Association, Crescent, Eclipse, GWL, Our Bus, Skylark and Universal. Bennett's own company, Admiral, which had by now grown into a business of substance owning 37 buses, sold its assets to the new company on 17th August 1927. By May 1928 the new company had absorbed 77 companies and 219 schedules on 41 routes operating from garages at Kilburn, Paddington, Waltham Cross and West Green. The LGOC's interest in LPOC was finally put on a formal footing at a special meeting of its Board on 6th February 1928, when it acquired enough shares to give it a controlling interest. This became public knowledge in March 1928. Public continued to work as a separate undertaking with little outward sign of its change of ownership and there was no apparent co-ordination of its activities until 6th February 1929 when the two companies entered into a new working agreement, resulting in an exchange of routes. The 20, 41B, 69 and 154 went from LGOC to Public and the Public operations on the 17, 217, 247, 263A, 263B, 297, 297A and 526D to General. This enabled Public to concentrate its work in its own West Green garage and the premises in Southbury Road, Ponders End, known as Enfield garage (E) which had been built by the LGOC for this purpose and to absorb the Redburn work from Enfield Highway. Staff passes were made available on both Public and General buses and, in the case of breakdown, passengers could use their tickets on either company's buses. The company was finally absorbed into the LGOC on 11th December 1929.

Representative of the large fleet built up very rapidly by the London Public Omnibus Company, this Strachan & Brown bodied Dennis 4-tonner was originally owned by James Hartley who named it Regina and ran it latterly on routes 21 and 36. First licensed on 8th October 1924, it was sold to Public on 27th July 1927. It was numbered D 16 by Public and is seen on route 299 at Edmonton. (W. Noel Jackson)

Havelock had been one of the earlier arrivals on the Independent scene, in December 1923, and had built up a fleet of seven Dennises, two double-deck and five single-deck by the summer of 1927, operating on the 6A, 42A. 263 and (Sundays only) the 551. The business was sold to Public on 4th August 1927 and this 1926 Dodson-bodied 2½-tonner became DS 8 in the LPOC fleet. It is at Stroud Green working a former Admiral schedule on route 201C to Edmonton. (W. Noel Jackson)

Another early starter, in September 1923 was Clarendon, whose base was in Rochester Mews Camden Town, near the British garage. Three double-deckers worked mainly on route 29 but two of these Dodson-bodied Dennis 2½-tonners pioneered route 297 (King's Cross–Tufnell Park) in 1925. Still at work on the route after the company's sale to Public, YL966 now bears the fleet number DS 15. It was to survive to join the LPTB fleet in 1933. (Alan Cross/W. Noel Jackson collection)

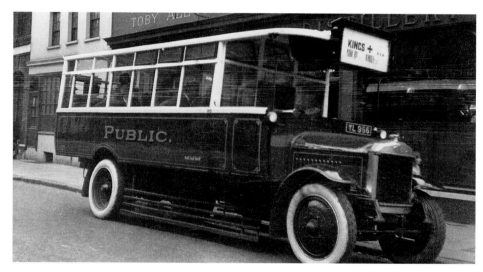

Another pillar of the Independent establishment, Walter Dangerfield, the early history of whose Carlton and Overground companies is described in chapter three, was also soon quietly plotting a sale to the LGOC. Before that happened two of the companies that closed down in 1926 sold to Dangerfield and as both worked on route 284A, his dominant position on that route was consolidated. Nulli Secundus, which had started in November 1923, was bought by Dangerfield on 2nd July 1926 and the Northern Omnibus Company, which started in September 1923, changed hands on 1st September 1926. Both continued to trade as separate companies. The buses were a Dodson-bodied Leyland LB4 and a Straker Squire respectively. Between these two events, on 23rd July 1926, Overground Ltd was incorporated. Dangerfield was appointed Managing Director on 26th November 1926 and he was authorised to hold the police licences on behalf of the company and the share issue on 30th December allotted 19,998 of the 19,999 to Dangerfield. It was not long before preparations were made for the sale of the business and the first step was to transfer 10,200 shares to Christopher Dodson on 20th May 1927, presumably in consideration of finance provided by Dodson for the purchase of the company's buses. The end of the company's independence came on 8th June 1927 when the Board appointed Frank Pick, Daniel Duff and Ernest Law of

*Top* Biss Brothers bought two maroon and cream Straker Squires in November 1923, mainly to run on route 69. At first they used a garage near Waltham Cross station but on 22nd January 1924 they bought Theobalds Garage in Waltham Cross High Street near what is now Theobalds Grove station. Subsequent purchases were exclusively Strachan & Brown-bodied Dennises, seven double-deck 4-tonners, two 2½-ton and two E-type single-deckers. With the two Strakers this was the fleet sold to Public on 3rd August 1927. RO1596 (BB No 11) is in Bowes Road, Palmers Green, on route 551 in which BB took a share from August 1925. (Norman Anscombe collection)

*Centre* Overington contributed three of these Strachan & Brown-bodied Dennis 4-tonners and one with Dodson body to the LPOC fleet when the business was sold on 29th September 1927. XU3752 (Public D 98) had been the first Overington bus to be registered, on 25th July 1924. Judging by the presence of the Morris 30cwt van, formerly owned by Admiral, advertising a service of solid tyre fitting, the bus is presumably in some trouble here. (The Omnibus Society)

*Left* One of the last companies to submit to the siren voice of A.T. Bennett before the real nature of London Public's activities became public knowledge, was Red Rose Motor Services Ltd, which was taken over on 3rd March 1928. Red Rose started on 4th January 1924 and built up a fleet of nine Dennis 4-tonners, to which they added four more by acquiring the Allber Omnibus Company and JH (The Trinity), which continued to trade separately but carried the full Red Rose livery. Allber ran mainly on route 49 and this is one of its pair of Dennis 4-tonners at Streatham Common. (Norman Anscombe collection)

the LGOC as directors and John Christopher Mitchell as Secretary in place of R.W. Smith who resigned. The Board of Dangerfield Ltd made similar appointments on the same day. Dangerfield resigned from his two Managing Director posts and as director of Dangerfield Ltd. A condition of the sale was that Walter Dangerfield should remain as manager of his former companies and he was duly appointed on 21st June. It is possible that this appointment was for life, in continuance of the terms on which he had been appointed to as the manager of Dangerfield Ltd but no evidence of this has yet been found. This condition created a unique subsidiary for the LGOC, which remained under Dangerfield's separate control until finally taken over by the LPTB in 1933 – significantly a week later than the other subsidiaries. Pick became Chairman of both companies on 12th December 1927 when an Emergency General Meeting of Dangerfield Ltd resolved to wind up the company, which was duly completed on 27th August 1928. The Overground meeting on the same day recorded arrangements for purchasing Nulli Secundus and the Northern Omnibus Company by agreements made on 1st December 1927. General used Overground as a tool for expansion in the north and its fleet was strengthened in 1928 by the allocation of Leyland LBs which had been acquired from Atlas and Horseshoe (6) and the LPOC (4). These were followed by another nine in 1930.

*Top* Overground 35, a Dodson-bodied Leyland LB5 first registered on 17th December 1925, is on route 284 at Potters Bar on 15th July 1927, just over five weeks after the LGOC had taken control. (W. Noel Jackson)

*Centre* One of Overground's competitors on the 284A was Drake, which had started as Drake & McCowen in August 1923 but adopted the simpler title when Robert McCowen left in 1926. The two primrose and black Leylands were housed at Dangerfield's Harmood Street garage until it was acquired by the LGOC, after which they were kept in Bridge Wharf Garage, next to the Regents Canal in Camden Town. Having escaped the clutches of General, Drake sold to Birch on 26th October 1928. On the stand at Hadley Highstone is XT4608 which achieved fame during the General Strike when it was overturned by rioters, only to be back in service the following day. (Alan Cross/W. Noel Jackson collection)

*Right* Nulli Secundus was acquired by Dangerfield in July 1926, bringing this Dodson-bodied Leyland LB4 under his control. This photograph was taken in the early days of its operation when it normally ran on route 29. (Ken Glazier collection)

General dealt with its other subsidiaries differently. All businesses acquired before 31st December 1927 were incorporated as limited companies so that the sales could be completed by transfer of shares, enabling them to retain their separate legal existence and continue to trade as apparently independent operators. This was necessary to overcome the refusal of the Police to allow schedules to be transferred between companies. The disguise was so effective in some cases that the staff of the acquired companies often were not aware that anything was happening until suddenly confronted by evidence of LGOC control. Most of the buses which came with the companies were gradually replaced by LGOC K-type vehicles, the first being Central in February 1926 and by December 1927 150 of the type were in use. All but two were double-deckers, the exceptions being those used by Uneedus on single-deck route 551.

Twenty of the acquired Dennises were allotted to Redburns, who already had eleven of their own, other Dennis operators being Cambrian, whose Thornycrofts and Strakers were gradually replaced by Ks, Alberta, Lea Valley and W & P. At first they were painted in the acquired company's colours but after November 1926 standard General red and white was used, evidence of different ownership being conveyed by the fleet name and legal lettering on the sides. The other exceptions were the companies in the 'Batten Group', already described. The final phase of this revolution was heralded at General's Board meeting on 3rd November 1927, when it was resolved to absorb the acquired companies into the LGOC (92 per cent) and

*Above* Bertram and Frederick Mason started Uneedus in June 1924 with a double-deck Dennis which, with another bought in October, ran on route 29. Later, three single-deckers, all like the double-deckers with Strachan & Brown bodies, were bought for operation on route 551 (Whetstone–Edmonton), two Guy BBs and this Dennis E (ML1169) seen at Edmonton, which became D 64 in the LGOC fleet. The Guy BBs were transferred by General to the National Omnibus and Transport Company once Uneedus was absorbed fully on 1st January 1928. (W. Noel Jackson)

*Centre* Redburn's Motor Services was the fifth largest Independent when the company and its 33 buses were sold to the LGOC on 18th October 1926. General leased part of the Redburn site in Green Street, Enfield Highway and erected a temporary building for the buses, giving the 'garage' the code RS. This can be seen on the side of Straker Squire 7 which, along with the other 21, was soon withdrawn and replaced by Dennises transferred from other acquired fleets. Green Street closed on 23rd May 1928, when the new garage at Enfield opened, and the LGOC operations were transferred to Tottenham. (Ken Glazier collection)

*Right* The Fairlop Dennis which had worked on route 511 since January 1925 was acquired by City on 30th January 1929 and immediately replaced by one of City's own vehicles. City's C 1 was a vehicle of unusual interest as it was the company's first foray into the extensive rebuilding of a vehicle. This had been A 18, an LB new in March 1925, and was rebuilt as a forward-control chassis, with a new, but surprisingly still open-top, 55-seat Dodson body in October 1928.

A.G. Summerskill started operating on 7th August 1924 and remained in business until being acquired by the LPTB in November 1933. Dennis YE6281 was the third bus and is on route 58E, which with 173E was the main weekday operation. (Ken Glazier collection)

Tramways (MET) Omnibus Company (8 per cent). These proportions were those laid down in the operational agreement between the two companies. This followed agreement by the Ministry of Transport to the amendment of the regulations to allow the operating licences to be transferred. The designated date was 1st January 1928, when all but one of the undertakings was absorbed. Those taken over by Metropolitan were Cosgrove, Direct, Primrose, Tottenham Hotspur, W & P, Grafton, Jockey, Lea Valley,

PC, Wellington and RA Motor Services. The South Metropolitan Electric Lighting & Tramways Company's buses were also absorbed by MET, whose fleet increased from 194 to 241. The odd-man-out was Cambrian, which was still in the hands of the receivers, but the stay of execution lasted only until 30th April, after which the name Cambrian also disappeared from London's streets.

At the beginning of 1928 the number of Independent companies operating in the Metropolitan Police District had fallen to 69

and one of those was Public. During 1928 another eight names disappeared from the scene, including one (Empires Best) which sold out to City and one (Victor) that was bought by Premier. Seven more went in 1929, three going to Birch (Tally Ho!, Brown and Drake), one (Fairlop) to City, one (Albert Ewer) to the LGOC and two just went out of business (Pickwick and Newlands District). Of the 54 left at the end of 1929, 51 were to survive until being compulsorily acquired by the LPTB.

Holliday & Bangs (H&B) started in August 1924 and applied for licences on routes 11, 27 and 37 but their main field of operation was the 59 group. Birch-bodied Dennis YU4689, new in November 1927, is at Thornton Heath Pond having completed a journey on the 59F from Camden Town, despite the number displayed. H&B remained in business until taken over by the LPTB on 5th December 1933, but continued to operate coach services to Kings Lynn and Fakenham until selling to Eastern Counties in 1934. (J.F. Higham)

## CHAPTER NINE

# Serving the Suburban Sprawl

Between the censuses of 1921 and 1931 the population of Greater London, broadly the area served by the LGOC, rose from 7,480,000 to 8,204,000 (9.7 per cent) but the whole of this increase was concentrated on the area outside the London County Council boundary. The number of people living inside the county of London went down slightly over the same period as the LCC's policy of building 'out-county' cottage estates took hold and the so-called 'slums' were cleared. This brought the increase in the 'outer ring' to 812,000, a remarkable inflation of 27 per cent. At the beginning of the decade a journey eastward would bring the traveller into open country or marshland once clear of Barking or Ilford, while to the west the countryside would start to appear beyond Ealing and Hounslow. There was very little in the way of settlement in the north-western quarter, where the main built-up area ended at White City, Willesden and Golders Green. In the south the outposts were Woolwich, Lee, Sydenham, Croydon and Mitcham, although not all the area immediately to the north was built. There were still green fields between Streatham and Croydon, for example.

Almost the entire population was dependent on public transport for all their travel needs and, until these areas were covered with houses, shops and factories, they were fruitful territory for the operation of leisure services. In the summer of 1922 apart from such obvious destinations as Hampton Court, Epping Forest and Dorking, the programme of special Sunday routes included services to Wanstead, Rippleside, Chadwell Heath, Bexley, West Wickham and Caterham. The Traffic Circular gave a list of country towns, villages and resorts served which included such places as Ashford (Middx), Barkingside, Cheam, Edgware and Shirley. The desire of the LGOC to develop these services led to a charming episode which showed Frank Pick's close interest in art and design and its application to everyday activities, like transport. In January 1922 Pick was approached by Harold Stabler, who had already done some work for the company, with an idea for a rabbit design which could be adapted as a radiator cap for display on buses operating into the countryside. Various designs were examined, including one with bent ears which Pick described as a 'very seedy affair' and 'looking

scared'. Pick wanted it to 'look intelligent and as though seeking the good things in life' but also made the practical point that it should not lean forward or it would get snapped off in traffic. There was a constant exchange of correspondence and a series of meetings which culminated in an upright design being chosen. It was announced in the *Daily Mirror* in April as 'Wilfred the Rabbit' who would appear on country buses the following month. The company's Easter poster added, teasingly, 'who knows perhaps Pip and Squeak will appear at Whitsun', a reference to a popular cartoon of the period.

The LGOC had run buses beyond Southgate to Hadley Woods for many years to serve leisure traffic but did not consider a daily service necessary until Admiral started one, the competition provoking General into putting its own daily service on from September 1923. This picture of S 172 was taken in Chase Side Southgate during 1928 when the road was being resurfaced, the tar boiler smoking away on the other side of the road, a steam roller faintly visible behind the bus and what looks like a railway-influenced traffic signal in the foreground. (Enfield Libraries)

There were production problems with the casts, the first examples of which would not fit onto the radiators and there was a dispute with Stabler about responsibility but the problem was solved early in May and 'Wilfred' began to appear on the radiators of buses on thirty routes almost immediately. The mascot so caught the public's imagination that Pick had proposed a pottery version for sale through W.H. Smith but was advised against it as Wilfred had become a drug on the market, having been represented in sorbo sponge, chocolate, china and in Easter eggs. Pottery versions were made for presentation to the members of the Board as souvenirs, however. Pick floated the idea of having a turtle mascot for city buses and asked Stabler to consider it but nothing came of this idea which seems more tongue-in-cheek than sound proposition, and the rabbit itself did not last for long.

On 4th January 1922 the LGOC opened a new garage at Kingston (K) and took the opportunity to spread its tentacles further into Surrey. New route 61 followed the existing 112 from Kingston as far as Weybridge and then continued through Addlestone to Chertsey. The 112 itself was renumbered 79

in General's usual cavalier manner, and extended from Weybridge to Woking via Byfleet and Old Woking. The former 79 was withdrawn, leaving the road from Church Cobham to Byfleet unserved until it was covered by the 162 in 1926. The other new route was the 62, which completed the trio operating between Kingston and Walton-on-Thames and then branching off over Walton Bridge to reach Shepperton. All three used single-deckers, initially the 26-seat B-type but later in the year these were replaced by the new S-type 30-seaters. The availability of the new vehicles may have been what made it possible to extend the 61 only three months later from Chertsey to Windsor via Egham, Englefield Green and Old Windsor, not serving Staines.

A lot of suburban expansion took place on 12th April 1922. The gaps between the existing developed areas of Finchley and Hendon had been filling in gradually and this brought buses to East End Road and Hendon Lane on route 43A which started running through from London Bridge via East Finchley and Finchley, at first to The Welsh Harp but later only as far as Church End (Hendon Garage). In the south-west, Roehampton Lane was served for the first time by route 74 which was introduced between Highgate Station (Archway) and Kingston Vale, following a route more akin to the 27 of later years, via Camden Town, Paddington, Kensington, Hammersmith and Barnes. Across the river in the sleepy glades of Chiswick, tucked out of sight of the world at large and protected by the sweeping U-bend of the Thames, secluded housing had been encroaching onto the riverside meadows.

Buses first penetrated the area on 12th April 1922 when new single-deck route 55 began running three times an hour from Acton to the Grove Park Hotel, via Sutton Court Road, at the same time putting buses into Southfield Road and The Avenue at Bedford Park. The development of the 55 beyond this, to serve Burlington Lane and Edensor Road was a complicated story. In essence, in the early years it operated to the riverside meadows on boat race days and to the Metropolitan Police Sports Ground for their sports days and then became a summer daily service to Edensor Road between 1926 and 1928. A full all-year-round daily service started on 18th July 1928, co-inciding with the route's being turned into a circular service serving Mawson Lane and Chiswick Lane.

Further upstream on 12th April 1922, the area west of Twickenham found itself host to route 27C, which introduced buses to Staines Road, Hanworth, Sunbury and to the section from Shepperton to Chertsey. It ran all the way from Highgate Station (Archway). The western end of the route was littered with hazards, four blind corners in Sunbury and Halliford, a weight restriction on Sunbury railway bridge and narrow sections of road in Staines Road (Longford River bridge), Green Street and Green Lane. The through operation lasted only until 23rd January 1923, after which it ran only from Richmond and was operated by single-deck buses.

Golders Green and Mill Hill, two areas which saw significant house building in 1922, were linked from 12th April by new single-deck route 104. Within a few months, on 12th July, it was extended along the edge of the extensive new LCC Watling Estate, via Deans Lane and Deansbrook Road to Edgware then on through Canons Park, Stanmore and Harrow to South Harrow serving Whitchurch Lane and Marsh Lane for the first time. Golders Green was reached from the other direction on 12th April by the new 110 from Finsbury Park which opened up long stretches of road to buses between Stroud Green and Hornsey Rise and along Hampstead Lane and North End Road.

A single-deck B on new route 110 negotiates the tricky narrow curve through Spaniards Gate at the Spaniards Inn, Hampstead Heath, a hostelry associated, among others, with Dick Turpin and the Gordon Rioters. (Ken Glazier collection)

LGOC buses reached Rainham for the first time on 7th September 1921, extended from Barking (Rippleside on Sundays) but only on Saturdays and Sundays until a full daily service started on 10th May 1922. Some time later, NS 1189 stands at the Clock Tower and War Memorial, with the Norman Church of St Helens and St Giles hidden by the trees. (David Brewster Collection)

The biggest single post-war development was the London County Council's Becontree estate which by 1930 had a population of 116,000 and covered an area of four square miles bounded by Barking, Goodmayes, the Great Eastern Railway line, and the Metropolitan Police boundary at Dagenham. Routes 23 and 23A had served the extreme southern boundary daily from September 1921 but the first route to penetrate the areas of new housing was the 25A. This was withdrawn from Seven Kings on 13th December 1922 and diverted through Green Lane to Becontree (Heavy Waters – near Mayfield Road) a point named after a farm that had been there. From 14th March 1923 it was extended another five minutes down the road to Becontree Heath (Three Travellers) but was cut back to Chittys Lane on 7th November. Another part of the estate was to have been served from the Barking direction from 9th January 1924 when new route 23B was to have run from Marylebone Station to Becontree (Bennetts Castle Lane) but the roads were not ready. Instead it terminated at Barking garage, which had just been built and had opened for business on 9th January. It got through to its intended terminus at the Longbridge Road and Bennetts Castle Lane junction on 18th June, although two Monday–Saturday morning journeys were extended there from 9th April 1924.

Other areas newly served during 1922 were Elder Road and Central Hill, Norwood (route 2 extended from West Norwood to Catford as 2A), Royal Hospital Road and Cheyne Walk (route 39 re-routed) and Crayford to Dartford (route 99 extended to Dartford).

The ancient farming village of Cheam quietly awaits the onslaught of suburban development, with only a few discreet bits of modern architecture to break the rural spell. S 439 is working the extension to Banstead of route 113 which started on 17th January 1923, having reached Cheam on its original route from Kingston through Coombe and Malden to Sutton, on 7th September 1921. (Ken Glazier collection)

From 17th January 1923 route 113 was extended from Sutton to take the hazardous journey through Sutton Lane and Banstead Road between Belmont and Banstead. There were so many overhead obstructions, trees on the downs, shop and inn signs in Banstead village, and the road so narrow, that only one bus was allowed in the section at a time. In the same part of Surrey, after a few false starts in earlier years, Lower Kingswood finally got a settled daily service on route 80 from 13th June 1923. A month earlier, it had been the turn of pastoral Middlesex to benefit from General's favours when route 62 was extended from Shepperton through Laleham to Staines. Drivers were cautioned to take special care through Laleham village with its narrow winding roads and the hazardous crossroads at the Bull Inn. A less trying extension for drivers was implemented from 13th June taking the 97 southward from Northfields to Brentford through virgin territory in Windmill Road, only a short section of which was too narrow for buses to pass.

Another of the LCC's cottage estates was being built at this time in the area west of White City and north of Uxbridge Road and there was also a council estate newly built on the old golf links at East Acton, in the wedge north-west of what later became known as Savoy Circus. The road layouts of the estates made them largely impassable for buses and the first services put on to serve them had to skirt around the edges, an arrangement that has changed only little in the intervening eighty years. The first was route 7 (with a Sunday service on route 15) which was extended from *The Pavilion Hotel* Wormwood Scrubs to East Acton (Goldsmiths Arms) via Ducane Road and East Acton Lane on 21st February 1923. The other side was served from Uxbridge Road and Old Oak Lane by route 12B (Lower Sydenham to Shepherd's Bush with journeys to Acton Vale), extended to East Acton Post Office on 24th October.

The first known example of an Independent opening up new territory occurred in August 1923 by an accident of history. Redburn had planned to start a new route entirely alongside Combine trams from (Enfield to Finsbury Park via Ponders End, Edmonton) but when they got wind of General's intention to put on competing buses, they invented route 69. This ran from London Bridge to Edmonton, again alongside trams for most of the way, both LCC and MET. They started running it on 2nd May 1923 and six weeks later the LGOC started an identical service. Redburn stayed the course, extended the route northward to Wormley and as an adjunct introduced two new routes in August 1923, the 515 from Enfield Highway to Brimsdown via Green Street and 516 Ponders End High Street to The Alma, both on hitherto unserved roads.

Route 62 was extended from Shepperton to Staines in May 1923, increasing the risk of drivers encountering flooding of this kind, a perennial feature of the Thames Valley. S 433 was one of the thirty-four 30-seaters built in September and October 1922. (Ken Glazier collection)

The first FA Cup Final at Wembley was staged on 28th April 1923 and six bus routes were extended there for the day, using newly-built roads through open country. The notice on the right reads 'Steam Roller at work' and this is believed to be the North Circular Road under construction. K 809 on the 53 has not attracted much custom, perhaps because it is advertising a rival establishment at Charlton, but neither has the other K on route 16. The two Private buses are B 1233 and 1816 and other traffic includes a taxi, a pony and trap and a char-a-banc. (Ken Glazier collection)

*Below* Clear publicity for the bus services is carried on totem poles, capped by illuminated 'GENERAL' signs and with platform numbers on similar fittings at a lower level. The design of the purpose-built shelters enters into the spirit of the occasion, with exotic decoration and roundels coloured green. The workaday paraphernalia of bus operation, the water point and cans on platform 6 and the wheel scotches on platform 5 somewhat spoil the effect. Platforms 1 to 4 face in the other direction on the right. (London's Transport Museum)

Old Kent Road's NS 642 has already attracted a good load in readiness for its two-hour trek across London to Grove Park but perhaps this was untypical because the route did not run again in 1925. Behind it K 270 can be glimpsed, working on route 6A to Hackney Wick. (London's Transport Museum)

The great national event of 1924 was the British Empire Exhibition at Wembley, which was staged in the grounds of Wembley Park, owned at that time by the Metropolitan Railway who operated it as a leisure park. To meet the road transport needs of the event the local network of country lanes was improved to the prevailing standard of new roads and these provided the wherewithal not only for the special services to the Exhibition but also for the development of new services afterwards. This enormous venture included Wembley Stadium which was ready in time for the FA Cup Final in 1923 and routes 11, 15, 16, 53, 68 and 68A were extended there for one day only on 28th April. The 11 and 15 approached Wembley from Harrow Road but the others all did so from the Cricklewood direction via the newly built North Circular Road and Forty Lane. This is the first recorded instance of service buses using the last two roads.

For the event itself General built a special bus station at the south-west entrance to the exhibition, generously laid out and provided with shelters for waiting passengers. The special arrangements for the Cup Final in 1924 were this time a prelude to the main event and were supplied by routes 6A, 18A, 49 and 93. When the Exhibition opened to the public on 23rd April the range of destinations offered was much wider and covered much of London with through services coming from as far afield as Walthamstow, Hackney Wick, Old Ford, Grove Park, Norwood Junction (West Wickham on Bank Holidays!) and Wimbledon. Buses ran

frequently, most routes having headways of between six and nine minutes. The routes were 6A, 8B, 18A, 36A, 43A, 49 (which started earlier than the others on 9th April), 58, 68A, 83, 92 and 93 and all ran only on Mondays to Saturdays and Bank Holiday Sundays at first. The 92 was a special local service from Sudbury Town station with through tickets to and from the District Railway. From mid-June onwards Sunday services were provided on routes 8B, 43D, 49A and 93 and six new routes added, the 1, 15A, 16A, 43D, 49A and 68. The exhibition was a resounding success and was repeated for a second season in 1925, the total attendance over the two years being 27 million. The bus services were much the same as in 1924, except that the 36A did not run and the 11 was added. As it was now the Bassom era, most routes carried the plain number but the 43A and 43D had become 143F and the 15A, 68 and 92 were now known as 151, 169C and 192 respectively.

At the end of the 1924 season routes 83 and 93 were not withdrawn from Wembley but were extended to Sudbury Town and became daily services. This ensured that Forty Lane, Kingsbury Lane and the section of North Circular Road between Hendon and Neasden, retained the service which had not existed before April 1924. The section of route 6 between Kensal Rise and Willesden was not so lucky. It enjoyed a frequent service while the exhibition was open but lost it again at the end of each season and had to wait until 19th May 1926 for the 6 to be extended daily to Blackbird Hill Farm.

The first daily bus service to approach West Wickham from the direction of Shirley arrived on 25th June 1924, when new route 34A started running between Liverpool Street and West Wickham. Such was the rural nature of the route that drivers were cautioned about the presence of a water pool just beyond Spring Park Road and another adjoining the White Hart P.H., as there was no street lighting. Not much more encroachment onto new ground took place during 1924 but new route 95 was introduced on 16th July from Hounslow to Hayes, the new section being from Harlington Corner northwards. The new Hampstead Railway station at Colindale which opened on 18th August was scheduled to have a connecting bus service from 3rd November but this had to be delayed until 7th January 1925 when route 60 was extended the short distance along Colindale Avenue from Edgware Road. The only other bus service improvements made in connection with the new Underground service were new routes 104A (Edgware to Pinner) and 142A (Edgware to Watford), neither of which reached any areas not already served.

Becontree estate continued to grow year by year and on 14th January 1925, Bennetts Castle Lane had been improved from its country lane status, edged by farms and cottages, to that of a modern estate road ready to receive an extension of route 123 (the Bassom manifestation of the 23B) as far as Chittys Lane. At the other end of the year, on 2nd December it was extended further through Becontree Heath and Rush Green to

Romford, the first Monday–Saturday service beyond Becontree. In Metroland, meanwhile, the small local company A & W had brought buses to Paines Lane and Uxbridge Road from 23rd January, on route 351 which ran from Harrow (Met Station) to Hatch End. The area was still quite rural and the little 14-seater brown and cream Crossleys were more than adequate to carry the meagre traffic offering. Yet more rural was Thames-side Buckinghamshire which was blessed with a new service from Slough to Staines via Datchet from 12th August 1925, numbered 162A as it entered the Metropolitan Police District at Staines and was caught by the Bassom rules. Two single-deck Ks were needed for its 50-minute service. For that summer only, until November, the service continued beyond Slough to Burnham Beeches on Wednesdays, Saturdays and Sundays, numbered 162. In March 1926 the 162A was extended from Staines right through to Leatherhead via Chertsey, Addlestone, Weybridge and Cobham on a route first offered to East Surrey, as mentioned in chapter four.

Two enterprising Independents, Admiral and Redburn joined forces on a new route in northern Middlesex during the summer of 1925. It started as the 280 running from Finsbury Park to Enfield (Chase Side), competing with the Metropolitan Electric trams, but a month later it struck out into new pastures through Lancaster Road to Forty Hill. The buses used were 26-seat 2½-ton Dennises and those fielded by Admiral were significant in having pneumatic tyres. In September the route was extended to Stroud

Green and renumbered 538, in which form it survived via LGOC ownership to be taken over by the LPTB. Another Independent enterprise in the same sector of Middlesex was started by Redburn's Motor Services in July 1925. Taking advantage of the newly opened North Circular Road, it ran from Whetstone to Edmonton (Aerator Works – later renamed Sparklet's) and was numbered 551. This proved to be a magnet to other operators and during the next couple of years became populated by buses from Astoria, BB, HHC, H.M. Merry, Prince, SB, Silver Star and Uneedus. All were single-deck because of the low bridge at Silver Street, Edmonton and were mainly 2½-ton Dennises but in later years there were also Dennis E, Leyland Lion and Guy BB. The year 1925 also saw the initiation of a daily service to Lonesome for the first time (route 50). There had been various weekend and afternoon operations for the cemetery in earlier years but it was now becoming a suburb for the living as well as the dead.

In Essex work on the building of the Southend Arterial Road (Eastern Avenue) had progressed to the point where it was possible to start running buses, although the traffic potential was still thin until the surrounding fields had been smothered in housing and industry. A small start was made on 14th October 1925 with route 66 running from Leytonstone to Romford Station. A solitary S-type double-decker ran every 105 minutes until the route was extended to Gidea Park on 10th February 1926, when it blossomed into a 30-minute service needing four buses. Two weeks later,

Route 263 was an example of the ingenuity inspired by the strict limitations of the London Traffic Act. By avoiding Restricted Streets it brought buses to areas of hinterland in Canonbury, Dalston, Hackney, Leyton and Leytonstone which otherwise may well have remained without until the midibus revolution of the 1980s and 1990s. It was started by Charles Batten's new ARO company and became home to buses of six Independents in total over the years. ARO's Dodson-bodied Dennis 2½-tonner HM7040 was photographed after being acquired by the LPOC but still in the former owner's colours. (W. Noel Jackson)

*Above right* Holloway's B 665 in the special livery of blue and cream, at work on the City & South London Railway 'Auxiliary Omnibus Service' when it ran between Moorgate and Euston. (Ken Glazier collection)

the Leytonstone to Gants Hill section was rewarded with an additional 30-minute peak service in the form of route 148 which also added to the weight of service down Bennetts Castle Lane, Becontree, on its journey from Leytonstone to Longbridge Road. Another Bennetts Castle Lane service that started on the same day was the 145B. This started from Woodford Wells and used the new Woodford Avenue from Gates Corner to Gants Hill. The 145 had run from there to Chittys Lane but it (renumbered 145C) and the new route, were extended along Bennetts Castle Lane to Longbridge Road. The intrusion of the suffix letters foreshadowed a summer Sunday operation to Epping Forest as 145. Two variants of the 66 were later developed by Independents. The 266 ran from Leytonstone to Billet Road, north of Little Heath and was started by Miller in May 1928, while the 366 ran the full length of Eastern Avenue and on to Brentwood and was started by Reliance in December 1928.

In west London there were two arterial roads, Western Avenue and Great West Road. The latter was completed in 1925 and there was an immediate rash of ribbon development in the area, which stretched north into Heston and Norwood Green. To serve this, route 120A was introduced on 27th January 1926, running between Hounslow Heath (The Hussar) and Southall and using three of the new single-deck Ks. The Southall terminus was 'The Victory' at the

green, by the junction of Western Road and King Street. The 120 was a Saturday afternoon and Sunday extension to Feltham. There were a number of infillings closer to town in the first half of 1926. From 3rd February Route 74 was rerouted to serve the LCC estate in Doverhouse Road, Roehampton instead of using Roehampton Lane, the rest of the route having by this time become the more familiar one from Camden Town via Baker Street, South Kensington and Fulham. The LCC estate at Roehampton was probably the most extreme example of Herbert Morrison's policy of putting working class housing into middle class areas, as there could hardly be a greater contrast between the living and working conditions of those who came to live in the Doverhouse Road estate and those occupying the plush detached villas further to the west and south.

A famous Independent initiative provided the most spectacular example of filling the gaps in inner London. Route 263, which started out running from London Fields to Leyton (Essex County Cricket Ground), weaved about on a course which kept it to unrestricted streets, through Victoria Park Road, Eastway, Ruckholt Road, Grove Green Road, Fairlop Road and Hainault Road. First on the scene, on 1st June 1926, was none other than Charles W Batten with his new ARO company, who bought seven new 2½-ton Dennises for the operation. Over the next two years he was to be joined by F&K, Havelock, HHC, Pro Bono Publico and Public, before the route was itself declared restricted. Some time after December 1926 it was extended to Finsbury Park, opening up more sections of road through Dalston, Kingsland, Canonbury and Highbury, most of which are still served at the time of writing by its successor, the 236. In 1928 the Approved Route allowed an extension to Chingford and by the summer of 1928 it was running between Finsbury Park and Chingford Mount.

Serious house building had begun to encroach on the countryside east of Eltham during the second half of the 1920s and the first recognition of its transport needs came on 16th June 1926 when new routes 132 and

132A started running from Eltham to Bexley Village via Blackfen (132A) with a Sunday extension to Dartford (132).

The big event for the Combine in 1926 was the extension of the City & South London Railway from Clapham Common to Morden, which opened to passengers on 13th September 1926. There had been a long prelude to this event because the project included the enlargement of the running tunnels on the original sections of the railway to enable standard tube stock to be used. The line was closed between Euston and Moorgate on 8th August 1922 and the LGOC provided a replacement service of B-type buses in a special blue and cream livery with City & South London Railway fleet names and labelled 'Auxiliary Omnibus Service'. Sunday buses were withdrawn on 1st January 1923 and the weekday service was extended to Clapham Common. A daytime service was kept going on the railway south of Moorgate until a catastrophic incident on 27th November 1923 closed the line completely and the bus service was then increased to every minute in peak hours. The garage in Milman's Street, Chelsea, was brought back from the dead to house some of the extra buses The section north of Moorgate re-opened on 20th April 1924, from which date the special service was curtailed to operate only from Moorgate to Clapham Common. Perhaps with the impending London Traffic Act in mind, the route was registered as a normal service, numbered 5B from 10th June 1924. The southern end of the railway resumed on 1st December 1924 and the bus service was not withdrawn but reduced substantially. Bassom decreed that it be renumbered 155 but it did not survive Bassom's cull and ran for the last time on 6th January 1925.

The number 155 was one of the three used for the first services put on as feeders to the new Underground line at Morden. The effects of the General Strike had delayed work on the line and it did not open for passengers until 13th September 1926 but the 155 (Wimbledon – South Wimbledon – Morden – North Cheam – Worcester Park), 156 (Wimbledon – Morden – North Cheam – Cheam) and the 164 (Wimbledon – Morden –

Silver-painted K 533 on route 156, one of the new feeder services for the City & South London Railway's newly extended tube at Morden. (Alan Cross/W. Noel Jackson collection)

St Helier – Sutton – Burgh Heath) nevertheless all started on 21st July. On the opening of the railway service, they were withdrawn between Wimbledon and Morden and joined by the 157 (Morden – Sutton – Wallington) and 165 (Morden to Walton on the Hill). The 157 and 165 ran at first via Wandle Road and London Road until the new 'bye-pass road' (St Helier Avenue) was ready on 25th September, after which they took the direct route. The 155 and 156 were

extended from Morden to Raynes Park via South Wimbledon on 19th January 1927. The LGOC made a big splash with these services, allocating a batch of the new K single-deckers decked out in a special livery of mainly silver, because the success of the Morden extension relied crucially on the growth of new housing in an area which was mainly still green fields. The routes were expanded and consolidated two years later (1st August 1928) when the 155 was

extended from Worcester Park along the new Kingston By-Pass to Raynes Park, South Wimbledon and Morden, becoming a circular route, the 156 through Sutton back to Morden also as a circular, the 164 from Banstead through Banstead village and Sutton to Morden as another circular and the 165B from Morden to Raynes Park via South Wimbledon, becoming 165D Raynes Park to Burgh Heath with a summer Sunday extension to Walton-on-the-Hill (165).

The through service on route 99 was split from 31st March 1926 to enable double-deckers to operate on the increasingly busy Woolwich–Erith section. This was numbered 99A and the single-deck Erith–Dartford service, 99C. NS 1298, at the Erith (Prince of Wales) terminus, was operating from Crayford garage, who shared the operation with Plumstead. (Ken Glazier collection)

*Above right* Bush House was still being built when this photograph was taken in Aldwych on Sunday 28th July 1929. Summer Sunday route 102 had started running to Hampton Court on 20th June 1926 and became the first bus route to use the new Great West Road, a Monday–Saturday service being added by route 32 as far as Lampton from 25th August. The three buses here are NS 2327, one of the ADC422s, on route 33B to Richmond, NS 721 on 33D to Hampton Court and NS 203 on the 102. (W. Noel Jackson)

*Right* Route 292 was the Poplar–Becontree Heath route via the East Ham and Barking By-Pass pioneered by Martin in March 1927 and also operated by Miller, Peraeque and Renown. Peraeque had started bus operation in May 1924 with two Daimlers and, like the other three, survived to have its seven buses taken over by London Transport. YT8381 was new in September 1927 and appears to be working a short which should be carrying the number 292A. (W. Noel Jackson)

*Right* S 268 at Chittys Lane, Becontree, reached by route 106B on an extension from Poplar on 19th September 1928, the number 106 applying to the full route through to Upminster which ran only on summer Sundays. The main allocation on the route was covered top NS but a minority of the Athol Street allocation, varying between six and nine buses, was S-type. (W. Noel Jackson)

Improved road conditions south of Alperton provided the opportunity for route 83 to be extended from Wembley to Kew Gardens on 7th July 1926, providing Alperton itself and Hanger Lane with their first regular daily service. On its southward journey it crossed the the stark new concrete of the Great West Road, which netted its own regular Monday–Saturday service on 25th August 1926 when part of route 32D was extended, as 32, from Turnham Green to Lampton (Black Horse) on a meagre 18-minute headway. It was not the first bus route to use the new road, however as the summer Sunday 102 (Aldwych to Windsor) had started on 20th June.

While hatching his plot to establish the London Public Omnibus Company, Alfred Bennett started another new Admiral service, the 201, in January 1927. It ran from Finsbury Park through Harringay and Westbury Avenue to another of the new arterial roads, the somewhat grandiosely titled Great Cambridge Road, to reach the London County Council's 'out-county' cottage estate at White Hart Lane. The route was extended on via *The Cambridge* to Edmonton (Sparklet's Works) the following month.

The East Ham and Barking By-Pass also opened at this time. It formed a branch off the older established Beckton Road and cut through between the housing areas of West and East Ham to the north and the East Ham and Eastbury levels to the south, to connect with New Road, Dagenham, on the southern boundary of the Becontree Estate. This unrestricted road was ignored or overlooked by the LGOC, who perhaps saw little potential in such a barren landscape but Martin thought differently and obtained two schedules on the 292, for which he bought two new Dennises which went onto the road in March 1927. Martin (Paterson Omnibus Company) was in fact the pioneer of the route, which ran from Poplar via the by-pass and Barking to Becontree Heath. Three other Independents joined him in the next three months, Miller, Peraeque and Renown and all four survived to be compulsorily acquired by the LPTB. The LGOC did not establish a presence on the road until the autumn of 1928 when route 106 was extended from Poplar to Becontree. Two other areas of Essex covered in 1927 were Collier Row and Cranham, both by General's G1 which linked them via Romford, Hornchurch and Upminster from 13th April.

Kingsbury and Kenton experienced spectacular growth in the 1920s, the village of Kenton alone increasing its population from 628 in 1921 to over 6,000 in 1931. By early 1927, road improvements to support the growing population provided the means for a major infusion of buses to add their touch of modernity to the scene. New route 183 started operating between Golders Green and Pinner on 9th February 1927 and route 83 was diverted away from North Circular Road and Neasden Lane to run via Kingsbury Green on 15th June. Both routes served Kingsbury Road, the 183 being a pioneer in Kenton Road and the 83 bringing the joys of the open-top NS to Church Lane. Both

routes were altered in July (20th) to run in Hendon via Vivian Avenue and Queens Road, formerly busless, instead of Church Road and The Burroughs, which were then served by extensions of routes 13 and 28.

Since the arrival of the Hampstead Railway in 1924, the area surrounding Edgware station had been built over gradually and the roads improved, making it possible for Hale Lane to be served by an extension of route 114 (pre-Bassom 104B) to the Green Man, Mill Hill from 19th October. A month later the new Edgwarebury Lane was served by route 141, which continued via the 'bye-pass road' (Watford Way), Stanmore Circus and Brockley Hill to Elstree and Borehamwood (The Crown). The two single-deck buses that were allocated had to be fitted with sprag gear for the stiff climb up Brockley Hill. Other changes during 1927 saw the 58 extended from Coulsdon to Chipstead Valley, new route 602 (Muswell Hill to Edmonton, extended to Chingford on 25th January 1928) bringing buses to Alexandra Park Road and Brownswood Road and to Hall

Lane, Chingford and the 154 being diverted through the northern end of Middle Lane Hornsey. Also in the Croydon area from 19th October 1927, the 194 was a new route from West Wickham to Cheam which took an indirect route between South Croydon and Waddon so as to serve new housing in Warham Road and Denning Avenue. The year ended with Birch at last getting his route 203 onto the road between Belsize Park and Kensal Rise, winding around the back streets through Englands Lane, Ordnance Hill, Hall Road and Maida Hill to avoid restricted streets.

*Above* London Public DE 24 at Finsbury Park on route 154 which began serving the northern end of Middle Lane from 28th July 1926. (W. Noel Jackson)

*Below* Under the watchful eye of a young boy dressed, like the driver, in summery white, NS 1215 operates a journey to Pinner Green (The Starling) on route 183 seventeen months after the route had started on 9th February 1927. (W. Noel Jackson)

Route 247 was the first to reach the village of Greenford in 1925, operated by Royal Blue. The busier part of the route between King's Cross and Sudbury (originally 247A but later renumbered 218E) attracted a number of Independents, including Ryan, whose Dennis MK403 is at the Sudbury terminus.
(The Mike Sutcliffe collection)

For a thousand years, the village of Greenford had straddled Oldfield Lane to the south of Greenford Green, surrounded by farm land and with its centre some way north of the modern shopping centre. This pastoral serenity was put to an end in the mid-1920s by the opening of Western Avenue and Greenford Road and other associated road improvements. Greenford Green had been reached from the Sudbury direction by Royal Blue on route 247 in 1925 and this was later extended to Greenford station but the first invasion from the south did not take place until 8th February 1928. Route 97 was extended from its Argyle Road terminus via the then London Road (Ruislip Road), Greenford Road, Western Avenue and Oldfield Lane to the station. It was extended on to Sudbury Hill station in July, when it became 97B as a Sunday extension to Northwood took the number 97. One of Birch's many thwarted attempts to pioneer new services had been for a Greenford Station to Ealing service, running via Greenford Avenue, Drayton Green and Castlebar Hill for which the company had sought a licence in July 1927. The attempt was frustrated by the Minister's decision to impose Restricted Streets Orders on Haven Green, Cleveland Road and Castlebar Hill, which not only kept Birch out but also protected the 97. The almost immediate extension of route 97 must have left a sour taste in the mouths of the Birch family but the residents of Cuckoo Hill and Drayton Green were left busless until Mrs Sayers's Royal Highlander started the 210B in November 1930.

Another of Birch's schemes was prompted by the opening of the Barnet By-Pass north of Hendon on 18th October 1928, which inspired the idea of a new service linking Hendon Central Station with the new estates between Mill Hill and Edgware. The resulting route was numbered 214 and registered as Canons Park to Hendon Central but when Birch started it later in October the main service ran as 214A between Edgware and Hendon Central with only three morning journeys going right through. An all-day through service was introduced on 2nd February 1929, a day before Hale Lane was declared a restricted road. The route was a great success and soon needed augmentation but it was to prove yet another of the company's collisions with the brick wall of the establishment and no dispensation was granted. All was eventually settled by a scheme of co-ordination with the LGOC which came into being in December 1930 but not before Birch's hackles were again raised by the grant of a licence to the LGOC for route 121 (Dulwich to Mill Hill) which covered the Finchley Road to Hendon section newly from 5th June 1929.

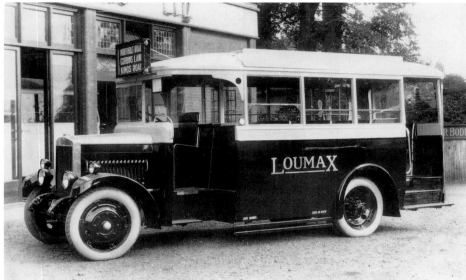

Another venture with which Mrs Sayers of Royal Highlander was to become involved later was the Loumax company, a latecomer started by the brothers Grundel in 1928. They started a short route between South Harrow Station and Harrow Council Estate in Eastcote Lane on 10th October 1928 but overlooked the need for a licence and soon had to withdraw it on the insistence of the police. They were nevertheless granted a licence for it a year later and it started its legal existence as route 206 on 8th October 1929.

Two other areas in opposite corners of London were served for the first time in 1928. One single-deck K supplied by Sidcup garage started running on new route 195 between Sidcup station and Chislehurst via Perry Street on 7th November 1928. On the same day route 8 had an important extension from Willesden through Kingsbury to Colindale, bringing buses to some of the more extravagantly designed reproduction architecture of the period in Roe Green and Hay Lane. The extension incidentally supplied an alternative route from Old Ford to Colindale, already linked by the 60!

The introduction of buses into new areas in 1929 comprised a number of individual changes which did not fall into neat packages although each had a local significance. For example, two changes in different parts of London early in the year introduced buses to large new populations. In the expanding Becontree estate from 20th February the 148 was rerouted and extended to serve Becontree Avenue and Valence Avenue to reach Heathway and Dagenham while in Norbury from 27th March the 159 was rerouted to run through a much transformed Green Lane and Parchmore Road, instead of London Road. In passing it is of interest to note that route 623 started running between Barking and Beckton Gas Works on 20th February, replacing the troubled Barking Council tram service which had ceased the day before.

*Top* When route G3 was extended from Romford to Chadwell Heath on 20th February 1929 it entered the Metropolitan Police District and therefore had to be renumbered 188. K 533 was photographed just before the route was was withdrawn just over six months later, being replaced from 4th September in part by new route G5 (Romford 'Parkside Hotel'–Hornchurch) and changes to route 187 (Chadwell Heath–Brentwood). (W Noel Jackson)

*Centre* Duple supplied the idiosyncratic 18-seat body for the Guy OND which operated on the new service from South Harrow to Harrow Council Estate started by the brothers Grundel legally on 8th October 1929, having run it illegally for a while in 1928. Unlike later operations into the area, the Loumax route ran via Corbin's Lane. (Ken Glazier collection)

*Left* Route 148 reached maturity on 20th February 1929 when it was extended to Dagenham (The Chequers) through Becontree Avenue, Valence Avenue and Heathway. NS 426 is passing the Wanstead Museum of Music preparatory to launching out onto the 'New Southend Road', as Eastern Avenue was described on the route board. (W. Noel Jackson)

The road from Banstead to Epsom via Drift Bridge and College Road had been served at weekends since 16th August 1923 when route 80B started but was still waiting for a Monday–Friday service at the end of 1929, apart from Firtree Road which had been served by the rerouted 164 from 1st August 1928. S 186 is at Trafalgar Square on the 181, the new number given to the 80B under the Bassom system. (Ken Glazier collection)

Despite the rapid growth of suburban housing in the 1920s, there was still plenty of virgin land awaiting the developers of the 1930s, as can be seen in this view of London Road, Morden just under three years after the Underground had arrived. The potential for developing leisure traffic by feeder services from the railhead was exploited in the summer of 1928 when route 131 ran on Sundays from Morden to Epsom Downs (Derby Arms) between 6th April and 9th September. In 1929 the Approved Route registration was altered to allow operation of a revised version on race days only to Epsom Downs (Yewtree Bottom Road), a service that still exists in 2002. The photograph shows how successful the operation was from the start and on Derby Day 5th June 1929 no fewer than 178 buses were operated from Cricklewood, Merton, Mortlake, Norwood, Old Kent Road, Sutton, Tottenham and Willesden garages. (Ken Glazier collection)

Route 104 reached Burnt Oak on 27th July 1929, serving the heart of the new LCC Watling estate. Twenty-four seat K 1055 is parked on the stand outside the block of shops at the front of Golders Green station. (The Mike Sutcliffe Collection)

Nunhead was an area that was already well developed at the end of the nineteenth century but had been ignored by bus operators for the first twenty-nine years of the twentieth, apart from an attempt by Newlands District whose F.H. Bruce was impatient, tried to work outwith the law and ended up in court for his trouble. Following exhaustive surveys the LGOC finally recognised the need in 1929 and introduced route 621 on 10th April 1929. This was a panhandle circular route from Peckham whose loop ran via Peckham Rye Ivydale Road and Nunhead Lane. Under the Bassom system it might have been expected to have different numbers for each direction of travel but the operators of the system at this late stage seem to have been happy to give them the suffixes A and B as though they were short workings. The route was destined to survive almost unchanged for over fifty years but managed in that period to carry four different route numbers.

The western end of North Circular Road had gradually been lined with a typical ribbon development mixture of housing and factories to the extent that route 608 had started to run from Stonebridge Park to Finchley (Regents Park Road) to serve them in May 1928. It was extended further on 19th June 1929, to terminate at the junction

of Addison Way with Barnet By-Pass, which was still under construction. When a little more of the road was available, on 28th August, it was pushed on as far as Hampstead Garden Suburb Market Place. To complete the story, it finally got through the rest of the new road on 9th April 1930 when it was extended to Hornsey Rise via Archway.

Two new Uxbridge routes started on 26th June and 17th July respectively. The first was the 505, a single-deck K-operated route serving the isolated Richings Park estate which had been built to the south of the Great Western Railway main line at Iver. In contrast, the 506 which started three weeks later ran down the existing 501 through Cowley and then branched off to run through Colnbrook and Horton to Staines.

It remains to record two small but contrasting changes in 1929 to round off this account of headlong expansion during the decade. A final piece of the Watling LCC Estate jigsaw was put in place by the 104E which was rerouted and extended in two stages completed on 24th July, to serve Orange Hill Road. The last change links two aspects of the 1920s story as it concerns route 551, once a haven for Independents free of interference from General but now operated in strength by that company through its acquisitions. In sharp contrast to the extension of the 104E, the 551 was projected through some of the most expensive housing in London to a new terminus at Totteridge War Memorial, on the edge of what remains to this day relatively open countryside.

Just as you might tow your small boat to the river or sea for a day's sailing, so apparently in 1925 you might tow your folded-up airplane to the aerodrome for some pleasure flying. This two-seater Morris is making its way along Colindale Avenue to Hendon Aerodrome, famous for its air displays between 1920 and 1937, passing K 379 on route 60. The 60 had arrived at Colindale (Edgware Road) on a Saturday extension from Cricklewood on 25th July 1923 and on Mondays-Fridays from 3rd November 1924, but did not reach Colindale Station until 7th January 1925. (Ken Glazier collection)

# Epilogue

In the eleven years between the end of World War 1 and the end of 1929, the motor bus grew to maturity from the still primitive horse-bus derived B-type to the first of the truly modern buses of the T, LT and ST classes which appeared just as the decade closed. These improvements took place amidst such a phenomenal growth in the population that the number of passenger journeys made by public transport in Greater London grew by 935m a year (38 per cent) between 1920 and 1929. Buses bore the brunt of this growth as both railways and tramways suffered a slump during the

mid-1920s from which they were only just recovering and buses were able to take immediate advantage of the opportunities offered by newly developing areas, without major investment. Passenger journeys by bus showed steady growth from 1921 onwards and more than doubled, rising from 936m in 1920 to 1,912m in 1929. In tune with these advances, the size of the bus fleet also more than doubled and the supporting infrastructure was developed, expanded and improved. Fifteen new garages were built for the LGOC's own services and another nine for services operated by its agents East Surrey and National and some of the Independents also provided themselves with new and improved garages as their operations grew and stabilised. The equipment in existing LGOC garages was improved and modernised and many were enlarged or rebuilt to house the extra buses and to make them suitable for the newer buses which were gradually getting larger and taller.

The biggest single project was the new central overhaul works at Chiswick which opened in stages during 1921 and 1922 as described briefly in chapter one. The creation of Chiswick Works provided the means by which the LGOC could build its own

buses if it chose and this became a matter of contention with AEC, which had suffered immediately from the loss of overhaul work and could see its principal market for new vehicles under threat. This fear was given substance when Chiswick started to assemble S and NS chassis in its earlier years and had become a real threat by 1929 when plans were in hand for a new range of chassis designed and built at Chiswick. This state of affairs seems strange when the two participants were wholly owned subsidiaries of the same Underground Group and shared the same top management, but it does demonstrate the remarkable way in which the different companies within the Group retained their own independence even when, outwardly, they appeared to be thoroughly subsumed into the organisation. AEC successfully negotiated an agreement to be allowed to sell more of its products on the open market outside London and this easement was to prove useful in later years when the company became wholly independent of any operator.

The state of public transport in the capital was a political issue throughout this period, spurred on in the immediate post-war years by the inadequacies caused by the

Whitsun Bank Holiday traffic at Hampton Court in 1928. The growth in popularity of the private car is evident but the importance of public transport is also clear. K 540 on the right is emerging from Bushy Park, on one of the many summer route extensions, partly masking an S on route 14. Among the other buses two Independents are passing the *Queen's Arms* on route 33D and 73, and the tram is a London County Council E1 which has come through from the Embankment on the summer extension of route 4, using LUT tracks from Merton. (Ken Glazier collection)

depredations of war. Lord Ashfield was a keen proponent of unification and made many public pronouncements on the subject. As early as 1919 he was having discussions with the London County Council about the possibility of setting up an organisation which would provide common management of local transport, without altering the pattern of ownership of the undertakings involved. A 'supreme traffic authority' for London had been recommended as far back as 1905 by the Royal Commission on London Traffic and the idea was put forward again by a Parliamentary Select Committee reporting in 1919. They recommended that such a body should direct the co-ordination of routes and services, carry out research and prepare a transit plan, while leaving the ownership of the undertakings in the hands of the individual companies and municipalities. The subject was discussed in various other forums but nothing came of the proposals until the sudden rise in bus competition after 1922 brought matters to a head and provoked the passage of the London Traffic Act in 1924. The main effects of that Act on bus operation have already been

New garages were built and extensions and alterations made to existing garages to accommodate the increasingly large fleet and make them suitable for the larger modern buses. Part of the grassed forecourt at Catford was paved in 1926 to increase parking space and the doorways widened to allow a more efficient arrangement of the petrol pumps, which is the work going on here. This photograph was taken during the General Strike, which is why the petrol-electric on route 36 has a chalked 'Marble Arch' and has a police constable alongside the driver. (The Omnibus Society)

During the 1920s many improvements to passenger facilities were made and the first steps taken towards installing technological help for controlling bus services. The forecourt of Victoria Southern Railway station was laid out with proper loading platforms and

in 1927 the control tower was built from which officials supervised the departure of buses by operating light signals on the bus stop posts. These can be seen just below the bus stop flags.

The second view shows the inspector's control desk at Victoria with a telephone handset worthy of an appearance in a Marx Brothers' film. The buttons which actuated the signal lamps are on the console below the phone. (London's Transport Museum)

described in earlier chapters but its importance in this context is that it was the first attempt at some form of co-ordinated public control of service planning and provision, in which respect it followed the principles espoused by the 1905 Royal Commission and the 1919 Select Committee.

It was the London & Home Counties Traffic Advisory Committee set up by that Act that eventually lit the touch paper that led to the formation of the LPTB. In March 1925 the Minister asked the committee to investigate travelling facilities in north and north-east London, east London and south-east London. Their report on north-east London criticised the wasteful competition between the various undertakings in the area and urged that the proposal to set up a common fund and common management should be studied immediately. In the east London report they expressed the belief that unified management of local passenger transport agencies was the only permanent solution. The Committee was then charged by the Minister to examine the proposal. Their report was published in July 1927 and again recommended a single unifying authority providing common management and common funding. It was a controversial proposal and was a particular blow to the smaller independent bus proprietors, who would have found it difficult to fit into such an arrangement, other than by some form of amalgamation. This was what the formation of the London Public Omnibus Company was alleged to provide but this proved to be a snare and a delusion. Nevertheless, the Underground Group and the LCC entered into negotiations which culminated in each undertaking submitting a Bill to Parliament seeking powers to set up common funding and management of their transport services. The Bills went through most of their stages and were awaiting third reading in the House of Lords when parliament was dissolved and a new Labour Government elected. The new Minister of Transport killed the Bills.

While these deliberations had been progressing, life had been continuing in the world outside and an entirely new ingredient had dropped into the London traffic pot, almost by stealth. Some operators had found what they believed to be loopholes in the 1924 Act which made it possible for them to operate some types of service not included in the Metropolitan Police List of Approved Routes but still remain within the law. They believed that the law only applied to services operating wholly within the London Traffic Area and that its provisions could also be side-stepped by selling tickets from an office and not on the bus. The latter belief was behind the operation of the Selsdon Garden Village route by East Surrey in 1925 (see chapter four) but that was never tested in the courts, although the Police had been prepared to prosecute. A number of operators used that principle to justify the operation of limited stop services to places of interest in outer London, such as Dalston to High Beach, causing established bus operators considerable concern as it was eating into their revenue. Worse still, these services were operating along roads where bus operators had been forced to reduce their own services under Restricted Street Orders or where permission to start new services had been refused. Much more far-reaching was the idea of running what became known as 'suburban coach services' from central London to country destinations, mainly in the Home Counties but also further afield, a form of operation that laid the foundation for the famous Green Line network.

The first operator to enter the field was Empress Motors, later New Empress Saloons who started operating their Wood Green to Southend service on 27th May 1927. When City acquired a controlling interest the route was extended first to Camden Town then to Kentish Town. Westcliff-on-Sea Motor Services Ltd joined them on the same route in late 1928 or early 1929. Redcar Services of Tunbridge Wells followed their lead on 16th September with a service from their home

town to Victoria (Buckingham Palace Road) and the other route to start that year was between Luton and King's Cross, operated by Imperial Motor services. Seven more routes were started during 1928: Lupus Street to Aylesbury via Amersham (West London Coaches); Marble Arch to Aylesbury via Tring (Red Rover Saloon Coaches); King's Cross to Baldock (Baldock Motor Transport and later Queen Line); London to Luton (Strawhatter); Liverpool Street to Bishops Stortford (Acme Pullman); Aldwych to Bedford (Birch); and Stratford to Brentwood (Hillman). Similar growth followed in 1929 with services to Farnham (Farnham Blue and Aldershot & District), East Ham to Grays (Amalgamated), East Ham to Aveley (Price's Super Coaches), Hemel Hempstead (West Herts), Watford (Bucks Expresses), Hertford (Priest, then Regent Motor Services) and Reading (Thackray's Way). These were the services that were successful enough to continue operating but there were also many that had brief lives. There were fourteen operators in this category between August 1927 and November 1929, most of whose services lasted only a year or two, if not less. Among them were such well-known names as Glenton Coaches, the Gordon Omnibus company and Renown Motor Coaches but many were small local concerns. Their services ran to Dunstable, Dartford, Egham, Hertford, Ongar, St Albans, Sevenoaks, Thame, Tilbury, Welwyn Garden City and Windsor, nearly all destinations which were to become a permanent part of the 'suburban coach' or Green Line map in subsequent years.

All this activity alarmed the traffic authorities but no formal action was taken despite Frank Pick, for one, pressing the Ministry and the London & Home Counties Traffic Advisory Committee to intervene. Having failed to ensure that, in their eyes, the law was obeyed, the LGOC finally decided that it could not ignore the competition and joined in the fun in a modest way. East Surrey had operated two routes to London for a time

The Amalgamated Omnibus Service and Supplies Ltd, a company owned by the ever-active Charles Batten, started running a coach service from East Ham to Grays and Tilbury Dock on 8th March 1929. This Duple-bodied 28-seat ADC 426 was one of the vehicles which launched the service and is seen at Barking after the route had been extended to Aldgate, later in 1929. (The Mike Sutcliffe Collection)

*Left and below* The leaflet advertising the new LGOC coach service from Watford to Golders Green which started on 2nd October 1929 with through coach/rail tickets to central London via the Underground. (Laurie Akehurst collection)

---

GENERAL **MOTOR COACHES**
**EVERY 15 MINUTES DAILY**

# WATFORD (MARKET STREET)
## Via Golders Green Station
# To LONDON

Through Tickets are issued to the following UNDERGROUND Stations in the City and West End.

| | | |
|---|---|---|
| Aldwych | Edgware Road | Oxford Circus |
| Angel | Euston | Paddington |
| Baker Street | Goodge Street | Piccadilly |
| Bank | Hampstead | Post Office |
| Belsize Park | Holborn | Regent Street |
| Blackfriars | Hyde Park Corner | Russell Square |
| Bond Street | King's Cross | Strand |
| British Museum | Leicester Square | St. James' Park |
| Camden Town | Mansion House | Temple |
| Chalk Farm | Marble Arch | Tottenham Court |
| Chancery Lane | Marylebone | Road |
| Charing Cross | Mornington | Trafalgar Square |
| Covent Garden | Crescent | Victoria |
| Dover Street | Moorgate | Warren Street |
| Down Street | Old Street | Westminster |

**THROUGHOUT FARE** 1/6 Single 2/- Return.

**Golders Green Station only** 1/- " 1/6 "

Available on day of issue only.

---

## TIMES OF DEPARTURE.

### FROM WATFORD (Market Street)

| First Coach. | | Last Coach. | |
|---|---|---|---|
| Weekdays. a.m. | Sundays. a.m. | Weekdays. p.m. | Sundays. p.m. |
| 7.0 | 9.0 | 11.30 | 10.30 |

### FROM GOLDERS GREEN Station

| First Coach. | | Last Coach. | |
|---|---|---|---|
| Weekdays. a.m. | Sundays. a.m. | Weekdays. a.m. | Sundays. p.m. |
| 7.35 | 9.35 | 12.5 | 11.5 |

Service every 15 minutes.

BOOKINGS FROM

NATIONAL OMNIBUS & TRANSPORT CO. LTD.
GARAGE, HIGH STREET, WATFORD
MARKET STREET, WATFORD } Telephone No.: WATFORD 1642

or

LONDON GENERAL OMNIBUS CO. LTD. GARAGE, LEAVESDEN ROAD, WATFORD, or
55, BROADWAY, WESTMINSTER, LONDON, S.W.1. Telephone, VICTORIA, No. 6800.

500. 2/10/29.

WATERLOW & SONS LIMITED, LONDON, DUNSTABLE & WATFORD

The growing traffic problem in the City of London 1929-style. Famous landmarks abound in this photograph, starting with the Mansion House on the left, the Mappin & Webb building on the corner of Poultry and Queen Victoria Street and, further on, the church of St Mary-le-Bow and St Paul's Cathedral. Buses also abound, predominantly covered-top NSs but with at least one K and possibly an S partially hidden behind an Independent Dennis on route 233 in the short Mansion House Street. Horse-drawn traffic is still to be found but there are also three of the much larger modern lorries, one looking as though it is on its way to Covent Garden, a brewer's dray and another delivering rolls of paper. (London's Transport Museum)

from Reigate via Sutton and from Redhill via Croydon but these ran only between 7th August 1928 and 2nd March 1929, and this was before the company had been taken over by General. Formal entry onto the stage by the LGOC took place on 2nd October 1929 when a small fleet of AEC Reliance all-weather coaches began running every fifteen minutes between Watford and Golders Green, with through bookings via the Underground to central London, initially for six weeks. It came back on 18th December but this time at half the former frequency, the rest of the service being provided by a second route which ran from Watford to Charing Cross via Stanmore, Edgware and Kilburn. That was as far as things had got by the end of 1929 but the LGOC soon expanded its services and a new company, Green Line coaches Ltd was formed in 1930 to operate them.

The authorities were alarmed by what they saw as unfettered operation by these coaches jamming the streets of central London and this was no doubt a major incentive in the drive towards some form of unified control. They did not have to wait long. The new Minister of Transport was Herbert Morrison who, having killed the private Bills of the LCC and the Underground Group, announced his own proposals in December 1929. Given his municipal background and general political philosophy most people expected that he would propose some form of municipal control but the content of his announcement surprised everybody. The proposals were far more extensive than anything that had gone before and envisaged nothing less than a publicly-owned authority run on commercial lines, which would take over and own all the existing undertakings within its monopoly area. The proposals

went through many changes before they finally became law in 1933 but the essentials were already established at the end of 1929, so leaving this turbulent period on the brink of the most fundamental change imaginable. The decade had started with Ashfield (then Sir Albert Stanley) seeking monopoly bus operating powers for the LGOC and now ended with the prospect of his heading an organisation with more power than even he would have dared suggest ten years earlier. Not only the motor bus but perhaps also public transport in London had reached maturity.

In September 1929 the LGOC painted NS 933 in this brighter livery with cream above the waist panels, in a style which was also used on the new T 1, LT 1 and ST 1 but which did not prevail. The official caption for this photograph says the bus is in Fleet Street but the building on the right suggests somewhere else, possibly Strand. (Popperfoto)

# APPENDIX 1
# GARAGES

(List A) At the end of the Great War, the LGOC and its Underground Group associate companies were operating buses from twenty-three garages, BAT from one, Thomas Tilling from two and National Steam from three. Sixteen other garages (fourteen LGOC and two Tilling) had been requisitioned for war service or closed for other reasons and were not operational. The complete list of operational garages is shown below. Garage premises acquired with the businesses of Independents but which were never operated as part of the LGOC, are not shown.

| GARAGE | CODE | GARAGE | CODE |
|---|---|---|---|
| **LGOC** | | | |
| Acton | E | Leyton | T |
| Athol Street | C | Merton | AL |
| Battersea | B | Middle Row | X |
| Chalk Farm | CF | Mortlake | M |
| Chelverton Road | AF | Norwood | N |
| Cricklewood | W | Old Kent Road | P |
| Dalston | D | Palmers Green | AD |
| Forest Gate | G | Seven Kings | AP |
| Hackney | H | Streatham | AK |
| Hammersmith | R | Turnham Green | V |
| Hendon | AE | Willesden | AC |
| Holloway | J | | |

**THOMAS TILLING**

| | | | |
|---|---|---|---|
| Croydon | TC | Lewisham | TL |

**NATIONAL STEAM CAR COMPANY**

Nunhead
Putney Bridge
Shepherd's Bush (Becklow Road)

**TILLING & BRITISH AUTOMOBILE TRACTION**

Camden Town    AQ

Total garages : 29

(List B) Between 1920 and 1929 the LGOC built 18 new garages to house the buses needed to supply the expanding network. Four of the garages acquired from other operators became part of the permanent stock and most garages which had closed during the war were also re-opened. The following list shows the opening or re-opening dates of these garages in chronological order. Some garages closed during this period, including a number of acquired premises which were operated for only a short time. Details of these can be found in the footnotes. In view of the closer relationship which developed between General and Tilling during this period, the garages of both companies are shown in one consolidated list.

| GARAGE | Code | Re-opening Date | Opening Date |
|---|---|---|---|
| Upton Park | U | 28.05.1919 | |
| Twickenham | AB | 04.06.1919[1] | |
| Tottenham | AR | 25.06.1919 | |
| Camberwell | Q | 09.07.1919 | |
| Clay Hall | Y | 09.07.1919[2] | |
| Hounslow | AV | 30.07.1919 | |
| Plumstead | AM | 19.11.1919 | |
| Putney Bridge | F | | 21.02.1920[3] |
| Nunhead | AH | | 21.04.1920[3] |
| Watford (Leavesden Road) | WT | | 25.08.1920[4] |
| Catford | (TL) | 03.10.1920[5] | |
| Crayford | CR | 10.08.1921 | |
| Kingston | K | | 04.01.1922 |
| Weybridge | WB | | 16.05.1923 |
| Shepherd's Bush | S | 04.07.1923[6] | |
| Loughton | L | | 11.07.1923 |
| Barking | BK | | 09.01.1924 |
| Sutton | A | | 09.01.1924 |
| Bromley (Tilling) | TB | | 16.04.1924 |
| Sidcup | SP | | 11.06.1924 |
| Romford | RD | | 16.07.1924[15] |
| Hanwell | HW | | 18.03.1925[7] |
| Edgware | EW | | 08.04.1925 |
| South Harrow | SH | | 08.04.1925 |
| Muswell Hill | MH | | 23.09.1925 |
| East Ham (Tilbury Road) | EH | | ??.04.1926[8] |
| East Ham (Invicta) | E | | 18.05.1926[9] |
| Slough (Langley Rd) | SL | | 08.09.1926 |
| Enfield (Green St) | RS | | 18.10.1926[10] |
| Upper Edmonton | UE | | 09.09.1926[11] |
| Uxbridge | UX | | 01.01.1929[12] |
| Elmers End | ED | | 27.03.1929 |
| Enfield | E | | 11.12.1929[13] |
| West Green | WG | | 11.12.1929[14] |

The following garages which closed during the war were not re-opened:

**LGOC**
Kingston, Ceres Street (AH) and Walworth, Penrose Street (AG), formerly London Central, Farm Lane (Fulham) (F), Kilburn (K)
The former Vanguard garage in Albany Street (A) also closed (in 1916) but was replaced by the new garage at Chalk Farm (CF) which opened at the same time.

**THOMAS TILLING**
Acorn Street, Camberwell.
Victory Place, Southwark also closed (in 1916) but was replaced by the new Croydon garage which opened at the same time.

# FOOTNOTES TO LIST B

[1] Twickenham garage was closed again between 04.05.1921 and 15.04.1924 inclusive during which time it was used for building bus bodies.

[2] Clay Hall was re-opened to house lorry buses and was later closed again, the last day of operation being 10.08.1920. Sometimes known as Old Ford, this was a different building from the later one with that name.

[3] Putney Bridge and Nunhead garages had been owned by the National Steam Car Company, who had closed them on 11.11.1919 and 18.11.1919 respectively, when the company withdrew from London.

[4] Watford garage was handed over to the National Omnibus and Transport Company on 25.05.1921 for the operation of services on behalf of LGOC.

[5] When Catford re-opened it was handed over to Tilling for the operation of services under their agreement with the LGOC, Tilling's Lewisham garage being closed from the same date. The pre-war code AN was discontinued but the new code TL (Tilling Lewisham) was not shown on buses until 1924.

[6] The premises at Shepherd's Bush had been open since 09.07.1919 but only for the turning of buses on route 11, not as an operational base.

[7] Acton garage closed on this date. It had also been closed for a short period between 31.05.1921 and 04.07.1922 inclusive, re-opening the following day. Cambrian buses operated from this garage but carrying the code CA from 24.02.1926 until the Cambrian business ceased to trade on 30.04.1928, after which they became part of the LGOC fleet.

[8] Acquired from Atlas and operated as part of the Batten group until the LGOC took control on 31.12.1926.

[9] Acquired from Invicta and operated as part of the Batten group until absorbed by the LGOC on 31.12.1926. It was closed at the end of traffic on 16.10.1928, when its operations were transferred to Tilbury Road garage (EH).

[10] The site in Green Street, Enfield Highway, was acquired from Redburn's Motor Services. LGOC operated services from a temporary building on the site until 22.05.1928, services being transferred to the London Public Omnibus Company at Enfield (Southbury Road) the following day.

[11] The premises in Claremont Street, Edmonton, which had been used by various Independents, were acquired from Howard C. Barrett and were operated as part of the 'Batten Group' until 08.02.1927, but under direct LGOC control after 31.12.1926. Services were transferred into Tottenham garage on 09.02.1927.

[12] Uxbridge garage was built by the LGOC but operated on its behalf by the Thames Valley Traction Company from 14.06.1922 to 31.12.1928 inclusive.

[13] Enfield (Southbury Road) garage was built by the LGOC for operation by the London Public Omnibus Company and opened on 23.05.1928. It became an LGOC garage when the LPOC was absorbed.

[14] The premises in Willow Walk had been used as a bus garage since December 1922, first by Admiral and later by the London Public Omnibus Company. They became an LGOC garage when the LPOC was absorbed, having been under LGOC control since 06.02.1928.

[15] This garage was renamed Hornchurch in 1935.

(List C) The following is a complete list of the garages from which the Combine companies were operating at the end of 1929.

| | | | |
|---|---|---|---|
| Athol Street (Poplar) | C | Merton | AL |
| Barking | BK | Middle Row | X |
| Battersea | B | Mortlake | M |
| Bromley | TB | Muswell Hill | MH |
| Camberwell | Q | Norwood | N |
| Camden Town | AQ | Nunhead | AH |
| Catford | TL | Old Kent Road | P |
| Chalk Farm | CF | Palmers Green | AD |
| Chelverton Road (Putney) | AF | Plumstead | AM |
| Crayford | CR | Putney Bridge | F |
| Cricklewood | W | Romford | RD |
| Croydon | TC | Seven Kings | AP |
| Dalston | D | Shepherd's Bush | S |
| East Ham | EH | Sidcup | SP |
| Edgware | EW | Slough (Langley Road) | SL |
| Elmers End | ED | South Harrow | SH |
| Enfield | E | Streatham | AK |
| Forest Gate | G | Sutton | A |
| Hackney | H | Tottenham | AR |
| Hammersmith | R | Turnham Green | V |
| Hanwell | HW | Twickenham | AB |
| Hendon | AE | Upton Park | U |
| Holloway | J | Uxbridge | UX |
| Hounslow | AV | West Green | WG |
| Kingston | K | Weybridge | WB |
| Leyton | T | Willesden | AC |
| Loughton | L | | |

Total garages : 53

The LGOC also owned or held leases for the following garages which were leased to the East Surrey Traction Company or the National Omnibus and Transport Company for operation of services on its behalf in the 'London Country Area'.

## EAST SURREY

Chelsham
Dunton Green
Godstone
Leatherhead
Swanley

## NATIONAL

Bishop's Stortford
Hatfield
Hemel Hempstead (Bury Road)
Luton (Castle Street)
Waltham Abbey
Ware (Town Hall)
Watford (High Street)
Watford (Leavesden Road)

# APPENDIX 2
# LORRY BUSES

Details of the operation of the lorry buses by the LGOC are hard to come by, as there was then no such thing as the 'Allocation of Scheduled Buses' (more commonly known as the Allocation Book), which first appeared in 1927. Instead, the information was normally promulgated in the Traffic Circulars but, particularly in their early years, these were fickle documents which left out a lot of vital information. Unfortunately, this included the lorry bus allocations which were not fully recorded. The following information is based mainly on research which was carried out for the Omnibus Society by J.D.P. House and George Robbins and published in a pamphlet entitled 'Traffic Emergency'.

## (A) ROUTES ON WHICH LORRY BUSES OPERATED

The following list is as complete as is possible from the sources available but there may have been other routes involved in the scheme from time to time. Lorry Buses did not operate simultaneously on all the routes shown as there were some changes made during their operation. The sections of route shown in the list, particularly where they are the full extent of the route, need to be treated with some caution as the full facts are not on record. The only routes for which there are positive entries in the LGOC Traffic Circulars are: from 3rd September 1919, routes 56 (18 lorries), 101 (10), and 142 (6); from 17th September, route 73 (14 lorries 'intermingled with Omnibuses', as the Traffic Circular said); and from 24th September route 103 was allocated 9 lorries when it took over the Cubitt Town to Poplar section of route 56, which was reduced to 11.

On most routes the lorry buses were additional to the main schedule and at first ran as limited stop supplementaries but following public requests it was announced by Frank Pick on 14th July 1919 that normal stopping arrangements would apply.

| | | |
|---|---|---|
| *1 | Kilburn – Tower Bridge Hotel | Cricklewood ++ |
| 3 | Charing Cross – Brixton | Chalk Farm |
| 11 | Ebury Bridge – Liverpool Street | Shepherd's Bush + |
| 13A | London Bridge – Finchley Road Station | Chalk Farm |
| *16 | Victoria – Cricklewood (Crown) | Cricklewood ++ |
| 17 | London Bridge – Ealing Broadway | Shepherd's Bush + |
| 21 | Wood Green – Sidcup | Palmers Green |
| *22 | Homerton – Putney Common | Putney Bridge or Leyton ++ |
| 23 | Oxford Circus – Barking | Clay Hall (Y) |
| #24 | Hampstead Heath – Pimlico | Chalk Farm |
| 26 | South Harrow – Watford Junction | Cricklewood |
| 27 | Archway Station (then known as Highgate) – Twickenham | Twickenham |
| 29 | Victoria – Palmers Green Garage | Palmers Green |
| 31 | Camden Town – Chelsea | Chalk Farm |
| #32 | Turnham Green – Wimbledon | Merton |
| 33 | Charing Cross – Barnes (Red Lion) | Mortlake |
| *35A | Clapham Common – Walthamstow (Wood St) | Leyton ++ |
| #38 | Victoria – Walthamstow (Hoe Street Station) | Leyton |
| *42 | Finsbury Park Station – Camberwell Green | Hackney ++ |
| 49 | Shepherd's Bush – Streatham Common | Shepherd's Bush + |
| 56 | Mile End Station – Millwall Docks/Poplar (Blackwall Tunnel) | Clay Hall (Y) |
| *73 | Highbury Station – Richmond | Tottenham |
| #76 | Victoria Station – Edmonton (Angel) | Tottenham |
| #77 | King's Cross – Tooting | Chalk Farm |
| #80 | Charing Cross – Belmont | Merton |
| #88 | Acton Green – Mitcham (Cricketer's Arms) | Merton |
| 101 | Wanstead – North Woolwich | Upton Park |
| *103 | Cubitt Town – Poplar (Blackwall Tunnel) | Clay Hall (Y) |
| *106 | Finsbury Park Station – Poplar (Blackwall Tunnel) | Athol St or Holloway ++ |
| 142 | Kilburn Park – Watford Junction | Cricklewood |

* Routes onto which lorry buses were transferred at some time during their operation.

+ Shepherd's Bush garage was not open as an operational garage at this time. It is believed that the lorry buses were kept in nearby railway arches.

++ This is assumed to have been the allocation as it is the garage which normally ran the route on Mondays to Saturdays but there is no concrete record to support the assumption.

# Routes from which lorry buses were removed and transferred to others at some time during their operation.

## (B) NUMBERS OF LORRY BUSES LICENSED FOR SERVICE

The first lorry bus (the prototype) went into service on route 33 from Mortlake garage on 2nd June 1919. The maximum number was reached on 5th July 1919 and remained at that level until all 180 were delicensed on 14th January 1920. The only routes on which lorry buses were still operating by that date were the 56, 101 and 103. The rate of introduction is shown in the following table.

| Date | Number licensed | Date | Number licensed | Date | Number licensed |
|---|---|---|---|---|---|
| 31st May | 1 | 16th June | 59 | 26th June | 124 |
| 3rd June | 7 | 17th June | 67 | 27th June | 133 |
| 6th June | 10 | 18th June | 73 | 28th June | 138 |
| 7th June | 20 | 19th June | 80 | 30th June | 142 |
| 10th June | 28 | 20th June | 87 | 1st July | 151 |
| 11th June | 31 | 21st June | 94 | 2nd July | 157 |
| 12th June | 38 | 23rd June | 97 | 3rd July | 166 |
| 13th June | 47 | 24th June | 106 | 4th July | 175 * |
| 14th June | 55 | 25th June | 115 | 5th July | 180 |

* Prototype delicensed and converted to breakdown lorry on this date.